Revolt of the Scribes

Revolt of the Scribes
Resistance and Apocalyptic Origins

Richard A. Horsley

Fortress Press
Minneapolis

REVOLT OF THE SCRIBES
Resistance and Apocalyptic Origins

Copyright © 2010 Fortress Press, an imprint of Augsburg Fortress. All rights reserved. Except for brief quotations in critical articles or reviews, no part of this book may be reproduced in any manner without prior written permission from the publisher. Visit http://www.augsburgfortress.org/copyrights/ or write to Permissions, Augsburg Fortress, Box 1209, Minneapolis, MN 55440.

Scripture marked NRSV is taken from the New Revised Standard Version of the Bible, copyright 1989, Division of Christian Education of the National Council of the Churches of Christ in the United States of America. Used by permission. All rights reserved.

Scripture marked RSV is taken from the Revised Standard Version of the Bible, copyright 1952 [2nd edition, 1971] by the Division of Christian Education of the National Council of the Churches of Christ in the United States of America. Used by permission. All rights reserved.

Cover images: Réunion des Musées Nationaux /Art Resource, N.Y.; iStock
Cover design: Paul Boehnke

Library of Congress Cataloging-in-Publication Data
Horsley, Richard A.
  Revolt of the scribes : resistance and apocalyptic origins / Richard A. Horsley.
    p. cm.
  Includes index.
  ISBN 978-0-8006-6296-7 (alk. paper)
  1. Apocalyptic literature. I. Title.
  BS646.H67 2009
  220'.046—dc22
                          2009022548

The paper used in this publication meets the minimum requirements of American National Standard for Information Sciences — Permanence of Paper for Printed Library Materials, ANSI Z329.48-1984.

Manufactured in the U.S.A.

Contents

Chronology of Imperial Rulers and Major Events	vi
Maps	vii
Introduction: "Clueless about Apocalypticism"?	1
Part I: Scribal Resistance to Hellenistic Imperial Rule	**19**
Map of Maccabean and Hasmonean Palestine	20
1. The Escalating Crisis in Judea under Hellenistic Rule	21
2. The Statue and the Stone: The Tales of Daniel	33
3. The Giants Who Kill and Devour: Enoch's Book of Watchers	47
4. Wolves and Sheep, Eagles and Lambs: Enoch's Animal Vision and Other Historical Surveys	63
5. A Terrifying Fourth Beast: The Visions of Daniel	81
Part II: Scribal Resistance to Roman Imperial Rule	**105**
Map of Palestine after the Death of Herod the Great	106
6. Roman Conquest and Roman Rule	107
7. The War against the "Kittim": The Covenant Community at Qumran	123
8. The Arrogance of the Dragon: Roman Conquest in the *Psalms of Solomon*	143
9. Visions of Vindication: The Parables of Enoch and the Updated *Testament of Moses*	159
10. Demonstration, Organization, and Assassination: Parallel Scribal Resistance	177
Conclusion: Rethinking "Apocalyptic" Texts	193
Abbreviations	208
Notes	209
Index	227

Chronology of Imperial Rulers and Major Events

587 B.C.E.	Babylonian destruction of Jerusalem and the Temple
530s–330s	Persian imperial rule over ancient Near East; rebuilding of Temple and establishment of a temple-state in Judea
330s	Alexander the Great establishes Hellenistic Empire over the ancient Near East
316–200	Ptolemaic empire over Judea; wars between Ptolemaic and Seleucid empires for control of Syria-Palestine
220s–150s	Factional conflict in the Judean aristocracy increases
200–130s	Seleucid Empire rules Judea
175–164	Reign of Antiochus IV Epiphanes
175–172	Jason high priest; Hellenizing reform begins
175–160s	Resistance by scribal groups
172	Menelaus high priest; continues Hellenizing reform
169–167	Scribal and other resistance intensifies in Jerusalem; Antiochus attacks Jerusalem, imposes a military colony, profanes the Temple
167–164	Maccabean Revolt
ca. 150	Jonathan the Hasmonean obtains high priesthood; "righteous teacher" leads dissident scribes and priests to Qumran
ca. 110–ca. 80	Hasmonean wars of expansion; opposition by Pharisees and others
63	Roman conquest of Judea
40–37	Romans impose Herod as king; Herod conquers his subjects
37–4	Herod's rule over Judea and other areas
4	Teachers and students cut down the Roman eagle; Herod dies; popular revolts
6 C.E.	Roman governors and high priests over Judea; resistance to tribute
50s–60s	*Sicarii* assassinate high-priestly figures
66–70	Roman war against Judea; destruction of Temple

Map of the Hellenistic World

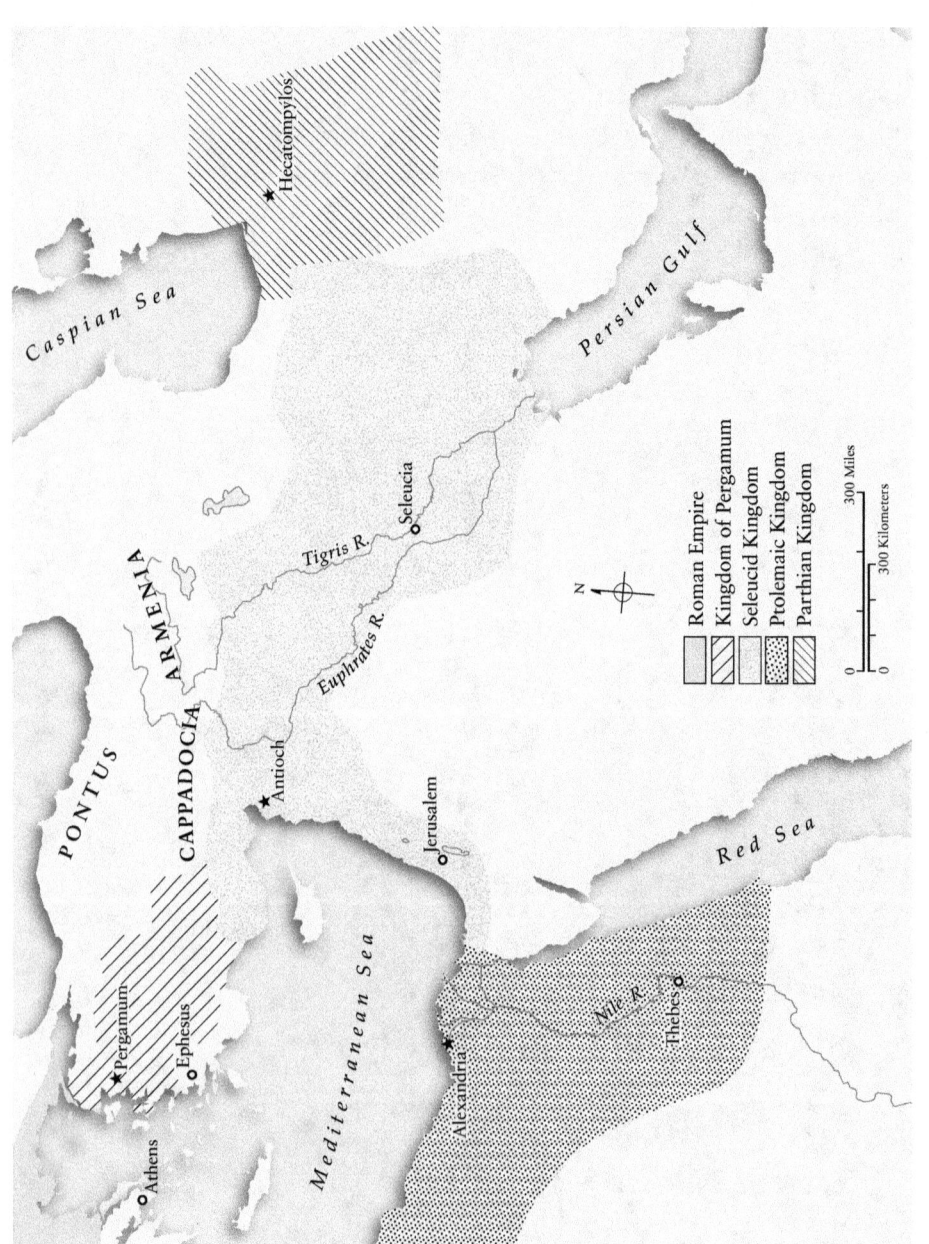

The Near East in 168 B.C.E.

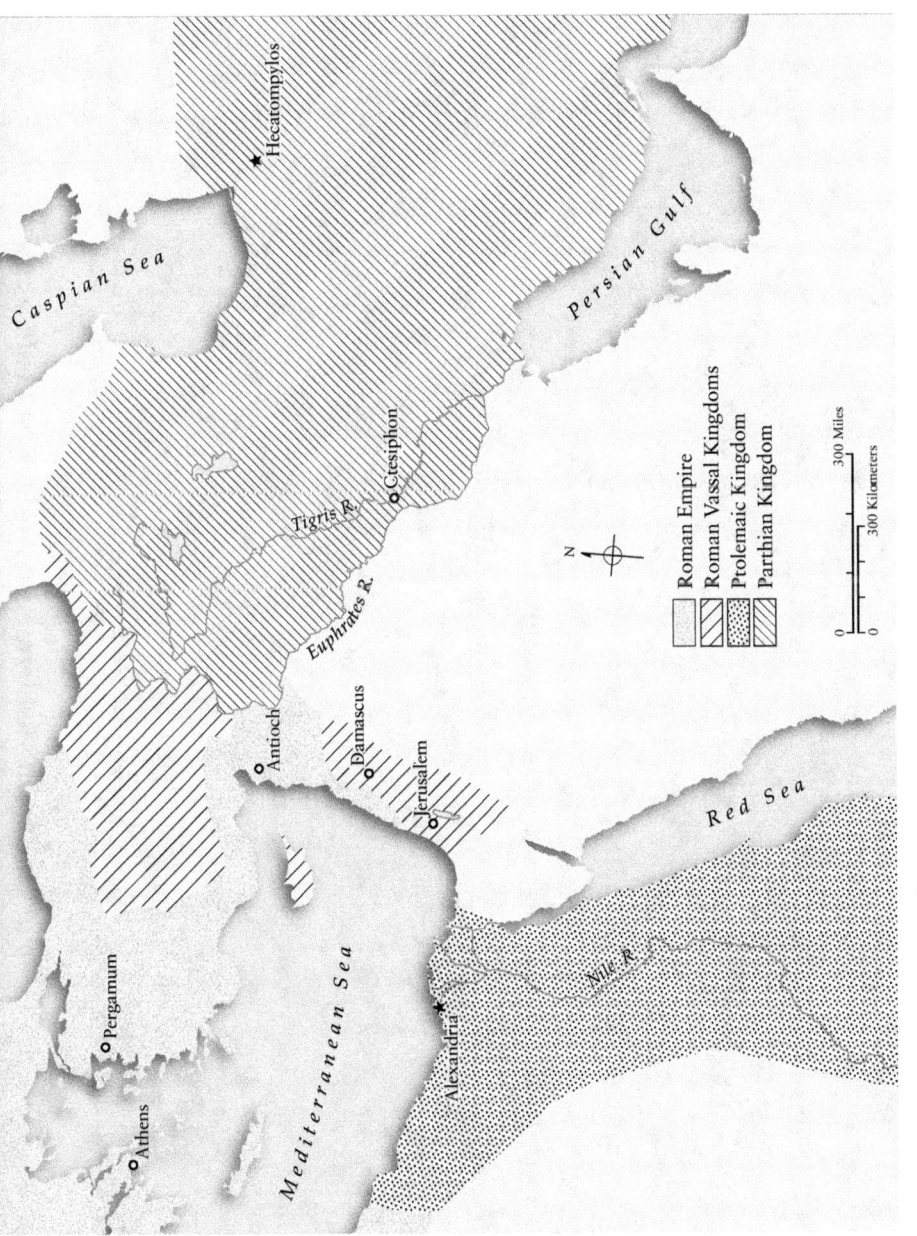

The Near East in 63 B.C.E.

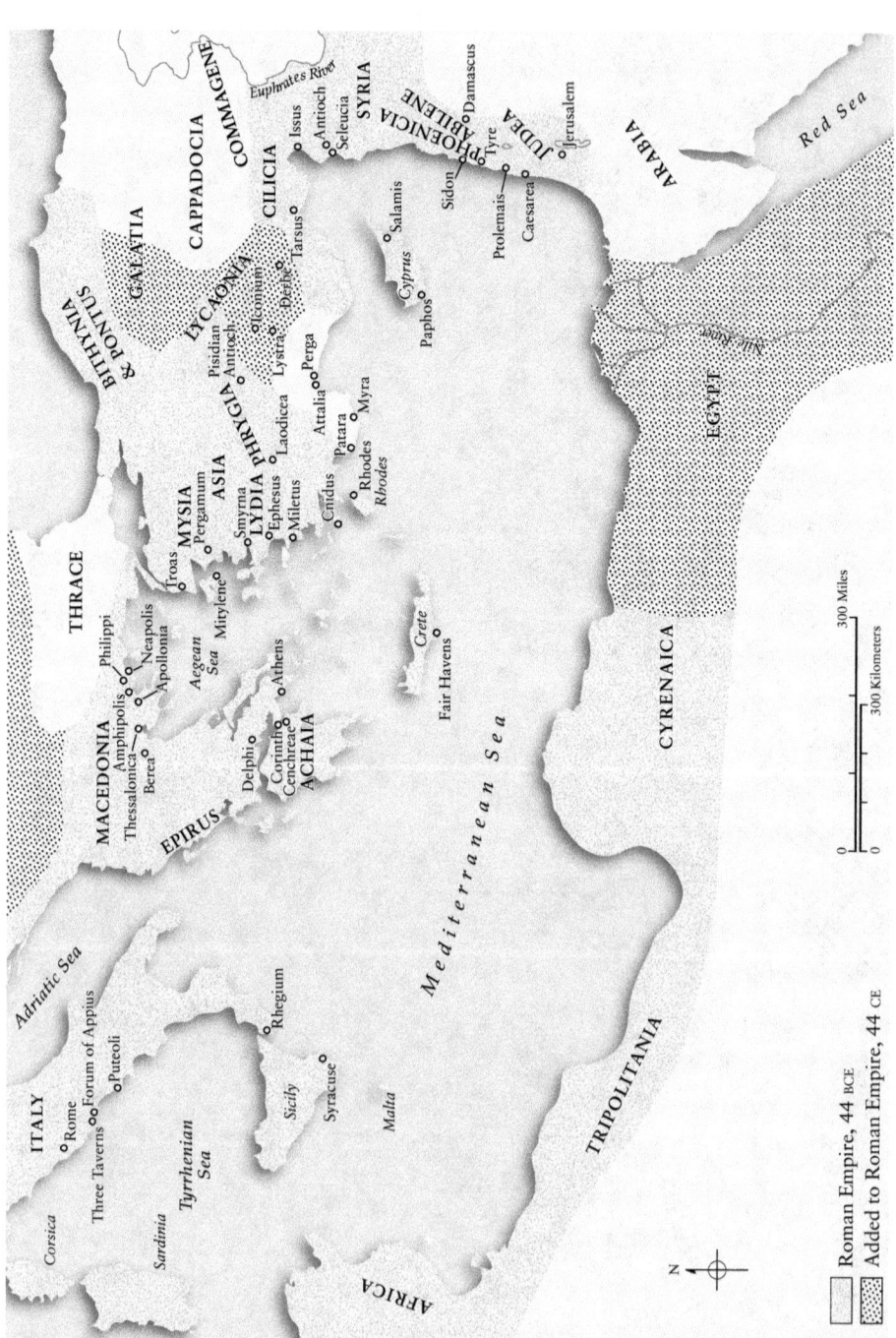

Map of the Roman Mediterranean World, First Century C.E.

Introduction
"Clueless about Apocalypticism"?

In the popular mind, "apocalypticism" is about the end of the world. Biblical interpreters have often reinforced this understanding. Albert Schweitzer and Rudolf Bultmann, the most influential New Testament interpreters of the twentieth century, claimed that Jesus believed that "cosmic catastrophe" was imminent. Expectation of "the end" supposedly pervaded Jewish society at the time. While interpreters have developed a more complicated and critical view in the past generation, even specialists still find "the end of the world" in a "cosmic dissolution" to be central to the message of "apocalyptic" texts.[1]

The textual passages usually cited to prove the point, however, cannot be taken literally. On the contrary, they are full of grand metaphor and hyperbole. They portray how awesome will be the appearance of God in judgment upon the foreign rulers who have been oppressing the people of Judea (*1 Enoch* 1:3-7; *T. Mos.* 10:3-7). The earthshaking pyrotechnics of God's appearance in judgment, moreover, are nothing new or distinctive to "apocalyptic" literature. Rather, they adapt earlier portrayals of God's coming by the prophets, to defeat oppressive domestic or foreign kings (Deut 33:1-2, 27, 29; Judg 5:4-5; Isa 13; 24:17-23; Jer 25:30-38; Mic 1:3-4). As exemplified in the vision and interpretation of Daniel 7, "apocalyptic" texts are not about the end of the world but the end of empires.

The discrepancies between standard interpretations and the texts themselves are many. Interpreters suggest, for example, that the texts are struggling with "the problem of evil." The texts, however, lack such abstract concepts but, instead, tell of rebel heavenly forces generating a race of giants who make war on the peoples of the earth and devour their livelihood. In the quintessential "apocalyptic" dream-vision in Daniel 7 interpreters see the ancient Canaanite "combat myth" of the battle between the Lord and the Chaos-monster Sea. The dream itself, however, focuses on increasingly violent and fearsome beasts, whose dominion is finally ended by "the ancient one" in a heavenly court of judgment. The application of the dream to ancient Near Eastern history that follows in the text explains that the beasts represent the sequence of imperial kings, the last of whom would attempt to "change the seasons and the law" but whose dominion would be terminated in divine judgment. Interpreters write of the conflict between "Jews" and "Gentiles." But the texts focus on "the kings and the mighty" or on the "shepherds" that supervise the beastly emperors who rule over Judeans. Interpreters find references to "resurrection." But the texts speak of God's restoration of the people and vindication of those martyred in their steadfast resistance to imperial domination.

Most of the standard generalizations about "apocalyptic" literature became well established in the field of biblical studies before the recent revival of literary criticism. In the past two or three decades, however, innovative interpreters began approaching biblical texts as if they were in an introductory course on prose fiction, starting with the characters, setting, and plot and then focusing particularly on the main conflict in the story. This approach, simple as it sounds, may help us discern the principal concerns of the texts from late Second Temple Judea that have been classified as "apocalyptic." A brief overview shows that the main conflict in each text focuses on imperial oppression and its control or termination by God's judgment, which usually includes restoration of the people.

The tales in Daniel 1–6 focus on Daniel and other learned Judean scribes who are working at the court of foreign empires. They interpret the dreams of the king and often come into conflict with arrogant rulers, over whom God asserts ultimate sovereignty. The Book of Watchers in *1 Enoch* 1–36 tells of how rebel heavenly "watchers" generated a race of giants who created violent warfare and exploitation on the earth, and the steps taken in the heavenly governance of the universe to control the rebel watchers and mitigate the damage they had done. Several of these texts are surveys of history, whether history in the Second Temple period or history since the beginning of the world. These surveys climax in an extreme crisis for the people under oppressive imperial rule. The Animal Vision in *1 Enoch* 85–90 tells of seventy heavenly "shepherds" set over the "wild beasts" (kings) who rule over the "sheep" (the people of Judea), until God sits in judgment on both the shepherds and beasts. The *Testament of Moses* focuses on the powerful kings who rule over the Judeans, especially the extremely violent last emperor, until God comes in judgment. The visions and historical surveys in Daniel 7–12 tell of the sequence of imperial kings, particularly the violent invasion by the last king and God's final restoration of the people. Similarly, the later Parables of Enoch, in *1 Enoch* 37–70, climax with the judgment of "the kings and mighty."

If the focal characters and plot of each of these texts are any indication, then their principal concerns would appear to be the desperate situation of the people of Judea under the domination of foreign rulers and the resulting question of God's sovereignty over history. These concerns are unmistakable in all of the texts. As the plot of the texts that survey history comes to a climax, moreover, additional characters play a crucial role that leads to God's action in resolving the historical crisis. The "lambs who have their eyes opened" or a certain "Taxo and his sons" or "the wise among the people" (in the Animal Vision, the *Testament of Moses*, and Daniel 10–12, respectively) engage in resistance to imperial oppression, for which they are martyred. In the overall sequence of events, their resistance leads finally to God's judgment against the empire, restoration of the people, and, in some cases, vindication of the martyrs. Resistance by people who are enlightened, or "instructors," is the turning point of the stories. It has long since been suspected that the attention given to these stalwart resisters constitutes the footprints of those who composed these texts.

That the plots of Judean "apocalyptic" texts in late Second Temple times focus on oppressive imperial rule and also, in many cases, on resistance to the point of martyrdom has led me to explore the texts as expressions and explanations of that resistance. Unless it is simply a historical accident, it is surely significant that no Second Temple Judean text classified as "apocalyptic" has survived that does *not* focus on imperial rule and the opposition to it. There were other forms of Judean opposition to imperial rule as well, which we will also explore. But the fact that all of these Second Temple Judean texts classified as "apocalyptic" focus on imperial rule and opposition to it suggest that their composition is closely related to the experience of that rule.

In anticipation of the examination of particular texts in the chapters below, my argument can be summarized briefly. The professional role of Judean intellectuals was to use their knowledge of Judean sacred traditions as advisers to the priestly aristocracy who headed the Temple. When imperial rulers and the priestly aristocracy's collaboration with that rule threatened the traditional Judean way of life, however, these intellectuals were caught in a conflict between loyalty to their patrons, who were in turn dependent on their imperial overlords and their loyalty to the traditions of which they were the guardians. At least some circles of dissident Judean intellectuals were led into resisting imperial rule. The Second Temple Judean texts that have been classified as apocalyptic are the expressions of their struggles to affirm that God was still in control of history and to resist Hellenistic or Roman rule that had become overly oppressive.

Exploration of these texts as resistance to imperial rule, however, will require a more comprehensive and often different approach than has been followed in standard interpretations of "apocalyptic" literature.

Devising a More Historical Approach

Standard scholarly interpretation does not necessarily deny that the texts are concerned with oppressive rule and the resistance to it among teachers or the enlightened. But its conceptual apparatus tends to block the recognition that these are the focal concerns of the texts. Standard interpretation of "apocalyptic" texts was shaped in the field(s) of biblical studies, where Christian or Jewish theological agendas and concepts have long been predominant. "Apocalyptic" texts, along with other Judean texts, are understood as expressions of and sources for "Judaism," a generalizing conception of the ancient Jewish *religion*. Just as the books of the Hebrew Bible are used as authoritative sources for constructing general theological doctrines or ideas, so Judean "apocalyptic" texts are treated as sources for the scholarly construction of a distinctive theology or worldview in ancient Judaism called "apocalypticism."

Of course, important aspects of modern Judaism do derive from scriptural texts, and biblical studies plays an important role in the interpretation of scripture. To impose the synthetic scholarly construct of "(early) Judaism" onto ancient Judean texts, however, obscures particular concerns of the texts and the complex realities of the society and the historical circumstances that they addressed. Religious expressions, ranging from collective prayers in local village assemblies to priestly sacrifices at the altar of the Temple, were important in Second Temple Judean society. But they were inseparable from the political economic structure, the dynamics of that society, and the political conflicts that flared into scribal resistance, widespread popular revolt, and the subsequent violent repressive measures by high-priestly rulers through the last three centuries of Second Temple Judea. The subjection of Judean society to imperial rule was often the most determinative factor in those persistent conflicts. To mention only the most obvious examples: the invasion of Jerusalem by the emperor Antiochus Epiphanes to enforce a Hellenizing "reform" led to the Maccabean Revolt; Herod was appointed "king of the Judeans" by the Roman Senate, which also loaned him Roman troops to conquer his subjects; and after Herod's death, the Roman governors appointed the high priests, who collaborated with the Romans to suppress popular protests. To discern the concerns of those texts standardly classified as "apocalyptic" requires consideration of the historical circumstances that they addressed, which are often obscured by the standard discourse of a synthetic "Judaism."

The modern scholarly construct of "apocalypticism" is similarly problematic for historical understanding. In the nineteenth century, discoveries of previously unknown manuscripts brought to light texts that seemed different from the well-known books of Torah, Prophets, and Writings in the Hebrew Bible. Partly because of their resemblances to images and motifs in the book of Revelation, which was the first book designated an *apokalypsis* ("revelation") in antiquity (see Rev 1:1), these texts were classified as "apocalyptic." Given their theological habits of mind, biblical scholars constructed a synthetic concept of "apocalypticism" from motifs, themes, and images found in texts from widely different times and historical contexts. Images, metaphors, and hyperboles were often taken somewhat literally and out of context as components of an "apocalyptic" scenario or worldview. The abstract construct of "apocalypticism," like that of "Judaism," tends to draw our attention away from the distinctive features of particular texts and their relationship with the historical contexts that they address.*

Intensive investigation of books such as Daniel and *1 Enoch* during the past generation has resulted in a wealth of valuable information about these texts.[2] Incorporating research on recently discovered manuscripts, scholarly studies provide a critical knowledge of the different translations and versions of the text, which is foundational for any inquiry. They also provide essential information on the background, meaning, and usage of key terms, phrases, motifs, and cultural forms. These critical investigations offer the necessary building blocks for further exploration of "apocalyptic" literature. Yet simply because of the way academic fields work, some aspects of these groundbreaking studies are also often embedded in the standard conceptual apparatus that, while serviceable for more traditional theological purposes, is problematic for investigation of these texts *in historical context*.

Specialists made an obvious but important distinction between the texts themselves and the theology or worldview they supposedly articulated and the cultural or social movement of which they were supposedly an expression as well. Taking a cue from one of the current interests in literary criticism, some specialists came up with a definition of a new macro-genre in Jewish literature that was supposedly followed by all "apocalypses."[3] This

---

* Because these texts are usually referred to as apocalyptic, I will continue to use the term, but in "scare quotes" because of the problematic connotations of the modern scholarly construct of apocalyptic/apocalypticism.

macro-genre, however, was a highly abstract definition intended to apply to texts from widely different times and circumstances. It was not at all clear how this macro-genre illuminated particular texts that are admittedly composites of other, smaller forms (other "genres"). More appropriate to the texts themselves was the distinction between "historical apocalypses" and "otherworldly journeys." Yet the latter label only serves to obscure the striking differences between the mystical texts of late antiquity, such as *2 Enoch* and *3 Baruch*, and the Book of Watchers, three to four centuries earlier. Defining the macro-genre was deemed important, however, because it supposedly involved "a new and distinctive worldview"—a phrase that brings us back to the theological interests of biblical scholars.[4]

The worldview that the more probing interpreters of the last few decades find expressed in the genre of "apocalypse" is no longer focused on the end of the world or a "cosmic catastrophe,"[5] but is still described in rather vague terms. Its key features are the belief in "supernatural beings" and in a heavenly world opposed to the earthly, and expectation of the final "eschatological" judgment. In perpetuation of the standard older construct of "apocalypticism," interpreters still characterize the relation of the heavenly or "supernatural" world to earthly life as a "fundamental antithesis" or "cosmic dualism."[6] The Second Temple texts, however, speak of a *correlation* between the heavens and the earth in a divinely created universe. Historical events in earthly life are influenced, and partly or largely explained, by what is happening among the "messengers," "holy ones," and "watchers," the heavenly forces involved in the divine governance of the universe. This, of course, is the point of the composers of these texts seeking and receiving heavenly "wisdom." The Second Temple texts portray God's judgment, moreover, not as an eschatological cosmic dissolution, leading to a state beyond historical earthly life, but as a resolution to a historical crisis that results in a renewal of Israel, on a renewed earth, under a restored heavenly governance (as we will see in the chapters below).

It is not clear how these two key elements constitute a "new and distinctive" worldview, since both are not only articulated in other kinds of texts but also stand in continuity with the Israelite prophetic tradition. The prophets understood historical events as the implementation of deliberations in God's heavenly council, and judgment as God's action against oppressive rulers and the restoration of the people on their land.

Scholars have generally agreed that these Judean texts are to be understood in social and historical context. Most of the attention to historical context has focused on the history of ideas, especially the impact of "Hellenism" (yet another abstract concept) on "Judaism."[7] Of course, a clash between the new Hellenistic political culture and the traditional Judean covenantal culture was clearly involved. And comparison with how texts from other ancient Near Eastern societies used the same or similar images or themes can surely lead to fuller appreciation of the distinctive message of particular Judean texts. But the Judean "apocalyptic" texts speak explicitly of imperial violence and exploitation as the historical circumstances they address. They give repeated indications that the imperial rulers were using violence to suppress the Judean way of life and replace it with Hellenistic forms that were inseparably political cultural. The texts themselves indicate that they are responding to particular historical circumstances of imperial domination. And that invites an investigation of imperial power relations, not just of a conflict of cultures.

In fact, this suggests a serious refocusing of investigation of particular texts, in two respects. First, instead of lumping Second Temple texts with all other texts that have previously been classified as "apocalyptic," we should more appropriately concentrate on the texts that are responding to the same definable historical circumstances. For the visions and interpretations in Daniel 7–12 and some of the early texts included in *1 Enoch*, for example, this happens to be the crisis of the Hellenizing reform and the violent invasion of Jerusalem by Antiochus Epiphanes in the early second century B.C.E. Second, instead of applying generic definitions and concepts derived from a synthesis of motifs and terms from an extremely wide range of literature, it would be more appropriate to investigate how the images and statements in each particular text may be related to *particular* historical circumstances.

In the last decade or so, interest has grown in the social origins and social context of these texts.[8] Discussion of social origins has focused on identifying a group that produced a given text or a movement that produced several texts. This discussion of texts and the supposed groups behind them, however, has not involved investigation into the political-economic-religious structure of Judean society, so shows little sense of the social location or contours of such "groups." The texts themselves speak of conflicts between the "righteous" and the "sinners," those who adhere to the covenant and those who abandon it, as well as between Judeans and their imperial rulers. Texts are not composed by a people collectively, but by particular persons with particular social locations, roles, and interests. In order to understand the conflicts indicated in the texts, it is necessary to investigate the conflicts inherent in the political-economic-religious structure of Judean society as well as the historical dynamics of imperial rule. The chapters below will focus on three interrelated lines of investigation.

The first step will be an elementary literary analysis of each text in its integrity (insofar as this is discernible from ancient versions and translations). Rather than looking for or applying the characteristic motifs, images, and themes of the standard concept of "apocalypticism," we will attend to each text's main plot, characters, climactic conflict, and the fundamental concerns and basic message of the text as a whole. With the integrity of each text in mind, we will also note how these texts are deeply rooted in Israelite and Judean traditions and build on and adapt them.

Second, understanding texts that are focused on imperial rule, resistance, and God's sovereignty over history requires at least an elementary sense of the historical situations they were addressing. This will further require moving past the previous reduction of the historical situation to a vague conflict between "Hellenism" and "Judaism," and moving beyond "religious persecution" to the concrete political-economic-religious conflicts between Judeans and their imperial overlords that, at points, escalated to periodic protest and resistance, military repression, and even to widespread revolt. Review of the historical situations addressed by the texts will be concentrated in chapters 2 and 6.

Third, understanding texts focused on imperial rule and resistance to it will also require critical attention to the political-economic-religious structure and dynamics within Judean society in the broader context of conflict with the dominant empires. Only in this way can we discern the social location and political conflicts that may have led the people who produced these texts into active resistance.

Who Produced These Texts?

The texts themselves indicate that they are the products of "sages," that is, wise scribes, the professional intellectuals and government advisers in the Judean temple-state. In the tales of Daniel 1–6, the legendary Daniel is characterized as "versed in every branch of wisdom, endowed with knowledge and insight, and competent to serve in the king's palace" (Dan 1:4). Those responsible for the visions and interpretations in Daniel 7–12 leave their footprints in the account of "the wise among the people" who instruct many, that is, sages and teachers (Dan 11:33; 12:10). The legendary figure to whom the various texts in the book of *1 Enoch* are attributed is "the scribe," "the righteous scribe," and "the scribe of truth" (*1 Enoch* 12:3-4). Like Daniel, he knows how to function in a royal court (13:4-7). He can read what is written on heavenly tablets, and he writes letters to communicate to his sons the wisdom he has acquired (81:1-6; 82:1-2; 92:1; 100:6). The recipients of his wisdom, moreover, are, like Enoch himself, wise scribes who have received wisdom and can read what he has written (5:8; 100:6; 104:11-13).

Even without these indications, it would be evident that scribes produced these "apocalyptic" texts. Although general literacy and the availability of books has been assumed in the fields of biblical studies and Jewish history, recent research has shown that in Judea, as in antiquity generally, literacy was limited largely to those specially trained to read and write, that is, the professional scribes.[9] Some scribes, of course, were involved in little more than copying documents or taking dictation (see the description of Baruch in Jer 36). At a higher level, scribes *(sopherim)* mastered the texts and lore of the society, hence were also "the wise" or "sages" *(hakhamim)*, that is, ancient "intellectuals." Insofar as the older generation of scribes trained the next generation of scribes, they were also teachers. With their mastery of legal, historical, prophetic, and other materials, professional scribes served as advisers to ancient rulers, administrators, and representatives in their regimes. As elsewhere in the ancient Near East, so in Judea, scribes were the only people who would have been capable of composing these texts and of making copies of them—so that they have survived, Daniel in the Bible and *1 Enoch* and the *Testament of Moses* outside it, to be (re)discovered in modern times.[10]

Recent studies have sketched out a far more complete and precise picture of scribal training, roles, and practices than previously available.[11] It is clearer, for example, that in composing new texts scribes drew heavily on and adapted the traditional forms that they cultivated as the professional guardians of the cultural repertoire. Barely begun, however, is investigation of the political-economic location and role of the intellectuals who produced all of the texts that professional intellectuals today are trained to analyze and interpret.

Caught in the Middle: The Social Location and Role of Scribes in Judea

The most familiar portrayal of scribes in the Second Temple period is found in the Synoptic Gospels: Matthew, Mark, and Luke. There the scribes work in tandem with the chief priests in command of the Temple, who in turn collaborate with the Roman governor (for example, Mark 14–15). The Gospels' picture of the scribes' close association with the priestly aristocracy at the end of the Second Temple period parallels Jesus Ben Sira's portrayal of the scribes' social location and role more than two centuries earlier. Ben Sira, moreover, offers a much fuller picture of the attitudes and orientation of scribes as well as their function in the political-economic-religious structure of the Judean temple-state.[12]

Ben Sira represents scribes as serving the priestly aristocracy, yet also as "caught in the middle" between those heads of the temple-state and the Judean people. "In the middle" does not mean that they were comparable to a "middle class" in modern Western society. Influential constructions by the last generation of scholars projected onto Second Temple Judea a rising middle class of merchants and entrepreneurs, analogous to those in early modern Europe. These scholars claimed that "Ben Sira frequently mentions merchants and their pursuit of profits, . . . reflect[ing] the new period which began in Judaea under Greek rule."[13] But Ben Sira mentions traders only at three points (26:29—27:2; 37:11; 42:5), where he articulates the negative view of merchants that was standard in traditional agrarian societies. His criticism of the stockpiling of "goods" *(chremata)* and wealth, and the use of other people's goods (11:10-19; 13:24-25; 21:8; 31:3-8) pertains not to merchants, but to the wealthy and powerful aristocracy. One key passage ("Whoever builds his house with other people's goods . . . ," 21:8) indicates more precisely how the wealthy and powerful in traditional agrarian society exploited the poor. That is, they took the produce of the peasants as tithes, taxes, or tribute, and when the poor were forced to borrow in order to survive, they charged interest on loans (which was prohibited by Israelite covenantal law; Exod 22:25). In Judea, those who took tithes, taxes, and tribute were not traders but the heads of the temple-state (and their imperial patrons, whom Ben Sira never mentions). The scribes, in Ben Sira's portrayal, stand in the middle between the aristocratic rulers of Judea and the rest of Judean society, the artisans and others who lived in Jerusalem and the peasants who lived in scores of villages.

Ben Sira uses a set of overlapping and synonymous Hebrew terms (which are translated by a similar set of overlapping and synonymous terms in the Greek translation known to us as the book of Sirach) in reference to the "chiefs, rulers, judges" who operate collectively at the head of the society. These "chiefs of the people" or "rulers of the assembly" (parallel in 30:27 [33:19] and 39:4) are the aristocracy among whom the wise scribes stand and speak (6:34; 7:14). In a more ceremonial passage, Ben Sira portrays what are evidently the same rulers and chiefs of the people presiding over sacrifices in the Temple. The high priest stands with "a garland of brothers around him . . . the sons of Aaron in their splendor holding out the Lord's offerings" (50:5-13). The Judean people are to serve "the Most High," who is understood as "the King of all." Since the high priests are their representatives to God, the people bring their offerings to the priests. And since, correspondingly, the high priests are God's representatives to the people, established by everlasting covenant, and given "authority and statutes and judgments" over the people, the people are to "honor the priest" with their tithes and offerings as the way of "fearing the Lord" (see esp. Sir 7:29-31; 35:1-12; 45:30-33; 50). From these statements by Ben Sira, it is clear that economics and politics are inseparable from and closely articulated with religion in the relationship between the priestly rulers and the people.

"Clueless about Apocalypticism"?

The scribes' principal role was to serve the "chiefs" (8:8), and it was for this responsibility that they acquired wisdom. In a lengthy, often-quoted reflection, Ben Sira focuses on the scribes' position and responsibilities in the larger political-economic-religious structure of society.

> The wisdom of the scribe depends on the opportunity of leisure;
>   only the one who is [not preoccupied with labor] can become wise.
> How can one who handles the plow become wise, . . .
>   who drives oxen . . . and whose talk is about bulls?
> He sets his heart on plowing furrows,
>   and he is careful about fodder for the heifers.
> So too is every artisan and . . . smith and . . . potter . . . .
> All these rely on their hands, . . .
> Without them no city can be inhabited,
>   and wherever they live they will not go hungry.
> Yet they are not sought out for the council of the people,
>   nor do any of them attain eminence in the public assembly.
> They do not sit on the seat of a court,
>   nor do they understand the decisions of courts;
> They cannot expound discipline or judgment,
>   and they are not found among the rulers.[13]
> How different the one who devotes himself
>   to the study of the law [Heb. *Torah*] of the Most High.
> He seeks out the wisdom of all the ancients, . . .
>   and is concerned with prophecies.
> He serves among the great ones [Gk. *megistanōn*]
>   and appears before the rulers [Gk. *hegoumenōn*];
> he travels in foreign lands
>   and learns what is good and evil in the human heart.
>   (Sir 38:25-35; 39:1, 4 abridged)

Free of the burdensome labors that preoccupy farmers in the countryside and artisans in the city, scribes acquired learning so that, "understanding decisions" and able to "expound judgments," they could serve as advisers to the ruling councils and courts and as members of embassies to foreign lands (38:24—39:11; cf. 4:9; 6:34; 7:14; 11:7-9; 15:5; 21:17; 34:12; 42:2).

In preparation for their responsibilities, they devoted themselves to intensive learning of the spectrum of Judean cultural traditions, including Torah, prophecies, and wisdom of various kinds. The cultivation of Torah, which had originated with Moses and was vested in the Aaronide priesthood (45:5, 17), had been delegated (perhaps gradually over the generations) to the learned scribes. Thus the scribes played a key role, as the ones who possessed knowledge of Judean laws and traditions, in advising and assisting the aristocracy in governing the society (8:8; 9:17—10:5; 38:32-33; 38:34—39:4).

In addition to the acquisition of knowledge of the Judean cultural tradition, scribal training entailed the formation of a certain kind of character and induction into a certain scribal ethos. The character requisite for service in the temple-state included rigorous personal discipline, obedience to higher authority, and patience with superiors reluctant to listen to legal traditions recalled and advice given. Scribes would thus have been conservative, both insofar as their role was to conserve traditional customs, laws, and cultural lore, and in the sense of obedience to authority.

Insofar as they served among the "great ones" and, for that purpose, were freed from physical labor, scribes must have been economically as well as politically dependent on patrons among the aristocracy. Not surprisingly, Ben Sira advises aspiring sages to bow low to their superiors (4:7). He also offers extensive advice on the proper deferential behavior for scribes when invited to dine with their patrons (13:9-11; 31:12-24). He warns about the potential dangers involved in dealing with the powerful (13:9). Particularly problematic would be "contending with the powerful" or "quarreling with the rich," lest the scribe "fall into their hands" (8:1-2, 14).

While their role was to serve the temple-state, however, learned scribes had a clear sense of their own authority independent of the authority derived from the priestly aristocracy. Their authority, certainly in their own minds, came from their wisdom and their faithful adherence to the Torah. Ben Sira repeatedly mentions the scribes' obedience to the covenantal laws. Ultimately their authority came directly from the Most High, the giver of the Torah and source of all wisdom. They also understood themselves as the successors of the prophets, as well as their interpreters, speaking by divine inspiration (39:1-3, 6). They thus had their own sense about how the temple-state should operate—that is, according to the sacred traditions of the people, of which they were the proper interpreters.

Ben Sira's instructional speeches to aspiring scribes show that at least some scribes, despite their vulnerability to their patrons, both criticized the aristocracy and saw it as part of their responsibility to mitigate the oppressions of the poor by the powerful. As evident in Ben Sira's reflection quoted just above, learned scribes saw themselves as a significant cut above farmers and artisans, both politically and culturally. People who worked with their hands did not enjoy the leisure necessary to acquire wisdom and counsel rulers (38:24-34). Yet Ben Sira inculcates in his scribal protégés a sympathy for the poor and a concern for their plight. He urges them to allay the exploitation of the poor by the wealthy and powerful. "Stretch out your hand to the poor" with almsgiving, and do not "cheat the poor" or "reject the supplicant" (29:1-2, 8-12, 14-15). For one who advises scribes to "watch their back" when around their patrons, Ben Sira has some cutting criticism of those who take advantage of the desperate situation of the poor to enhance their own wealth.

> A rich person will exploit you if you can be of use to him,
>   but if you are in need he will abandon you . . .
> What peace is there between a hyena and a dog?
>   And what peace between the rich and the poor?
> Wild asses in the wilderness are the prey of lions;
>   Likewise the poor are feeding grounds for the rich. (13:3-4, 18-19)

Couched in the style of wise observations about life, these lines are an indictment of the perpetual economic exploitation inherent in a system in which the peasant producers were the "prey" of the powerful.

The scribes' role with regard to tithes and offerings are a telling illustration of their position in the middle between priestly aristocracy and people. Tithes and offerings were the revenues that supported the Temple and priesthood and, indirectly, the scribes, as well as expressions of gratitude to God. One of the scribes' responsibilities as representatives of the temple-state was to exhort the people to render up tithes and offerings. In a lengthy discussion of sacrifices and offerings (35:1-26), however, Ben Sira includes a declaration that the Most High will heed the supplication and appeal of the oppressed and "break the scepters of the unrighteous." From the learned scribe's viewpoint, in commitment to covenantal Torah, commandment-keeping and almsgiving are the equivalents of temple sacrifices. In another exhortation to make sacrifices and offerings, Ben Sira includes an ominous warning to the "rulers" about exploiting the poor and humble.

> If one sacrifices ill-gotten goods, the offering is blemished . . .
> Like one who kills a son before his fathers' eyes
>   is the person who offers a sacrifice from the property of the poor . . .
> To take away a neighbor's living is to commit murder;
>   to deprive an employee of wages is to shed blood. (34:21-27)

The sharpness of this criticism is all the more striking since it comes from a well-established Jerusalem scribe who composed the elaborate praise of the ancestral officeholders that provides a legitimating ideology for the high priesthood, and in particular the incumbent Oniad high-priestly dynasty (Sir 44–50).

The book of Ben Sira's wisdom, one of the only other books contemporary with the first "apocalyptic" literature such as Daniel and *1 Enoch*, thus portrays scribes as "in the middle" in two interrelated senses. As advisers and representatives in the service of the temple-state, they stood in between the priestly aristocracy and the people whose tithes and offerings supported it. As professional guardians of the sacred Judean cultural tradition, they developed a personal commitment to covenantal commandments and a sense of their own authority under the Most High, independent of the high priesthood. This left them "caught in the middle," in conflict between their loyalty to the aristocracy on whom they were economically dependent and their commitment to the covenant commandments.

The Conflicts Inherent in Imperial Rule

Ben Sira's portrayal of Judean society and the role of the scribes conveniently leaves unmentioned the most important factor of all. In his long hymn of praise of the glorious Israelite-Judean line of officeholders from Moses to Simon (Sir 44–50), he grounds the current Oniad high priesthood that he himself served. The Judean temple-state, however, was not autonomous, not sovereign over its own affairs. Indeed, the original establishment of the temple-state had been sponsored by the Persian Empire. The Temple and the high priesthood were, in effect, imperial instruments to maintain order and collect revenues in Judea. After Alexander the Great's conquest of the Persian Empire, Judea and other territories came under the Hellenistic empires that brought new Greek political and cultural forms to the ancient Near East. Yet they retained the temple-state as the local institution by which they controlled and gathered revenues from Judea.

The subordination of the Judean temple-state to imperial rule set up several major conflicts that involved Judean scribes directly or indirectly. First was the fundamental conflict between the ideal of God as the ruler of the Judean people, and the reality of imperial rule. As professional custodians of Israelite cultural tradition, scribes were steeped in the conviction that God was Lord not only of Israel but of all peoples. The prophets had interpreted major international events in terms of God using imperial kings for divine purposes, such as punishing Judean kings for violation of covenantal principles or other kings for their inhumane violence against conquered peoples. The "second" Isaiah (chs. 40–55) welcomed the Persian king Cyrus's defeat of the Babylonian Empire, anticipating that it would mean the restoration of the previously exiled Jerusalem elite to their positions of power in Jerusalem. Later, however, the restored Judeans, who had adopted a Deuteronomic understanding that the previous kings, officers, and priests had broken the covenant, lamented that they were "slaves in the land" that God had given to their ancestors, as its "rich yield" of "fruit and good gifts" were going "to the kings who have power over [their] bodies and livestock" (Neh 9:36-37). There was an inherent contradiction and conflict between God's being sovereign over history and the claims to sovereignty by imperial kings. And there was always at least the possibility that imperial violence and exploitation could no longer be explained as God's just punishment, when the people were suffering in spite of their rigorous adherence to the covenant commandments.

Second, given the conflict just discussed, the subjugation of the temple-state to imperial rule compounded the conflict between the scribes and the priestly aristocracy whom they served and on whom they were dependent. The heads of the temple-state were vulnerable to influence and pressures from the imperial rulers on whose approval their positions depended. The aristocracy's collaboration with imperial policies and practices could and did move in directions that compromised or violated the covenantal Torah of which Judean scribes were the committed guardians. Although accommodated to Persian rule, the legal collections and historical traditions later incorporated into what we now know as the books of the Pentateuch became the basis of the traditional Judean way of life to which scribes were personally as well as professionally committed.[14] A change of empire, imperial policy, and/or dominant imperial culture, however, could set up serious potential conflict with what had become the sacred traditions of Judean life to which the scribes were personally committed, which is exactly what happened under the Hellenistic empires.

Third, subjection of the temple-state to imperial rule set up potential conflicts between rival factions within the aristocracy. The books of Ezra and Nehemiah attest to conflicts between priestly and other factions under Persian rule, some of which Nehemiah mediated as the governor, with troops to bolster his authority. As we shall see in chapter 1, the Ptolemaic practice of collecting the imperial tribute led to power struggles between aristocratic factions in Jerusalem. The struggle between the Ptolemaic and Seleucid Empires over control of Syria-Palestine set up a situation in which rival factions in the Jerusalem aristocracy could make alliances with one or another imperial regime. Scribes who had no independent economic base would be tempted to associate with one or another rival faction among the aristocracy, leading to rival scribal circles that paralleled the aristocratic factions. Thus, while the most fundamental divide in Second Temple Judea was between the rulers and ruled, more complex conflicts developed in the relations between imperial rulers, rival factions in the priestly aristocracy, and various circles of scribes.

The Cultural Repertoire of Judean Scribes

Insofar as Judean scribes were the professional intellectuals who cultivated Judean cultural tradition, they had a rich repertoire from which to draw in the articulation of their opposition to imperial rule.[15] The standard correlation of literature with social roles in biblical studies may have prevented us from recognizing the breadth of the cultural repertoire that Judean scribes cultivated. The books of the Hebrew Bible have traditionally been grouped into Torah (Law), the Prophets, and the Writings. Also traditional has been the division of "offices" in the Bible into priest, prophet, and king. With recent recognition of the importance of learned scribes, they have been added to the list. This division of offices is then matched up with the division of literature: priests cultivated law codes, prophets composed prophetic oracles, and wise scribes produced the collections of wisdom that comprise most of the Writings. This scheme, however, does not correspond with the "division of labor" in Second Temple Judea, as evident in Sirach and other sources. Prophetic oracles had indeed been composed and delivered by prophets. But scribes, as the professionals trained in writing and reading, were the ones who compiled collections of prophecies as well as books of Torah, and continued to develop them.

Ben Sira is clear that scribes devoted their leisure to learning not only the "wisdom of all the ancients," but also "the torah of the Most High" and "prophecies" (38:33—39:4). They could then, on the basis of their knowledge of legal traditions and prophecies, "expound discipline and judgment" in public assembly before the rulers. The wisdom that scribes cultivated, moreover, had several traditional forms, as Ben Sira indicates in other passages. What is usually understood by "wisdom" in biblical studies is proverbial wisdom (mentioned in 39:1-3), which takes the form of speeches of *instructional wisdom* in Proverbs 1–9 and most of Sirach. But scribes such as Ben Sira also cultivated *cosmological wisdom* and *reflection on wisdom* (several psalms of which are included in Sirach), and *mantic wisdom* (predictive, often hidden wisdom, about which Ben Sira himself was uneasy).[16] Scribes commanded the full spectrum of this cultural repertoire, ready for use in their political-religious role in the temple-state. They could thus draw upon the forms and themes of all segments of this repertoire in their opposition to imperial domination and struggles to understand the wisdom of God in a history that seemed to have run amok. We should not imagine, moreover, that the cultural repertoire they had mastered consisted solely of texts written on scrolls. Recent studies of scribal practice in Judea and other societies of the ancient Near East have shown that scribes learned texts by recitation, so that they were "written on the tablets of their hearts." They cultivated authoritative texts in their memory. In addition the Judean cultural repertoire also included oral-traditional legal, legendary, historical, and prophetic materials that were not included in texts (also) written on scrolls.

It should be evident by now, finally, that much of the Judean cultural repertoire consisted of material that was political as well as religious, just as the role of scribes in the temple-state was political as well as religious. The prophetic oracles of Isaiah, Micah, and Jeremiah condemned political-economic exploitation by rulers and their officers. Oracles by Malachi and Haggai supported the rebuilding of the Temple and the priestly faction in charge. Scrolls of Torah were written and recited publicly in support of the consolidation of power by Josiah and, later, by Ezra. Scribes such as Ben Sira thus stood in a long tradition of texts that were fully political in their purposes.

Outline of the Book

This book focuses mainly on the texts classified as "apocalyptic" that were composed in Judea in the second half of the Second Temple period, between the third century B.C.E. and the Roman destruction of Jerusalem and the Temple in 70 C.E. The chapters in part 1 deal with the texts that addressed the escalating crisis under Hellenistic imperial rule, climaxing with resistance to the invasion of Jerusalem by Antiochus Epiphanes. Chapter 1 reviews the historical conflicts and events to which these texts respond. Chapter 2 focuses on the tales in Daniel 1–6 that, while not "apocalypses," portray Judean scribes resisting the arrogant pretentions of ancient emperors. Chapter 3 examines the Book of Watchers, one of the earliest texts subsequently included in *1 Enoch* (chs. 1–36) and usually considered the first "apocalyptic" text. Chapters 4 and 5 investigate the surveys of history leading up to the crisis of the Hellenizing reform and the invasion of Antiochus Epiphanes, the classic cases of "historical apocalypses": the Animal Vision (*1 Enoch* 85–90) and the ten-week summary of history (*1 Enoch* 93:1-10 with 91:11-17), along with the *Testament of Moses* (chapter 4 below), and the visions and interpretations in Daniel 7–12 (ch. 5 below).

The chapters in part 2 discuss "apocalyptic" texts that oppose Roman imperial rule but also, for comparative purposes, other forms of opposition to Roman rule, in other kinds of literature (psalms) and in organized protests by scribal circles. Chapter 6 provides a summary of key events in the historical context, especially the Maccabean Revolt against Antiochus Epiphanes, the Roman conquest of Judea, the rule of the Roman client-king Herod, and direct Roman rule in Judea. The examination of the Qumran community that left the Dead Sea Scrolls and its key texts in chapter 7 is included because, while the Qumranites produced no "apocalypse," they are often considered an "apocalyptic" community and they anticipated fighting against the Romans. Chapter 8 on the *Psalms of Solomon* (often thought of as "apocalyptic") is another form of literature used to express opposition to Roman rule. Chapter 9 focuses on the two known late Second Temple Judean "apocalyptic" texts: the Parables of Enoch (*1 Enoch* 37–71), announcing God's judgment of the (Roman) "kings and mighty," and an updating of the *Testament of Moses*, recasting it as resistance to Roman rule. Chapter 10, on the scribes and teachers who carried out protests against Herod, the Roman tribute, and the high-priestly collaborators with Roman rule, shows how common scribal resistance to Roman rule became in late Second Temple times, and offers a comparison to textual resistance. The conclusion pulls together some of the implications of the exploration of "apocalyptic" texts as statements of opposition to imperial rule.

Part I

Scribal Resistance to Hellenistic Imperial Rule

Maccabean and Hasmonean Palestine

Chapter 1

The Escalating Crisis in Judea under Hellenistic Rule

The Judean texts classified as "apocalyptic" are generally understood as responses to crises. In the standard interpretation, the crisis with which Daniel 7–12, some of the *"Enoch"* texts, and the *Testament of Moses* were struggling is conceptualized as "religious persecution." More critical historical investigation into Hellenistic imperial culture, however, is discovering that what modern biblical scholars have termed religious persecution was virtually nonexistent and cannot explain how or why a Hellenistic emperor, even the notorious Antiochus IV Epiphanes, would have mounted such a program against "the Jews."

Obviously, the crisis that evoked these texts was more complex than the standard interpretation has allowed, and requires more detailed investigation and conceptualization. Not only do particular historical events emerge out of previous historical events, but all events in antiquity are determined by political, economic, and religious structures and dynamics. Particular historical conflicts are often rooted in what are almost inherent structural conflicts. It is clear, even from the limited sources for the history of Second Temple Judea, that Judea was not just a place where a religion, "Judaism," was practiced, and was not even an independent temple-state. Judean society was subject to, indeed a subordinate unit of, a succession of empires. Events and conflicts seemingly internal to Judean society were related to, and even determined by, imperial policy and initiatives. Careful attention to such complex historical factors reveals that the scribal circles who produced "apocalyptic" texts were responding to an escalating conflict between rival factions in the ruling Jerusalem aristocracy that were closely related to rival Hellenistic empires.[1]

Rival Hellenistic Empires

After Alexander the Great completed his rapid conquest of the Persian imperial armies in the 330s B.C.E., his successors *(diadochoi)* divided up the territories into what became rival empires. Judeans had been ruled for over two centuries by the relatively stable Persian Empire. But Judea now lay in the contested frontier area between the Ptolemies, who ruled Egypt and initially Palestine as well, and the Seleucids, who ruled Syria. These two imperial regimes fought five major wars for control of the contested area in the course of the third century B.C.E.[2] In the course of these prolonged wars, imperial armies moved back and forth through the area, with the resultant destruction of crops, towns, and people in their wake. Daniel 11:5-9 may attest to a scribal memory of the uncertainty over which empire would prevail in the third of these wars (246–241 B.C.E.). In the fourth war (221–219), the Seleucid emperor Antiochus III did take control of some areas of western Syria for a few years. The reference in Daniel 11:10-12 indicates that Judean scribes were still thinking about this conflict over two generations later. In the fifth war (201–200), Antiochus III finally gained control of Palestine, thus bringing Judea under Seleucid rule.

The obvious impact of these prolonged wars on affairs in Judea was compounded by periodic conflicts between rivals for the throne within each empire, as well as regular rebellions of subject peoples, especially against the Seleucid regime. As the Seleucids took control over Judea, moreover, the Romans began intervening more actively in the inter-imperial politics of the eastern Mediterranean. And in what became a central factor in the crisis in Judea, the chronic warfare and extortion by the Romans left the imperial regimes, particularly the Seleucids, desperate for funds.

The Emergence of Rival Aristocratic Factions under the Ptolemies

The priestly aristocracy, headed by a high priest, that had consolidated its power in Judea under the Persian Empire continued under the Hellenistic empires. The outside observer Hecataeus provides a sketch of the "constitution" *(politeia)* of the Judeans at the beginning of the Ptolemaic period.[3]

> [Having] established the Temple that they hold in chief veneration . . . [Moses] drew up their laws and ordered their political institutions. . . . He picked out the men of most refinement and with the greatest ability to head the entire people, and appointed them priests . . . [and] judges in all major disputes, and entrusted to them the guardianship of the laws and customs. For this reason the Judeans never have a king, and representation *(prostasia)* of the people is regularly vested in whichever priest is regarded as superior to his colleagues

in wisdom and virtue, . . . the high priest, who in their assemblies and other gatherings announces what is ordained. (Hecataeus, in Diodorus Siculus, *Bibliotheca Historica* 40.3.3-6)

This sketch is similar to Ben Sira's portrayal of the high priest surrounded by the priestly aristocracy in ceremonial assembly at the end of the Ptolemaic period (Sir 50). While the temple-state hardly appears to have been a priestly monarchy under the Ptolemies,[4] the high priest appears to have stood preeminently at the center of a priestly aristocracy.

While the Ptolemies set a military governor over the larger area of Phoenicia and western Syria, they did not continue the Persian practice of assigning a governor to supervise affairs in Judea.[5] Yet while they let the high priesthood run affairs in Judea, there is no evidence that the Ptolemies appointed or formally approved the high priesthood as head of the temple-state to rule Judea. This left the high priesthood vulnerable to the maneuvers of local magnates, just as it stood vulnerable to actions by the imperial regime affecting matters in Judea, as evident from the Judean historian Josephus and from the Zenon papyri discovered in Egypt.

While the Ptolemaic regime attempted to establish a centralized political economy in Egypt, it adapted to local circumstances in Syria-Palestine. To control upland areas, the Ptolemies used military colonies and local "sheikhs" such as Tobiah, in Ammon across the Jordan River. This was presumably the latest head of the Tobiah family that had intermarried with the high-priestly family in Persian times (Neh 2:10, 19; 6:1-9; 13:4-5). According to certain Zenon papyri, Tobiah sent gifts of rare animals, young slaves, and a eunuch to Ptolemy Philadelphus, beginning one letter with "Many thanks to the gods."[6] Clearly this wealthy sheikh had learned how to play the game of Hellenistic imperial politics, including the importance of knowing Greek language and culture. In its drive to maximize its revenues from its subject peoples as well, the Ptolemaic regime made special arrangements through ambitious local power-holders, as evident in the highly romanticized "Tobiad romance" that Josephus reproduces in his account of Judea under the Ptolemies (*Ant.* 12.156–222, 228–36).[7] The source is evidently most credible on the tax-farming practices of the Ptolemaic regime (*Ant.* 12:168–69, 177–78, 181–83), which are confirmed by other evidence.[8]

Some time in the third quarter of the third century B.C.E., Joseph, son of Tobiah by a sister of the high priest Onias and thus already a player in Jerusalem politics, ingratiated himself at the Ptolemaic court with lavish gifts. When the time came for "all the chief men and magistrates of the cities of Syria and Phoenicia to bid for the tax-farming rights which the king used to sell every year to the wealthy men in each city," Joseph outbid them all. Having offered to double the regime's revenue, he was granted the tax-farming rights to all of Syria. In Judea, this meant that he displaced the high priest (his uncle Onias) as the "representative" of the Judeans to the Ptolemies with regard to the imperial revenues. He used his expanding wealth to consolidate his power in Judea and beyond, continuing his lavish gifts to the imperial court. Acutely aware of the importance of Hellenistic culture under the "Greek" Empire, he had all of his sons tutored by the best-known teachers of the day.

The career of Joseph dramatizes both the loss of power by the high priestly office in the Judean temple-state and the rise to power of other ambitious members of the Jerusalem aristocracy. In displacing the high priest as the representative of the Judeans who sent up the tribute, Joseph significantly reduced the high priesthood's political and economic power within Judea, and the Ptolemies' reason to support the office. Collection of the imperial tribute by the Tobiad Joseph, and no longer through the high priesthood, now competed with the Temple's and priesthood's demands for tithes and offerings. Both in Jerusalem and in his relation with the imperial regime, Joseph came to rival the power of the high priest. More ominously, Joseph's machinations in the Hellenistic imperial court opened the way for further maneuvering by rival factions that developed in the Jerusalem aristocracy just at the time when the Seleucid regime mounted another bid to take control of the area.

In judgments far more romantic than the "Tobiad romance," previous interpreters have greeted Joseph as a paradigm of the "young enterprising forces [that] endeavored to break through the constraints of their native land,"[9] and yet also as a powerful Judean who was "able to protect his countrymen from excessive exploitation."[10] But the only way that Joseph could have expanded the Ptolemaic regime's revenues from the districts of Syria was to have extracted additional amounts from the peasants, whose produce supported both the temple-state and the imperial regime. Joseph's new wealth and lifestyle, moreover, can only have raised the horizons of other Jerusalem aristocrats, who in turn sought enhanced revenues to fund a more lavish and cosmopolitan lifestyle. And the only source from which they could generate the desired increase was the need of peasants to obtain loans to meet Joseph's higher demands for taxes. The added pressures on the peasantry can only have exacerbated indebtedness and accelerated loss of land. The situation would likely have been similar to the Judean aristocracy's exploitation of the peasants that Nehemiah had attempted to check over two centuries earlier (Neh 5:1-13).

It is not difficult to imagine the impact of the factional rivalry in the aristocracy on scribes who served the temple-state. Not only was it unclear who would be calling the shots in the aristocracy for whom they worked, but the scribes may have been caught in a conflict between their service to the aristocrats on whom they were economically dependent and their loyalty to the covenantal law of which they were the professional interpreters.

Aristocratic Factions and the Seleucid Takeover

Conflict between factions in the aristocracy increased just before the Seleucid regime took control of Judea, and intensified afterward. There was a clear relationship between the conflict between the rival imperial regimes and the conflict among aristocratic factions for control in Jerusalem. A prominent previous construction of Second Temple Judean history held that long before the Hellenizing reform in 175 B.C.E., the Jerusalem aristocracy was divided between a Hellenizing party that was pro-Seleucid and a more traditionalist party that remained pro-Ptolemaic.[11] Even the fragmentary sources, however, indicate that matters were not so simple. There may well have been more than two factions in the aristocracy; none is identifiably more pro-Hellenistic than another, and their loyalty to one imperial regime or another was determined by shifting power politics at both the imperial and local levels.

According to the "Tobiad romance" included in Josephus's historical account, Joseph's youngest son (by a different mother from the other seven sons) picked up where his father left off in skillfully manipulating the imperial regime to his own advantage (*Ant.* 12.186–224, 228–36). Through his father's "finance agent" *(oikonomos)* at the imperial court in Alexandria, Hyrcanus diverted large amounts of the funds his father was sending to the imperial treasury to pay for lavish gifts to the king and his high-ranking advisers, thus gaining favor for himself at court. Upon his return to Jerusalem, however, his brothers attacked him, each side commanding gangs of armed men. Forced to withdraw from Jerusalem politics, Hyrcanus retreated to the traditional family stronghold across the Jordan, where he gathered tribute from "the barbarians," presumably as agent of the Ptolemies. Josephus writes of further "factional conflict" between Hyrcanus and the older Tobiad brothers, who were joined by the high priest Simon, son of Onias. This may indicate that some of the older brothers held important positions in the administration of the temple-state.

In the last decades of the Ptolemaic control of Jerusalem, the Tobiads were thus divided, with the Oniad high priest on one side. There is nothing to indicate that one side was more ideologically "Hellenistic" than the other. All of the Tobiads had received tutoring in Greek *paideia*. Their conflict was more likely a simple struggle for power in Jerusalem. And there may well have been other factions within the aristocracy. Hyrcanus's favor at the court in Alexandria left his rivals little room to maneuver with the Ptolemies, and so long as the latter held control of Palestine, too blatant an overture to the Seleucids would have been ill-advised.

The situation changed with the new Seleucid move to take control of the area in 201 B.C.E. In response to the "rumors of war," some of the aristocracy, perhaps the majority (but not necessarily the Tobiad brothers and Onias), evidently cast their lot with the advancing Seleucids, while others (evidently more than just Hyrcanus) remained pro-Ptolemaic. The key indicator that a move toward the Seleucids was advisable was the defection to the Seleucids of Ptolemy, successor to his father Thraseus as the Ptolemaic governor of Phoenicia and Syria. Leading figures in Jerusalem, like other local rulers, would have had contacts with him and known which direction the imperial wind was blowing.[12] Josephus's account of the war indicates that those in control in Jerusalem decided to support the Seleucids. When a Ptolemaic army under Scopas went to secure control of Jerusalem, they had to defeat the force that was resisting them and install a garrison (*Ant.* 12.132–33, 135). When the now Seleucid governor Ptolemy came to expel the Ptolemaic garrison in Jerusalem after Antiochus III's victory over the Ptolemaic army at Panion, "the Judeans of their own will went over to him and admitted him to their city and made abundant provision for his entire army and his elephants; and they readily joined his forces in besieging the garrison left by Scopas" (*Ant.* 12.133). The only "Judeans" who could have supplied provisions for a whole army would have been the now pro-Seleucid faction of the Jerusalem aristocracy.

Whether in gratitude for the aristocrats' support or as a more general arrangement, Antiochus went back to what had been the Persian policy of supporting the temple-state as the instrument of imperial control and taxation of Judea. In a passage that critics deem authentic, in the main,[13] Josephus reproduces Antiochus III's decree to his governor regarding the Judean temple-state.

> Inasmuch as the Judeans . . . gave us a splendid reception and met us with their council *(gerousia)* and furnished an abundance of provisions . . . and helped us to expel the Egyptian garrison in the citadel, . . . we requite them for these acts and we restore their city which has been destroyed by the ravages of war. . . . We have decided, on account of their piety, to furnish them for their sacrifices an allowance of sacrificial animals [etc.]. . . . It is my will that . . . work on the Temple be completed. . . . The timber shall be brought from Lebanon . . . and other materials needed for restoration. . . . And all members of the people *(ethnos)* shall be governed according to their ancestral laws, and the council *(gerousia)*, priests, the scribes of the Temple and the temple-singers shall be relieved from the

poll-tax and crown-tax and the salt-tax which they pay. And . . . the inhabitants of the city . . . we shall also relieve from the third part of their tribute, so that their losses may be made good. (Josephus, *Ant.* 12.138–44)

Antiochus thus placed the temple-state in charge of Judea and the gerousia in charge of the temple-state. In Hellenistic political arrangements, the term gerousia referred to the elders or aristocracy of a city or people. Insofar as "the priests, the temple-scribes, and the temple-singers" were all clearly staff working in the Temple, the gerousia must refer to the officers who headed the temple-state. Antiochus makes a significant change from the Ptolemies' practice of assigning a powerful figure other than the high priest to collect the imperial revenues. The Seleucids thus set the Jerusalem gerousia in charge of collecting the tribute from the Judean peasantry. Besides granting them a third of the revenue for rebuilding the city, they gave tax relief (to enable the temple-state to recover) to the temple functionaries (who surely comprised most of the "inhabitants" of Jerusalem), with the Judean peasants expected to render up tribute as usual.

Conspicuous by his absence in Antiochus's decree is the high priest. This may be merely an accident, or perhaps Simon II, son of Onias II, had been among the leaders of the faction that Scopas had deported to Egypt just before Antiochus marched up to Jerusalem. Ben Sira, on the other hand, praises Simon for rebuilding the Temple and city fortifications as he stands at the head of his brothers, "the sons of Aaron," in ceremonial formation in the Temple (Sir 50:1-4). So the Seleucids had evidently placed Judea under the control of the priestly aristocracy headed by the high priest. Yet not only did some of the older factions continue, but new configurations and alliances may have emerged. Prominent priestly aristocrats had not only acquired a desire to participate in the broader Hellenistic imperial culture, but they had learned how to maneuver in imperial politics for position and power. And since the Temple headed the Judean economy, and the priestly aristocracy had charge of both temple and imperial revenues in Judea, and the Seleucid regime was chronically in need of more revenues, factional maneuvering focused on control of the revenue.

In a crucial step that prepared the way for more ominous dealings, the "temple-captain" *(prostates tou hierou)* Simon, of the priestly family of Bilgah (Neh 12:5, 18),[14] invited the Seleucids to expropriate more funds from the temple treasury, although it is not clear what he and those he represented wanted in return (2 Macc 3:4-12). The conflict involved some violence, including some "murders." In return for his defense of the sacred funds, however, the high priest Onias III, son of Simon II, was retained at the imperial court (2 Macc 4:1-7). One faction could maneuver the high priest who belonged to another faction into imperial house arrest, and the imperial regime was now intervening far more directly in the affairs of the temple-state.

Hellenizing Reform and Traditionalist Resistance

In what was probably the most important and brazen step escalating the simmering conflicts in Jerusalem into major crisis, a large faction of the aristocracy took the accession to power of Antiochus IV Epiphanes in 175 B.C.E. as an occasion to implement a Hellenizing "reform." The new emperor was desperate for funds. Jason, the brother of Onias III, heading a sizable party that included some Tobiads, secured appointment as high priest by promising an increase in tribute, from 300 to 360 talents, along with an additional 80 talents. Rivals could now obtain the high priesthood by bidding up the tribute from Judea. Even more troubling to scribal circles as well as to the ordinary priests and Levites, however, was the new "constitution" that Jason and his allies obtained in return for additional funds.[15]

> In addition to this he promised to pay one hundred fifty more if permission were given to establish by his authority a gymnasium and a body of youth *(ephebeion)* for [the city], and to enroll the Jerusalemites as citizens of Antioch. When the emperor assented and Jason came to office, he at once shifted his compatriots over to the Greek way of life *(pros tōn Hellēnikōn charaktēra)*. He set aside the existing royal concessions to the Judeans . . . and he dissolved the laws of the constitution *(tas nomimous politeias)* and set up new customs contrary to the laws. He took delight in establishing a gymnasium right under the citadel, and he had the noblest of the young men *(tōn ephebōn)* exercise with the broad-brimmed felt [Greek] hat. (2 Macc 4:9-12)

Judeans committed to the sacred ancestral traditions would have been horrified that the dominant priestly elite had so brazenly "abandoned the holy covenant" for the alien customs of the imperial political culture, as indicated by the accounts in both 1 Maccabees (1:11–15) and 2 Maccabees (4:9–17). This move, headed by Jason, has been interpreted as a *religious* reform or a change in culture, a shift from "Judaism" to "Hellenism."[16] There were indeed religious aspects of it, such as the neglect of the sacrifices, and the forms instituted were indeed from Hellenistic culture. But Jason's project was fully political. Hellenistic political culture was an imperial continuation of earlier forms of the Greek city-states. The *gymnasion* was the (mainly athletic) training facility for young men preparing to become citizens, that is, members of the corporation of citizens that constituted the *polis*. The *ephebion* was the corresponding group of young men in training for citizenship.[17] The "ancestral laws" *(patrioi nomoi)* or "constitution" *(politeia)* were the regulations

The Escalating Crisis in Judea under Hellenistic Rule

that governed these and other institutions of the city-state (Herodotus 2:91; Diodorus Siculus 1.81.7; Xenephon, *Cyropaideia* 1.2.2–15).

By instituting the new training system for citizens, Jason and company were changing the *politeia* or constitution of Judea, its "constitutive" stamp *(charaktera)*. The account in 2 Maccabees is instructive on this point: Jason had dissolved the ancestral laws of the Judean people and substituted a new way of life and an imperially recognized legal basis for the city corporation thus founded, Antioch (named presumably after its official "founder," Antiochus IV). Yet while the "reformers" may have "neglected" the sacrifices, they did not abandon the Temple and its sacrifices and did not suppress observance of Judean laws and customs and the traditional way of life of the people. Like other native elites in the Hellenistic empires, they were interested in transforming the political culture of their city. Such indigenous aristocracies established new city institutions following Greek patterns and gave Greek names to local gods and temples in dozens of "new" Hellenistic cities founded under the Hellenistic empires.[18] The subject peoples living on the land that became the territory belonging to the city effectively lost certain traditional "rights" but were otherwise allowed to continue their customary way of life. The Hellenizing re-forming of Jerusalem in 175 was similar.

Yet the change of constitution had ominous implications for the priests, Levites, and scribes. Political rights as well as political power were now monopolized by the elite, "enrolled" as citizens of "Antioch." Others, including presumably other priestly aristocrats as well as regular priests and scribes, were now mere residents of the city.[19] They were in effect "demoted," and their professional service in the altar or as scribes was relativized. And a cultural gulf, as well as an economic gap, widened between those who participated in the "reform" and others. What now was to be the role of the scribes who, like their fathers and grandfathers before them, had gone through rigorous learning of the Judean cultural repertoire of Torah, Prophets, and various kinds of wisdom to prepare for their service in the temple-state? At least some of them, like Ben Sira, had been critical—within the sequestered sites of scribal instruction, of course—of their aristocratic patrons for exploiting the poor. Now, however, it was unclear that there was any role for the custodians of ancestral traditions that no longer mattered to the new Hellenistic city-state and its elite citizens. In effect, their positions had been eliminated and their economic support from the aristocrats thrown into question. It would not be surprising if some circles of scribes reacted with at least some sort of resistance to the Hellenizing reform, as hinted in some of the texts to be examined, especially "Enoch's" Animal Vision.

The powerful Hellenizing faction in "Antioch," however, now had a more secure base from which they could participate in the dominant imperial culture. Shortly after the change of constitutions, Jason sent a delegation to the quadrennial games in Tyre, presided over by Antiochus (2 Macc 4:18-20). "Antioch" then staged a grand celebration to welcome Antiochus to the city (4:21-22).

Imperial Suppression, Scribal Resistance, and Popular Revolt

Conflict within the reforming faction led to an escalating series of events, climaxing in Antiochus's invasion of Jerusalem and his violent repression of resistance by Judeans who insisted on their traditional way of life. Three years into the reform and the high priesthood of Jason, Menelaus, brother of the temple captain Simon (of the Bilgah priestly family), in a delivery of tribute to Antiochus, obtained the high priestly office for himself in return for raising the tribute by another 300 talents (2 Macc 4:23-24). The high priesthood was thus removed from the Oniad lineage in which it had been hereditary for generations. The dominant reforming faction in the aristocracy was thus split, as Jason fled across the Jordan, and Menelaus plundered the Temple treasury and continued to wriggle his way around charges by other Jerusalem aristocrats by bribing imperial officials (4:30-50).

Affairs in Jerusalem now rapidly escalated into armed conflict. Despite differences in detail, the accounts in the principal sources agree on a basic outline of events (1 Macc 1:16-23; 2 Macc 5–7; Josephus, *Ant.* 12.242–56).[20] The sequence of events becomes clearer once it is recognized that Antiochus must have invaded Egypt twice. He evidently intervened successfully in Egypt late in 170 (1 Macc 1:16-24). Coming through Jerusalem on his way back, he looted the Temple in an invasion that did not involve any significant violent attack or resistance (Dan 11:28). In the spring of 168, he invaded Egypt again, but this time was checked by Romans and withdrew. Probably during Antiochus's disastrous confrontation with the Romans in Egypt (had there been a rumor that Antiochus had been killed?), Jason returned to Jerusalem at the head of a sizable force and forced Menelaus and his followers to take refuge in the fortress (2 Macc 5:1–7). Perhaps taking Jason's successful seizure of Jerusalem as a revolt, Antiochus then sent a large military force, under the command of Apollonius, to suppress the revolt and restore Jerusalem to the control of the highly cooperative Menelaus.

But matters were clearly out of control in Jerusalem and Judea. The now armed conflict between the two factions of the Hellenizing aristocrats is what appears in the books of the Maccabees and Josephus. What does not appear, except perhaps for hints here and there, but is strongly suggested in some of the texts that will be examined in the chapters below, is that other Judeans were also engaged in resistance of some form. It must have appeared to Antiochus that, since Menelaus and his faction could not hold Jerusalem by themselves, he needed to send in occupying troops to establish a military colony in the city. The military settlers, probably from Syria or Asia Minor, would have brought with them a cult of Baal Shamem, the Lord of Heaven, often identified with Zeus in other Hellenistic cities and sometimes with Yahweh/the Most High. And if the occupying troops either shared or took over the Temple, their sacrifices to the Lord of Heaven would surely have appeared to traditionally oriented Judean priests and scribes as an abominable profanation of the altar.

Although it is not clear just what measures he took, it seems likely that at this point Antiochus ordered the suppression of ancestral law and sacrifices in Jerusalem and Judea. And it also seems likely that these measures were an attempt to counter the continuing resistance of scribal circles and others that was deeply rooted in those ancestral laws and rites. Whatever motivated Antiochus to suppress Judean observances, his measures were counterproductive. In the escalating spiral of violence, the response to Antiochus's repressive measures was wider insurrection and the guerrilla warfare known as the Maccabean Revolt.

The Contradiction Confronting the Judean Scribes

In the late third and early second centuries B.C.E., Judean scribes faced an escalating crisis that they were forced to make sense of. Their role was to serve the temple-state and the priestly aristocrats who headed it from their knowledge of the Judean cultural repertoire of which they were the professional guardians, and to which they had become personally committed. They had devoted their lives to learning Mosaic covenantal Torah, the oracles of the prophets, and the different kinds of wisdom so that they could advise the presiding priests of the Temple, supply knowledge of "the laws of the Judeans" by which the temple-state operated, and coordinate the calendar of festivals in sync with the movement of the heavenly bodies. In the official imperial ideology that informed the establishment of the Jerusalem temple-state, their God was local, "the god who is in Jerusalem" (Ezra 1:3). But Judean scribes were firm in their worldview, deeply rooted in Mosaic Torah and prophetic tradition, that the God of Israel was the creator of the universe and the Lord of history.

The very structure of Judean society under imperial rule placed scribes in a conflict between their loyalty to Judean tradition and their role in the temple administration. There were inevitably circumstances and situations in which the policies or actions of local and/or imperial rulers went against the laws and traditions to which they were committed. And there were conflicts aplenty in the Judean temple-state, between predatory power-holders and the people, or between rival priestly factions. Much of the Persian imperial interference that we know of (through the books of Ezra and Nehemiah), however, was to favor the dominance of one priestly party over others, or to insist on compromises between rival priesthoods, or to force the powerful elite into at least minimal observance of Judean socioeconomic principles.

Under the Hellenistic empires, however, imperial policies and interactions between imperial regimes and the members of the Jerusalem aristocracy touched off an escalating series of processes and events that posed severe contradictions for the Judean scribes. Rival empires now periodically devastated the countryside and occasionally attacked Jerusalem as they battled back and forth for control of the territories of Syria-Palestine. The Ptolemaic practice of farming out tribute collection to the highest bidders encouraged Jerusalem power brokers, such as the Tobiads Joseph and Hyrcanus, to become more exploitative of Judean villagers than the priestly aristocracy had been previously. Aristocrats developed a desire for a lavish alien lifestyle and fuller participation in Hellenistic political culture. The desire to join the dominant Hellenistic imperial culture became so strong among many of the priestly aristocrats that they obtained imperial blessings on a new Hellenistic "constitution" for "Antioch" in Jerusalem. This abandonment of the traditional covenantal laws as the "constitution" of the temple-state demoted, and perhaps even eliminated, the traditional roles of the scribes, along with those of the ordinary priests. And all of these developments violated the traditional values as well as the laws of the Judeans, of which the scribes were the professional guardians. Finally, the Seleucid emperor imposed an occupying foreign military colony on Jerusalem, along with the cult of an alien god, and took measures to suppress observance of the traditional covenantal way of life. With every one of these major events, the crisis deepened in Judean society, and Judean scribes struggled to understand what was happening in the mysterious ways of God, and how they should respond to the ever-escalating crisis.

Chapter 2
The Statue and the Stone: The Tales of Daniel

The tales of Daniel and his friends in Daniel 1–6 tell of Judean intellectuals caught in a conflict between loyalty to their God and their professional service in the governance of the Babylonian (chs. 2–5) or Median-Persian (ch. 6) Empire. These tales (in Aramaic) about the legendary wise man Daniel (see Ezek 14:14; 28:3) come from a time well before the Seleucid regime launched violent repressive measures against the resistance by Judean scribes in Jerusalem. But they display the conflict that already existed between imperial claims to sovereignty and the Judean intellectuals' commitment to the God of Israel as holding ultimate sovereignty. That the tales conclude with God's vindication of Daniel's disobedience of the emperor in steadfast loyalty to his divine sovereign, unrealistic as it seems, would have encouraged the Judean scribes who cultivated them to maintain their ultimate loyalty in situations of conflict.*

The Tales and their Cultivators

The Greek historian Herodotus repeats a number of court legends focused on Croesus and derived apparently from intellectuals serving under the Lydian and Persian empires.[1] In these tales, an educated nobleman from a subject people becomes an adviser and administrator in the imperial court. The context of several of these legends is the Persian court,[2] in which scribes from subject peoples are known to have served as advisers. Told from the

---

* I urge readers to read through the tales in Daniel 1–6 in their Bibles and to consult the text regularly while working through this chapter. I sometimes offer alternative translations of key terms and phrases.

viewpoint of the ethnic scribes, these legends portray the wisdom and astute actions of the hero, and thus tout the values and identity of the subject people. Evidently, the tales were generated among circles of intellectuals serving the Persian imperial administration. Their many forms and features similar to the legends repeated by Herodotus indicate that the tales in Daniel 1–6 are parallel in origin and function.[3] The tales of Daniel are also set in the context of "Eastern" imperial courts. The reference to the fourth empire in Daniel 2, however, and the term "Chaldeans" for diviners and astrologers (Dan 2:2-5, 10; cf., for example, Diodorus Siculus 2.29–31) indicate that the tales as we have them in Daniel 1–6 come from Hellenistic times.[4]

Like the parallel legends of other intellectuals in the Persian court, the tales in Daniel 1–6 are of two related types. The tales in Daniel 2, 4, and 5 tell of a "court contest" in which rival scribes vie to divine the meaning of the king's dream or the writing on the wall; here the rivals fail, whereupon Daniel discerns the meaning clearly and is rewarded with high position. Daniel 3 and 6 tell, in contrast, of "court conflict" in which rivals set up a threat to Daniel's life, or his friends' lives, from which they escape only through God's intervention. While the tales of each type display a common pattern, the emphases in each one are distinctive. See further the discussion in Wills, *Jew in the Court*, ch. 3; and Collins, *Daniel* (1993), 36-38.

The point of noting the parallels between the tales in Daniel 1–6 and other court legends lies less in determining the form itself than in discerning the special emphases and distinctive features of these tales. Other forms and themes are woven together in legends of Daniel. Mixed with the "court contest" in Daniel 2 are Daniel's discernment of King Nebuchadnezzar's dream and his true interpretation, as well as a political oracle and a hymnic doxology. The "court conflict" tale in Daniel 3 has affinities with martyr legends, including the interrogation by the king (cf. 2 Macc 7), and a doxology. The contest story in Daniel 4 takes the outward form of an epistle from the king and includes a symbolic vision. Mysterious writing replaces the dream motif in the Daniel 5 contest story, and a prophetic indictment follows Daniel's interpretation of the numinous writing. While Daniel's skill as a learned scribe lies specifically in dream interpretation in Daniel 2 and 4, he and his friends display wider advising skills in Daniel 3, 5, and 6 (problem solving and explanation of riddles, as well as dream interpretation in Dan 5:1).

Most distinctive and striking in all of these tales are the ominous anti-imperial pronouncements that are not standard features in court legends. In his interpretation of the statue in the king's dream, Daniel pronounces God's judgment on all empires. The tales in Daniel 3, 4, and 5 all announce judgment against the emperor(s).[5] The composition of the tales in Daniel 1–6 has transformed court legends by combining them with several other forms in ways that focus on political conflict.[6] From the distinctive Judean theological perspective of the universal sovereignty of God, the tales of Daniel use court legends as vehicles to present prophetic indictments of arrogant imperial rule that are deeply rooted in Israelite prophetic tradition.

The context in which these tales were developed and cultivated will have been the Judean scribal circles. Mainline biblical interpreters have argued that the Daniel tales were addressed more widely to Jewish communities in the Diaspora. In rather vague terms, they read them as models of a "life-style for diaspora" and "the possibility of participating fully in the life of a foreign nation."[7] The prominence in the tales of advanced learning cultivated in royal administrations, and of skills for maneuvering in the intrigue of court politics, however, suggests, rather, that these legends comprised some of the lore more specifically of Judean scribes.

The "local color" of the Persian imperial court suggests that the Daniel tales may have originated and developed in circles of Judean scribes serving in the Persian imperial court, or in scribal circles descended from exiled families who had been reestablished in Jerusalem when the Temple was rebuilt. The fact that the tales were eventually joined with the visions of the Jerusalem intellectuals known as the *maskilim* in Daniel 7-12, however, indicates that they were (also) cultivated by circles of scribes in Jerusalem. The legends of Daniel, moreover, illustrate the conflict in the relations between Judean scribes and the dominant imperial culture that was inherent also in the Jerusalem temple-state as an instrument of the imperial rule of Judea. They would thus have resonated with scribes serving in the temple-state as well as those serving directly in the imperial court. While the Babylonian and Persian kings have a direct impact on Daniel in the tales, the Hellenistic emperors' impact on the later Jerusalem scribes, such as the maskilim, was indirect, mediated through the Judean aristocracy. But imperial policy and practice, as well as periodic crises within or between imperial regimes, steadily threatened and interfered with the scribes' practice of the traditional Judean way of life. Presumably at some point before the crisis that generated the visions-and-interpretations now found in Daniel 7-12, the tales now found in Daniel 1-6 were being cultivated by the maskilim, who left their footprints in 11:33-35.

To Serve in the King's Palace: Daniel 1

The introductory tale about Daniel and his associates provides almost a mirror of the training and responsibilities of learned scribes, whether they were serving in the imperial regime itself or in the Jerusalem temple-state. A professional cadre of scribes was trained in literacy, including record keeping and the composition and copying of (written) texts. They also mastered a wide-ranging repertoire of high culture, so that they became "versed in every branch of wisdom, endowed with knowledge and insight," and were thus "competent to serve in the king's palace" (1:4). The range of "wisdom" that they mastered included skill in interpreting dreams and visions.[8] So trained, these intellectuals served as administrators and advisers both in the central administration and in the local institutions of imperial rule, such as the Jerusalem temple-state. The introduction to the tales in Daniel 1–6 portrays "Daniel" and his friends as trained to serve alongside other learned scribes "stationed in the king's court" and supported economically in their service at the court (Dan 1:4-5, 6, 8, 19). Daniel proved more skillful than all "the dream-interpreters and exorcists" of Babylon (1:17, 20; 5:12; cf. Sir 39:1-2).[9]

The imperial regimes, however, evidently allowed the cultivation of indigenous Judean (Israelite) culture, including relations with the God of Israel. The scribal custodians of culture developed expressions of a distinctively Judean political and religious identity that conflicted with the culture and practices of the empire. Insofar as Judean scribes were the professional custodians of such culture, they developed a sense of their own authority separate from and independent of their authority as representatives of the rulers. This is evident in Daniel and his associates' insistence on observing their distinctively Judean rules regarding food (1:8-16). This meant also, however, that Judean intellectuals such as Daniel could use their own Judean wisdom to express the interests of the subjugated Judean people that conflicted with the interests and claims to authority of the imperial regime. In fact, in a crisis of authority, Judean scribes/sages might choose to resist orders and practices of the imperial regime, as happened in the ensuing tales in Daniel 2–6.

Our exploration of the tales set in the imperial court will thus look for the political conflict (criticism of and/or accommodation to the empire) in each story and its principal message or main point. Because of their social location and role, learned scribes were always in a position of serving the interest and will of the rulers on whom they were dependent economically. Imperial rule of Judea and Judeans only reinforced and complicated their position, whether at the imperial court or in the Jerusalem temple-state. The tales of Daniel and others in the Babylonian imperial court reflect how professional intellectuals had no choice but to accommodate to the imperial situation. Whether they came from longtime scribal families, or were former Jerusalem nobles now deployed as administrators and advisers in the imperial court (as in Dan 1:1–4), professional scribes (such as "Daniel" or Ben Sira) had no choice but to play their roles in the imperial administration or its local representative, the Judean temple-state. They occupied positions of privilege as well as dependency (1:5), even of favor and influence (1:18-21; 2:48-49; 3:30; et al.). On the other hand, however, they had their own source of authority separate from and often in conflict with the authority and power of the rulers in whose service they worked (3:12; 4:25; 6:5). And that conflict, usually covert and latent, could lead to overt conflict between Judean intellectuals and the imperial rulers they served.

The Statue and the Stone: Daniel 2

Nebuchadnezzar dreams of a statue with a head of gold, a chest of silver, a midsection of bronze, and legs and feet of iron and clay, which is destroyed by a huge stone. The king is so troubled by his dream that he becomes an irrational monster, utterly out of control. When his dream interpreters, exorcists, and Chaldeans insist that the king must tell them the dream before they discern its proper interpretation *(pesher)*, he flies into a rage and orders them destroyed. Then the Judean sage Daniel interprets the dream to mean that a succession of four empires will be crushed by the coming kingdom of God. The main message of the tale is twofold: God is ultimately in charge of the empires that currently control the lives of subject peoples, and God reveals the overall plan for the course of history, which is ultimately "under control," despite appearances. The doxology in the middle of the tale (2:21) proclaims these same interrelated points.

> [God] changes times and seasons,
>   deposes kings and sets up kings;
> he gives wisdom to the wise,
>   and knowledge to those who have understanding.[10]

At the end of the tale, Nebuchadnezzar himself articulates them again: "Truly your God (of Israel) is God of gods and Lord of kings and a revealer of mysteries" (2:47).

The "mystery" of the dream that is finally revealed to Daniel, that is, God's plan behind the succession of empires ruling the peoples of the earth, is that God's kingdom will finally destroy all the empires. In accordance with the standard notion that Daniel is an "apocalyptic" book, Daniel 2 has commonly been given an eschatological interpretation, as though it indicates that history was to come to an end. But there is no basis for this interpretation, either in the dream itself or in Daniel's interpretation. The phrase in 2:28 on which such an interpretation is often based (cf. Isa 2:2; Ezek 38:16; Dan 10:14; Hos 3:5; and Mic 4:1) can be approximated in English as "what will be at the end of the era," which suggests a period of history, not "end of days," as if history itself were to end.[11]

Scholars have discerned, behind Nebuchadnezzar's dream, two originally different schemes of a succession of ages or empires that were evidently well known in the eastern Mediterranean and ancient Near East in Hellenistic times. Sources that date from later than the book of Daniel attest traditional schemes that were apparently widely cultivated prior to the tales of Daniel. One was a scheme of four successive empires (originally Assyrians, Babylonians, Persians, and Macedonians), succeeded by a fifth.[12] Several kingdoms that had been subjected by one or another of the Hellenistic empires adapted this scheme as an assurance that they might finally regain their own sovereignty. The other scheme used the imagery of four metals to represent a declining sequence of world ages, to be succeeded by a better age in the future.[13] Fused with the scheme of four kingdoms, as in Nebuchadnezzar's dream in Daniel 2, the sequence of four metals signifies a declining series of empires to be replaced by a new golden age. The adapted scheme of the four metals probably goes back to a Babylonian version in which the declining sequence of the Persian, and especially the Seleucid, empires would be replaced by a renewed Babylonian Empire. The stone that smashes all the metals, of course, must be the kingdom of the God of the Judeans. Daniel's interpretation of the sequence of metals and the stone is thus a subversion of the Babylonian political ideology and expectations. More significantly, however, it also portrays the Seleucid Empire(s) as sharply escalating violence against subject peoples, as it "crushes and smashes everything" (Dan 2:40).

Measured by the pattern of a "court contest" legend, the ending of the tale does not fit Daniel's interpretation of the king's dream. This may be a significant clue to the tale's message. In the tale, after Daniel discerns and interprets his dream, Nebuchadnezzar not only promotes Daniel to be "ruler of the province and chief prefect over all the wise men," the chief administrative officer in the empire, but also confesses that Daniel's God holds sovereignty over kings. In his interpretation, however, Daniel had said that the sovereign God was about to crush Nebuchadnezzar's empire (2:44-45). If Nebuchadnezzar had been paying attention, he would have had Daniel executed for treason. Like his Babylonian diviners, he "does not have a clue" about what is really about to happen.

But the Judean intellectuals who repeatedly told the story understood. The portrayal of the king as clueless at the close of the tale matches his portrayal as utterly irrational at the outset, refusing to relate his dream to his professional dream interpreters so that they can interpret it, and then flying into a violent rage (2:4-12).[14] Judean intellectuals would presumably have enjoyed portraying the emperor who had destroyed Jerusalem as an irrational fool, as well as about to have his kingdom terminated by God.

The tale ends with Daniel exalted to the highest position in the imperial administration. However, to argue that the tale therefore serves mainly to establish Daniel's status as recipient of heavenly revelation separates the Judean scribes and the revelation they received from their political situation and the content of their wisdom. This tale may not advocate active subversion. But the wisdom that God has just given to the wise Daniel is that the king of Babylon is to be crushed along with the Hellenistic emperors who "crush and smash everything," when the God of heaven sets up a kingdom that will not be destroyed. Far from being "almost incidental to the message of the chapter,"[15] the political content of the dream and its interpretation are another expression of the God of the Judeans as true sovereign over history. The wisdom he gives to the wise is that He "deposes kings."

The Golden Statue and the Fiery Furnace: Daniel 3

The legend in Daniel 3, which is not focused on the figure of Daniel, tells of God providing protection for Shadrach, Meshach, and Abednego when they are thrown into the fiery furnace. This mightily impresses the previously arrogant and violent King Nebuchadnezzar: "no other god is able to deliver in this way," leading him to proclaim protection for their God and a promotion for them. Modern biblical interpretation has a tendency to reduce this story, like the other tales, to its religious dimension and even to impose the modern Western assumption of the separation of religion and politics. Claiming that the tale propounds the belief that religious fidelity was compatible with service in the imperial court, and could even lead to professional promotion, not only assumes the modern separation of religion and politics, but reduces religion to personal faith. Such a reading misses the significance of the focal symbol, the colossal statue to test loyalty to the empire, but also the all-important issue on which the story focuses.

Idolatry was a political and economic issue, not merely a religious matter. "Idols" in ancient Near Eastern societies were symbolic representations of personified divinized Powers that determined people's lives in a society such as the Babylonian Empire, that is, natural and civilizational forces, such as River, Sea, Storm (an aspect of kingship), and Irrigation (representing technology). As indicated in the second commandment in the Mosaic covenant (Exod 20:4), the people were not simply "worshiping" but serving these Forces in a political economic sense as well, with their obedience and their labor and offerings.

Nebuchadnezzar erected the colossal golden statue as a symbol of his imperial rule, his kingship. We cannot miss the point when he summons all of the imperial officers at every level of administration in all the provinces to the dedication of the statue (the elaborate list in 3:2-3) and orders the herald to proclaim that all the subject peoples are to prostrate themselves before the statue in obeisance (3:4-6). This elaborate ceremony is an exaggerated, highly symbolic political as well as religious act of loyalty to the emperor.

The Judean scribal intellectuals serving at court, however, refuse to participate in this ceremony of religious-political loyalty and service to the imperial kingship. The "Chaldeans" who denounce them recognize precisely the roots of the conflict, in a way that modern Western interpreters often do not: "they do not serve your gods," that is, the gods of the empire (3:12; cf. Esth 3:8). The Judeans are traitors; they are subversives. Precisely because they serve their own God, who holds political sovereignty over human kings, they cannot worship the symbol of his imperial rule (3:16-18, 28).

Nebuchadnezzar is not punished for his presumptuous arrogance. The tale, however, clearly condemns his arrogant imperial rule symbolized in the colossal statue. The telling and retelling of this tale would surely have prepared Judean intellectuals for potential resistance to measures and institutions intended to cultivate and enforce loyalty to the empire.[16]

Eating Grass Like an Ox: Daniel 4

The longer tale in Daniel 4 also indicts the imperial arrogance of King Nebuchadnezzar. In this tale, however, the king is punished under divine sentence until he acknowledges the sovereignty of God. Indeed, God's sovereignty is the dominating theme of the story. The hymnic confession of Nebuchadnezzar, placed toward the beginning and the end (4:3, 34-35, 37), frames the tale as a whole. It is the decisive message of the decree by the divine council of holy ones in the king's dream and its interpretation (4:17, 25). With all these pointed assertions about the ultimate sovereignty, it is impossible to miss the point of the tale, that the Most High God humiliated the king for his pretentious expansion of his rule (4:22). To reduce the issue to that of "Gentile rule" is to blunt the condemnation of arrogant *imperial* rule that is the point of this and other Daniel tales.[17]

Arrogant imperial rule is also the point of the central image of the tale. Nebuchadnezzar dreams about a tree at the center of the earth that grows to immense proportions, reaching to the heavens and the ends of the earth (4:10-12). But by divine decree it is cut down (4:14-17). This image (and text) often gets labeled as distinctively "apocalyptic." But the image and the message it carries had become deeply rooted in Israelite prophetic tradition. Earlier in the ancient Near East, it had been a positive symbol for empire. In the building inscription of Nebuchadnezzar, for example, imperial Babylon is compared to a great tree.[18] In late Judahite prophetic oracles, the symbol was turned against

The Statue and the Stone

empires. Ezekiel presents to the Pharaoh of Egypt an elaborate image of the Assyrian Empire as a great cedar of Lebanon. But when it had expanded its reach into the clouds of heaven, God delivered it into the hand of another empire because of the arrogance of its power (Ezek 31:2-14). Ezekiel uses a similar image of a great tree-like vine that grows huge and strong but is then destroyed in a prophecy against the last representative of the Davidic monarchy in Judah (Ezek 17:10). A standard message of earlier prophets such as Isaiah had been the declaration that YHWH struck down rulers for their arrogance and oppression (e.g., Isa 14:4-11, 12-17). Another example of this tale's deep roots in Israelite prophetic tradition is Daniel's admonition that the king atone for his sins with mercy to the oppressed (4:27; cf. Isa 1:17).

The tale mocks the pretentious use of power by Nebuchadnezzar, who was famous for his massive building projects that required vast expenditures and extensive use of forced labor. "Is this not magnificent Babylon, which I have built as a royal capital by my mighty power and for my glorious majesty?" he says with pride as he walks on the roof of his royal palace (4:29-30). As punishment, the king is exiled from society and transformed into an ox, the most docile and obedient beast of burden that labors under the lash in the construction of imperial palaces and temples (4:25, 33). Nebuchadnezzar's expulsion from society was derived from a tradition about the later emperor Nabonidus, which was also known in Judea, as attested by the Prayer of Nabonidus (4QPrNab) found among the Dead Sea Scrolls at Qumran.[19] The humiliation of Nebuchadnezzar reverses an earlier prophetic image. Jeremiah declared that God had "given him even the wild animals of the field to serve him" (Jer 27:6). The tale in Daniel 4 has him transformed into the humblest domesticated animal.

This transformation of the emperor into a beast of burden mirrors the transformation of a Mesopotamian myth of a primordial human, according to recent research. In the Gilgamesh epic and other Mesopotamian texts, a primordial animal-like human (for example, Enkidu) was transformed into the founder of civilization. In the imperial ideology of Babylon, this founder was the king of Babylon, builder of cities.[20] The tale in Daniel 4 turns this imperial ideology on its head. It portrays Nebuchadnezzar, the great builder of cities, particularly of the magnificent imperial capital Babylon, as eating grass like an ox. The principal message of the tale is a condemnation of imperial rule.

The Hand Writing on the Wall: Daniel 5

The tale of Daniel's interpretation of the hand writing on the wall of the royal palace at "Belshazzar's feast" (5:5-6, 24) brings yet another prophetic indictment and a sentence for arrogance and indulgence. The courtly contest legend in Daniel 5 provides little more than an awkward framework for the message. Insofar as Daniel here interprets an omen instead of a dream, this tale portrays a Judean intellectual engaged in a scribal practice that was particularly prominent at the Babylonian imperial court. Daniel's interpretation, however, stands in the tradition of lawsuits pronounced by the Hebrew prophets rather than the tradition of omen interpretation by Babylonian diviners. Against the background of a recitation of the history of God's favor, juxtaposed with the previous king's (Nebuchadnezzar's) abuse of his subjects (5:18-21), Daniel delivers an indictment against Belshazzar for similar arrogance (5:22-23). He pronounces the sentence finally in his interpretation of the words written on the wall (5:26-28):

> MENE, God has numbered the days of your kingdom and brought it to an end;
> TEKEL, you have been weighed on the scales and found wanting;
> PERES, your kingdom is divided and given to the Medes and Persians.

Both the form and message central to this tale are thus deeply rooted in, and a continuation of, prophetic indictments and sentences of oppressive rulers. The rulers in this case, however, are not the kings of Israel or Judah, but imperial rulers. The symbol of royal abuse and indulgence in this case is the sacred spoil that the conquering Babylonian armies had taken from the Jerusalem Temple. What was sacred to the conquered Judean elite was not only taken, but is now defiled in the debauchery of imperial court life (5:2-4).[21]

Again in this tale, Daniel is promoted to high rank, following the pattern of the court contest legend (5:29). But the ending that goes with the core of the story is that the prophesied judgment is executed on Belshazzar (5:30). Despite his compromised position of service to the regime, however, Daniel does not mince any words. He pronounces a severe prophetic indictment and judgment against empire.

Daniel in the Lions' Den: Daniel 6

Again in the story of "Daniel in the lions' den," the distinguished Judean scribe comes into severe conflict with the imperial regime. The king himself, Darius the Mede (historically a Persian emperor), is highly favorable to Daniel. But the institutionalized forms of an imperial regime can drive the centralization of power and the demands of loyalty to the regime in ways that override the mere personal disposition of an emperor. Indeed, the assumption at the beginning that Daniel's loyalty to his God should have no effect on his service in the imperial regime sets up the main point of the tale. But it does have an effect, as the sequence of events demonstrates. The imperial regime claims ultimate authority, as in the story of the fiery furnace (Dan 3). Even if the emperor himself does not demand it, the imperial regime insists that subject people pray to and otherwise express exclusive ritual loyalty to the emperor.

Previous interpretation, based in the assumption of the separation of religion and politics, that "Daniel's religion poses no problem in his service to the king," simply misses what the story is about. From the outset, the tale indicates explicitly that the point of vulnerability for Daniel, as the exemplary and distinguished Judean involved in the imperial regime, was his determination to adhere to "the law of his God" (6:5, 10-13). Observing the Torah of God meant not just personal piety, but a whole way of life, inseparably political and religious. The tale in Daniel 6 thus provided a model of the great sage who remained unflinchingly faithful to his God despite the threat of death—with the fantasy resolution that the emperor himself came to recognize and decreed that the God of Daniel has the true, eternal sovereignty.

Judean Scribes in Conflict with Imperial Rule

These tales are about more than issues of religion. They are also about imperial politics, or perhaps we should say, the religious and political pretensions of imperial politics. The best illustration lies in the importance of dreams and omens to imperial regimes of the ancient Near East. They viewed dreams and omens as the means by which the divine forces that determined political and economic affairs communicated about present and future events. Emperors thus maintained specialists in dream interpretation on their extensive staff of scribes. The tales of Daniel reflect precisely this all-important practice in imperial politics. In fact, the dream image of the statue signifying a declining sequence of empires destroyed by a more powerful empire is known from other sources to have been interpreted previously to indicate the restoration of empire to Babylon. Daniel's interpretation was clearly subversive. In the other tales, as well as the one in Daniel 2, the great Judean hero of dream interpretation, empowered by God-given wisdom, virtually reverses the usual interpretation of dreams and omens in the imperial court. Because of imperial overreach, the Most High God will humiliate the emperor or even destroy the empire.

The underlying assumption, as well as the main point articulated in all of the tales in Daniel 2–6, especially in the doxologies, is that the Most High God of the Judeans is sovereign over history. And the divine sovereign stands in judgment over the rulers who so arrogantly wield imperial power. That point, moreover, could not be made more strongly than it is in Daniel's interpretation of Nebuchadnezzar's dream in Daniel 2. Nebuchadnezzar insists that all subject peoples do obeisance to the colossal statue as a demonstration of loyalty to his glorious rule. And in arrogant self-satisfaction, he gloats in the magnificence of the city of Babylon, "which I have built as imperial capital by my mighty power and for my glorious majesty" (4:30). His son Belshazzar presides over extravagantly lavish banqueting by his entire imperial court, greedily consuming the rich supply of goods that the imperial armies have expropriated from the peoples they have conquered. Both emperors have thus exalted themselves against the Lord of heaven in some of the standard institutional forms of ancient Near Eastern empire, in which imperial rulers used their military might to seize goods and produce from subject peoples to augment their own glory in monumental building and lavish spectacle. The tales in Daniel 3, 4, and 5 thus prefigure Antiochus Epiphanes' arrogant self-exaltation in rivaling the divine in the visionary accounts in Daniel 8 and 10–12 (see ch. 5 below). The scribal hero Daniel to whom God's "mystery" has been revealed, standing firmly in the tradition of the Hebrew prophets, repeatedly turns the tables on the imperial interpretation of dreams and omens. The real interpretation of the dreams is that the empires stand under God's judgment.

The tales also portray dramatically how Daniel and the other Judean scribes who served in the imperial regime but remained loyal to their God lived in a situation of conflict. Their very role in life placed them between two claims to sovereignty that were perpetually in conflict. As the tales indicate, they lived in "an unresolved tension between . . . cooperation and opposition."[22] Because the regime had overwhelming coercive power, they had no choice about their geographical and social location (Dan 1:1-2 and 1:3-7, respectively). They could only refuse to go along with certain institutional expressions of exclusive loyalty to the imperial regime, and hope for the divine termination of overweening empire.

Cultivation of these tales of Judean scribes struggling with the conflict between loyalty to God and loyalty to the rulers in whose regimes they served was thus surely important in certain scribal circles in Jerusalem as they attempted to maintain their values, culture, and commitment.[23] It hardly seems likely that the tales' inclusion of the kings' approval or elevation of Daniel helped to resolve the conflict at the cultural level. The very existence of many such stories that came together in a whole cycle of tales suggests that the fundamental conflict came to a head again and again. Even though Daniel and those who cultivated tales about him were an intellectual elite who served the rulers, they were also members of a subject people and guardians of the elite culture of that people.[24] The main point in the tales is that ultimate sovereignty belongs to God, to whom the intellectuals should be loyal even when the conflict becomes overt, placing them in danger.

Besides this major conflict around which the tales revolve, another, interrelated conflict compounded the difficulties of the Judean scribes' situation. Both the "court contest" legends and the "court conflict" legends reflect rivalry and maneuvering between different factions of scribal administrators and advisers at imperial courts. This was often exacerbated, surely, by conflict between factions within the royal family and among the highest ranking officers of imperial regimes. Wise scribes in the service of the Jerusalem temple-state under the rival Hellenistic empires would have been well acquainted with both of these conflicts. The repeated wars for control of Palestine between the Ptolemies and Seleucids, the maneuvering between factions of the Jerusalem aristocracy, and the increasing Hellenistic influence in the temple-state in the late-third century could only have increased the difficulties of Judean sages attempting to maintain their commitment to "the law of their God."

The tales of Daniel offered a model to Judean scribes whose role as advisers in the Judean temple-state brought them into conflict between their commitment to the Judean traditions of which they were the guardians and the imperial demands to which they were subject. Daniel offered an example of steadfast loyalty to the Most High God. More dramatically, he was also a model of "speaking truth to power," even under threat of punishment or death. The tales also articulated the faith that the Most High God was still in control of history. Although their professional role involved considerable accommodation to imperial rule, they could follow Daniel's example in resisting imperial rule when it overreached or claimed exclusive loyalty. It is surely not accidental that these tales were placed together with the visions and interpretations of the Jerusalem intellectuals now in Daniel 7–12. The tales of Daniel would have reinforced the commitment of the maskilim, those dissident Jerusalem scribes who finally mounted active resistance to Antiochus Epiphanes' attempt to suppress the traditional Judean way of life.

Chapter 3
The Giants Who Kill and Devour: Enoch's Book of Watchers

The Book of Watchers is judged to be the oldest Judean text that is usually classified as an "apocalypse." Specialists have recently pushed its date back into the third century B.C.E. Previous interpreters have argued that, "as in all the Jewish apocalypses," the historical situation that the book addresses is concealed, that it "does not explicitly address any crisis of the Hellenistic age."[1] A close reading against what we know of the history of Judea under the Hellenistic empires in the third century, however, suggests that in fact, the Book of Watchers is focused on the effects of Hellenistic imperial rule. The book brings a sharp prophetic condemnation of the imperial violence and oppression to which the Ptolemaic and Seleucid regimes subjected the Judean people in the third century.*

A Composite Book of a Prototypical Scribe: 1 Enoch 1–36

The Book of Watchers is the first of at least five books that comprise what is known as *1 Enoch*. Attributed to the antediluvian figure Enoch, these books were originally composed in Aramaic, then translated into Greek, from which they were translated into Ethiopic, from which they became known to European scholars in the nineteenth and twentieth centuries. The oldest, the Book of the Luminaries (*1 Enoch* 72–82), is a collection of astronomical descriptions of the movements of the sun, moon, and stars, evidently

---

*A new translation of the Book of Watchers, *1 Enoch* 1–36, is available in George W. E. Nickelsburg and James C. VanderKam, *1 Enoch: A New Translation* (Minneapolis: Fortress Press, 2004). I strongly recommend reading the text in connection with reading this chapter.

standard cosmological wisdom cultivated by the Enoch circle of scribes in the third century B.C.E. The youngest, the Book of Parables (*1 Enoch* 37–71) presents a series of heavenly tableaux of the judgment over which a figure named variously as Righteous One, Elect One, Anointed One, and Son of Man presides. Since this book is usually dated to Roman times, we will discuss it in part 2, below. The Animal Vision that comprises most of the fourth "book" (*1 Enoch* 83–90) and the ten-week survey of history at the beginning of the fifth book (the Epistle of Enoch, *1 Enoch* 92–105, consisting largely of woes against the wealthy and reassurance for the righteous), both of which are usually classified as "apocalypses," evidently address the climax of the crisis in Jerusalem just prior to the Maccabean Revolt and will be discussed in the next chapter.

Although it is usually categorized as an "apocalyptic" text, the Book of Watchers presents itself as wisdom. Like Ben Sira and the "Daniel" of the tales, Enoch is represented as a scribe: the "righteous scribe" (12:3) and "the scribe of truth" (15:1). His scribal operation in the heavenly court must be based on his knowledge of how scribes function in an earthly court (13:4-7; 15:2). The recipients of his message are also learned scribes, to whom he is disclosing wisdom (5:8; see 32:3-6). Unlike Ben Sira, however, "Enoch" claims to have received his wisdom through heavenly "communications media": a vision that God showed him and "the words of the watchers and holy ones" (1:2). In substance as well, the righteous scribe Enoch's wisdom is broader than Ben Sira's. The Book of Watchers exhibits little or none of the instructional wisdom in which Ben Sira specializes. Instead, it draws heavily on the astronomical, meteorological, and other wisdom evident in the earlier Enochic Book of Luminaries, which was evident but not prominent in Sirach. Like Ben Sira, Enoch also knows the prophetic traditions and the historical traditions of Israel. Yet while Ben Sira cultivates the Israelite prophetic tradition as well as various kinds of wisdom, Enoch even undergoes a prophetic calling, assumes a prophetic role, and takes on a prophetic voice.

According to his résumé in Israelite tradition, Enoch was well qualified to become a revealer of wisdom from primordial times. Since he had "walked with God" (Gen 5:22), he must have received divine revelation. And insofar as "God took him" (Gen 5:24), he had taken up residence in heaven; hence, he could be a source of knowledge about the future through visions that the scribes had learned from the prophets. The genealogy of the ancestors of humankind in Judean tradition (Genesis 5–6) contained two further features that were intriguing to the scribes who cultivated Israelite tradition. Enoch, the seventh ancestor, died at age 365, remarkably young for one of the long-lived primordial ancients (Gen 5:23; see 5:11, 14, 17, 20, 27). This was attractive to the scribal circles whose astronomical wisdom led them to prefer the solar calendar of 364 or 365 days over the official lunar calendar of the temple-state, which was based on different astronomical wisdom. Enoch, moreover, was the seventh in the sequence of ten antediluvian figures. Given the communication between scribes in Jerusalem and the Assyrian, Babylonian, and Persian imperial regimes that had ruled the ancient Near East for centuries, the various kinds of wisdom were "international." Judean scribal speculation about Enoch is strikingly similar to the lore focused on Enmeduranki in Mesopotamian culture, the seventh antediluvian king. He was king of the city of Sippar, whose deity was Shamash, the sun god. Having received divinely revealed divinatory techniques for discerning omens, he had founded the elite *baru* guild of scribes who specialized in interpretation of dreams and omens.[2]

The book of *Jubilees*, composed a few generations after the Book of Watchers, offers a window onto Judean tradition of Enoch as the prototypical scribe-sage who specialized in visionary astronomical wisdom and knowledge of the future.

> He was the first among men . . . who learned writing and knowledge and wisdom and who wrote down the signs of heaven according to the order of their months in a book, that men might know the seasons of the years according to the order of their separate months. And . . . what was and will be he saw in a vision of his sleep, as it will happen to the children of men throughout their generations until the day of judgment; and he saw and understood everything, and wrote his testimony, and placed the testimony on earth for all the children of men and for their generations. (*Jub.* 4:15-19)

It could not have been by accident that a scribal circle whose wisdom included extensive cultivation of cosmology and visions identified with Enoch as the prototypical, primordial scribe, sage, and revealer. We recognize, of course, that the "Enoch" scribes' portrayal of Enoch as a wise scribe who had received revealed wisdom and then communicated it reflects their own role and compositional activity.

The Book of Watchers is clearly a composite text. Several sections of material have been placed in sequence within which it is difficult to discern a "plot" or an organizing scheme. The opening prophetic oracle of judgment has no particular link with the rest of the book other than the double theme of blessing for the righteous and punishment of the wicked, and may have been the introduction to the whole collection of texts that comprise *1 Enoch*. The story of the watchers' rebellion, chapters 6–11, is not narrated by Enoch and does not refer to him, yet is presupposed by his interaction with them in chapters 12–16. Enoch's two journeys, in chapters 17–36, are linked only by the theme of judgment of the watchers.

The composite character of the Book of Watchers suggests a collective product through a process of development for which the concept of "author" is anachronistic. The book's composite character also raises questions about categorization according to a "framing genre," especially when both of the alternatives, "apocalypse" and "testament," have been defined by scholars on the basis of later Judean texts.[3] The composition and cultivation of the different sections of the Book of Watchers appears to have involved a creative process of the mixing and transformation of materials that were standard in the Judean scribal repertoire into new combinations and composite forms. In fact, the different sections of the Book of Watchers assume several such composite cultural forms: cosmological wisdom framed by a prophetic oracle of judgment, narrative myth as embellishment of traditional legend, prophetic commissioning juxtaposed with prophetic oracle, and astronomical wisdom juxtaposed with heavenly journey.

The Introduction to the Book of Watchers

Earlier interpreters who thought that the situation addressed in the Book of Watchers was concealed were apparently not yet aware of how to detect the clues in the text. Thanks to intensive recent analysis of the Book of Watchers and other texts collected in *1 Enoch*, we are now better able to discern these clues.[4] They often result from the juxtaposition of allusions to Israelite tradition with the historical situation that the text addresses or tacitly assumes. The superscription of the Book of Watchers (also that of *1 Enoch* as a whole), Enoch's "words of blessing . . . [on] the righteous chosen who will be present on the day of tribulation, to remove all the enemies" (1:1), offers just such an allusion and hence a decisive clue to the text's agenda.

The "words of blessing" clearly allude to "the Blessing of Moses" in Deuteronomy 33 and other such prophetic blessings pronounced on Israel. The superscription thus evokes memories of Yahweh coming from Sinai with "myriads of holy ones" to fight for Judah "against his adversaries" and to deliver Israel from its enemies so that it might live in a land of plenty (Deut 33:2-3, 7, 26-29). "The day of tribulation" was a standard term in Israelite tradition for the time of distress in which God would finally intervene to rescue the people (2 Kings 19:3; Ps. 50:15).[5] The same term refers to unprecedented imperial oppression and the struggle against it as God intervenes to deliver the people at the end of Daniel 10–12 (12:1). Insofar as the Book of Watchers is now dated to the third century by specialists, Enoch's "words of blessing" evidently address the imperial political situation of Judea under the Hellenistic empires, and looks for the "removal" of imperial rule.

The introductory lines of the book (*1 Enoch* 1:2-3) also indicate that it stands squarely in the tradition of prophetic pronouncements against unjust rulers, which came from heavenly visions or auditions in which the prophet heard the words of God and/or other holy ones. These lines introduce the immediately ensuing prophetic oracle in 1:3c—5:9 and the rest of the Book of Watchers, much of which consists of two long travel visions.

Both the form and the language of Enoch's introductory declaration resemble those of the oracles of the diviner Balaam (see esp. Num 15–17; 24:3-4).[6] Presumably, the oracles of Balaam as framed by the narrative in Numbers 22–24 were already in the Judean cultural repertoire and known to the scribes who produced Enoch texts. These oracles would have been an obvious model for a prophetic announcement of blessings to Judeans who were feeling threatened by foreign rulers. When a foreign king solicited Balaam to pronounce curses on the Israelites, God repeatedly constrained him to pronounce blessings instead. Most prophetic oracles in the traditional Israelite repertoire were derived from the words of the Lord heard in an audition, with some being (also) from a vision of God or the divine court. The Balaam oracles would appear to be at least one possible model from the traditional Israelite prophetic repertoire of a double source of revelation, that is, both vision and words.[7] In "Enoch's" more complicated universe of heavenly beings, the words come not from God himself, but from "the watchers and the holy ones" and, more specifically in the second travel vision, from the divine messengers such as Uriel, Raphael, Michael, and Gabriel (*1 Enoch* 21–32).

Treatments of this passage introducing the Book of Watchers generally focus mainly on the oracles of Balaam as a prototype of literary features. But the representation of Balaam and his delivery of oracles in Numbers 22–24 and perhaps the "Balaam lore" behind this text are also suggestive for the political role of seers/diviners in Judea and its ancient Near Eastern environment. Interpreters of Enoch-texts now recognize the considerable influence of the Mesopotamian culture of divination on the basis of the astronomical wisdom and visions that lie behind the Book of Luminaries and the Book of Watchers. Balaam was known as a professional diviner from Pethor, on the Euphrates River, who received messages from the divine world in visions during the night (Num 22:5, 8-12, 20; the Hebrew word *ptr*, derived from a Mesopotamian word, can also mean "dream interpreter").

The story that frames the oracles clearly portrays his political role and relationships. A king, through his high-ranking court officers, pays fees to

Balaam for divination, in this case, curses against the Israelites (Num 22:1-7, 15-17; 24:10-14). And he follows the well-attested practice of performing elaborate sacrifices with the king to appease the divine prior to seeking communication from the divine (23:1-6, 14-17, 29-30).[8] In Mesopotamia, as noted, such diviners were among the scribal staff who served the royal court, with special expertise in revelations about the divine favor and about how current royal policies or future events might turn out.[9]

Considering the amount of astronomical, meteorological, and visionary material in Enoch texts, it seems likely that the producers of Enoch books had just such a background, however adapted in Second Temple Judea. Just as Ben Sira understood himself and other scribes as responsible for cultivating prophetic materials, so the "Enoch" scribes appear to have understood themselves as the custodians of prophetic-divinatory materials and even heirs of diviner-prophets such as Balaam—and projected that role and heritage onto the prototypical prophetic diviner-scribe Enoch. Balaam would thus have been an appropriate model for prophet-scribes who found themselves prophesying against their erstwhile patrons, the established aristocratic priests, and their patrons, the imperial rulers.

Enoch's Oracle of Judgment and Blessing

The first section of the book (1:3c—5:9) is a prophetic oracle of blessings on the righteous and of curses on the sinners patterned after the oracles of the Hebrew prophets. The four steps of the oracle are clearly indicated. After an opening announcement of God's appearance with his heavenly army (1:3c-7) comes an opening declaration of the blessings and destruction (1:8-9). The main, longest step brings an indictment of the disobedience of the sinners ("you"), in contrast to the obedience of the heavenly bodies and earthly cycle of seasons (2:1—5:4), followed by a final declaration that the sinners will be destroyed while the chosen will inherit the earth (5:5-9).

In some earlier constructions of "apocalypticism," images such as a great earthquake, a mountain melted by fire, and the earth rent asunder were taken in an almost literal sense as typical "apocalyptic" predictions of a "cosmic catastrophe," as if the created order were about to be destroyed.[10] But that is a misunderstanding of such language. It is simply the standard traditional language of theophany, of the terrifying, "earthshaking" effects on the created order of God's appearance in judgment of enemies. The prophets had used such language in oracles that announced God's judgment on oppressive rulers or on the foreign kings who had conquered Israel (Jer 25:30-31, 32, 34-38; Mic 1:2-7; cf. Deut 33:1-2, 27-29; and the early victory song in Judges 5:4-5). The images of sinners being a curse while the righteous are blessed with joy and fullness of days upon the earth is also rooted in prophetic tradition, as can be seen in Isaiah 65:15-16, 18, 20.

In the field of biblical studies that tends to focus narrowly on the religious dimension of life, it may be difficult to remember that the tradition of prophetic oracles in which the Book of Watchers was rooted (including Jer 25:30-38; Mic 1:2-7) was sharply political. In this type of oracles, prophets such as Micah, Isaiah, and Jeremiah had pronounced the defeat of exploitative Judean or imperial rulers by God and the heavenly armies. The prophetic oracle in Isaiah 24:17-23 provides a precedent for this oracle in the Book of Watchers by including the "host of heaven" along with "the kings of the earth" in the divine punishment.

Scribal shaping of the prophetic oracle is evident, particularly in the way that the indictment section (2:1—5:4) has been fleshed out from astronomical and meteorological wisdom (evident in the Book of Luminaries, the oldest section of *1 Enoch*). Several other texts produced around the same time offer other examples of how the regularity of astronomical-meteorological phenomena was used as a contrast to the disobedience of humans (see especially the hymn about "the works of the Lord" in Sir 16:26-28; cf. TNaph 3:2—4:1; *Psalm of Solomon* 18:10-12).[11] The luminaries' and the seasons' adherence to their appointed order provide the foil for the accusation in 5:4 that "you" have not acted according to God's commandments, the point of the indictment.

But who are the "you"? Starting with the indictment and extending into the verdict (5:5-9), the prophetic oracle is addressed, somewhat vaguely, to "the wicked/sinners." They have spoken "proud and hard words" against God and have not acted according to the commandments (1:9; 5:4). On the surface of the text, this would appear to indicate humans. In prophetic oracles, the indictment was usually addressed to political rulers for having oppressed the people in violation of particular commandments of the Mosaic covenant. This leads us to suspect that the "you" (5:4) and the sinners who are a curse in the ensuing verdict (5:5-7) might be the Jerusalem rulers who cooperate with the imperial "enemies." If the oracle is intended as the introduction to the rest of the Book of Watchers, which focuses on the disobedience of the watchers and holy ones, then perhaps the "you" also includes the rebels against the divine governance of the universe.[12]

The Story of the Watchers

The story of the rebel watchers (*1 Enoch* 6–11), which does not even mention Enoch, focuses on their generation of destructive giants and the steps taken to control them in the divine administration of the universe. Rebel heavenly watchers led by Shemihazah, taking human wives, produced a race of giants.[13] The giants devoured the labor of humans and killed the humans until the whole earth cried out. They then attacked and destroyed one another. They and Asael brought military weapons and introduced superhuman skills and spells into earthly society. The highest officers in the heavenly governance of the universe brought the violence and bloodshed to the attention of the Lord of Ages. The King of kings then ordered Sariel to warn Noah, Raphael to bind the rebel heavenly watchers until the day of judgment, Gabriel to destroy the giants by inducing them to war against each other, and Michael to cleanse the earth from impurity so that the righteous could live in peace.

Scholarly classification of the watchers and other heavenly forces into Enlightenment concepts such as "supernatural" or "otherworldly" may be blocking understanding of texts such as the Book of Watchers. Israelite, Judean, and other ancient Near Eastern cultures understood the heavens and the earth as complementary parts of the same universe. Earthly affairs were affected, even determined, by heavenly forces. Drought and famine, like rain and productivity, were determined by heavenly forces. Israel in particular, but evidently other cultures as well, even extended the influence of the divine world to historical affairs. The God of Israel had sent imperial armies to punish the kings of Judah for oppressing the people. The prophets' role was to hear or see, in the heavenly council of Yahweh, what God's verdict was on particular matters. Somewhat similarly, the purpose of those who composed the Book of Watchers was to understand what the connection might be between what was happening on earth and the actions among the heavenly forces that governed the universe.[14] As learned scribes, however, they sought understanding of the connections between heaven and earth in the astronomy and meteorology of their cosmological wisdom, as well as through prophetic visions. And not surprisingly, as we have already seen in the opening oracle of the Book of Watchers, Judean and other scribes did not keep cosmological wisdom and prophetic lore separate, but mixed them.

The story of the rebel watchers focuses on superhuman forces, as do some other sections of Enoch literature. In the Book of the Luminaries (*1 Enoch* 72–82) and in the prophetic oracle (*1 Enoch* 2:1—5:4), the astronomical and meteorological forces are somewhat personified, with wills of their own, which is presupposed in their ability to be obedient to the commandments of God. In the story of the watchers and giants, however, they are fully personified and semidivine forces with humanlike desire, as well as wills of their own with which they rebel against the divine order. That the names of the watchers are usually not translated in editions of the text of *1 Enoch* may partially obscure this. The ending particle *-el* (in Hebrew and other ancient

The Giants Who Kill and Devour 55

Near Eastern languages) indicates their divine nature or status. The heavenly watchers listed in 6:7 thus include such semidivine natural forces as Star-god, Thunder-god, Shooting-star-god, Lightning-god, Rain-god, Cloud-god, Winter-god, Sun-god, and Moon-god. Similarly, the transliteration rather than the translation of their names in our texts may hide the correlation between their identity (or area of jurisdiction and responsibility in the divine governance of the universe) and the problematic divinatory knowledge that they taught to humans (8:3):

> Lightning-god taught the signs of the lightning flashes.
> Star-god taught the signs of the stars. . . .
> Sun-god taught the signs of the sun.
> Moon-god taught the signs of the moon.

The listing of these named "sons of heaven" as "chiefs/commanders (of tens)" (6:7-8) suggests their military character, in formation of tens. The juxtaposition of their "commander," Shemihazah, whose name makes allusions to heaven, with the second, Arteqoph, "the earth is power," with connotations of military fortifications, points to the problematic pairing of heavenly and earthly power in the giants, who launched the warfare that destroyed the earth and its people (7:3).

The story of the watchers focuses on two principal concerns, the one being the solution to the problem of the other. The driving concern of the story of the watchers' rebellion is to explain the origin of imperial military violence that destroys human life and leads to the devouring of people's produce. The second part of the story provides reassurance that God is still in control of the world, albeit only through the chief officers of the heavenly governance, and will eventually eliminate the destructive forces and make a peaceable earthly life possible again. The superhuman power of the giants is symbolized by their fathers being the superhuman "sons of heaven," and by their great size (7:2). With their overwhelming power,

> they were devouring the labor of all the sons of men, and men were not able to supply them. And the giants began to kill men and to devour them. And they began to sin against the birds and beasts and creeping things and the fish, and to devour one another's flesh. And they drank the blood. (7:3)

In addition, one of the rebel commanders, Asael ("maker/fabricator-god") taught people to manufacture "swords of iron and weapons and shields and breastplates and every instrument of war" (8:1). Again the focus is on the military and warfare. That Asael and other "sons of heaven" also taught the processing of precious metals and all manner of astronomical knowledge, both of which were concentrated in the regimes of empires and their client rulers, indicates that the giants' military power and destructive warfare represented imperial power, conquest, and the exploitation of subject peoples.

Discerning just this allusion, George Nickelsburg suggested that the mutual destruction of the giants represented the wars of the Diadochoi, the successors of Alexander the Great who fought for control of territory in the late fourth century.[15] This surely fits with the dating, of the Book of Watchers to the third century on other grounds. Although iron weapons useable by infantry had been around for nearly a millennium (the Philistines), moreover, the armies of Alexander and his successors used swords of iron, shields, and breastplates (8:1).

The actions of the giants, however, need not be confined to the Diadochoi. They might rather pertain generally to the effects of Hellenistic rule on the people of Judea. That the fourth beast in the vision of Daniel 7 is so much more violent and devouring than the previous beasts suggests that Judeans experienced Hellenistic rule as more destructive and oppressive than Babylonian and Persian rule (ch. 5 below). As noted in chapter 1, the Ptolemies extracted maximum revenues from the agrarian economy of Judea and other areas they controlled—"devouring the labor of all the sons of men and men were not able to supply them" (7:3). Periodically through the course of the third century, moreover, the Ptolemies based in Egypt and the Seleucids based in Syria fought major wars for control of western Syria and Palestine, wars destructive and draining for Judeans and others in that area.[16] The giants' killing people and devouring one another, and the repeated theme of the giants' violence and bloodshed upon the earth (9:1, 9; 10:15), appears transparent to these recurrent imperial wars for the control of subject peoples.

It would have been intolerable for scribes such as those in the Enoch circle, who thought of themselves as obedient to God and faithful keepers of the traditional way of life, to believe that the imperial violence was punishment that they deserved for violating God's law. They sought another explanation for the imperial exploitation, violence, and destruction in the story of the rebel superhuman heavenly forces' generation of the giants upon the earth.[17]

With destructive imperial warfare and economic exploitation out of control, it is not surprising that the "Enoch" scribes devote most of the story to reassuring the audience (themselves) that, contrary to appearances, God is ultimately still in control. But here, too, the story of the watchers represents the imperial situation with which the "Enoch" scribes were struggling. The story portrays the universe as a great empire over which the God of gods presides as the great emperor. But "the King of kings," like the Persian emperor, seems to be "out of touch" with what is happening in his universal empire. Responsibility for governing has been delegated to officers who have jurisdiction over various aspects of the orderly operations of the universe.

So remote was "the King of kings" that when the earth and people cried out in their distress, it was not God who heard their cry, as in Exodus 2–3. Rather, the earth and people made their plea to high-ranking sons of heaven, who in turn brought the giants' violence and destruction to the attention of the now remote imperial "King of kings" (9:1-11). Only then did God delegate them to bind and destroy the violent and destructive giants (10:1—11:2). That God was remote helps explain why Judeans were suffering exploitation by the Ptolemaic regime and repeated warfare between the Ptolemaic and Seleucid empires. This situation, however, required the reassuring revelation that God was still ultimately in control in the governance of the universe that seemed so out of control. Accordingly, God instructed those four ranking officers of his imperial heavenly administration to bind the (leaders of the) rebel watchers (10:4-6, 11-12) and to renew the earth (10:7-8, 17-19). Gabriel was delegated to "destroy the sons of the watchers from among the sons of men" by "sending them against one another in a war of destruction" (10:9; cf. 12:6; 14:6). And here, for the "Enoch" scribes, was further explanation for the wars between the rival imperial regimes over control of Judea and other districts of Palestine.

Enoch's Prophetic Commission to Announce Judgment on the Rebel Watchers

While the story of the rebel watchers did not even mention Enoch, the next section of the Book of Watchers (*1 Enoch* 12–16) places "the scribe of righteousness" in the central role of a prophet pronouncing God's judgment on the watchers whose action led to violence and destruction on the earth. In the first step of his commissioning as a prophet, the loyal watchers of the Great Holy One charge the scribe to deliver an oracle of punishment to the rebel watchers (12:3—13:3). The next steps of his commissioning happen in dream visions. After he writes and presents a petition to God on behalf of the rebel watchers, he recites the visions of God's wrath to the watchers (13:4-10). "The book of the words of truth and the reprimand of the watchers" (14:1-7) appears to be a report, to the actual audience of the Book of Watchers as well as to the rebel watchers, about his vision of their sons' destruction (14:6). In the decisive step, Enoch goes through an elaborate account of his visionary ascent through heavenly mansions to the throne of the Great Glory (14:8-23).[18] There, God commissions him to indict the watchers for the destruction they have wrought and (briefly) to repeat their punishment (14:24—16:4).

Enoch is already established in the role of a scribe when he receives the prophetic commission (13:4-7; 15:1). Moreover, he carries out the prophetic commission in scribal form, producing a "book of the words of truth" (14:1-7 and elsewhere). Along with his prophetic oracle in *1 Enoch* 2–5, however, his commissioning, in a vision of God the king holding judgment in the heavenly court, establishes Enoch's primary role in the Book of Watchers as that of a prophet of divine judgment. The final scene in Enoch's commissioning bears close resemblances to the visions of prophets such as Micaiah ben Imlah (1 Kings 22:19-22), Isaiah (6; 40), and especially Ezekiel (1–2). It also has similarities to the scene of heavenly judgment in Daniel 7.[19] This portrayal of Enoch's commissioning as a prophet, like the prophetic forms in chapters 1–5, strongly suggests that the "Enoch" scribes who composed the Book of Watchers understood themselves as heirs of the Israelite prophetic *role*, as well as of the prophetic *tradition*. Whether they experienced visions themselves, or simply worked creatively from the tradition of revelatory visions in which prophets were commissioned, they had a sense of being called to deliver messages of God's judgment from the divine court.[20]

This whole section of the Book of Watchers has been driving toward the indictment that Enoch is to deliver to the disobedient sons of heaven (15:2—16:4). It focuses on the disastrous result of the watchers' mating with women (15:3bc, 4b): the giants who wrought desolation on the earth (15:3; 5–7). Enoch's indictment, however, encompasses an even greater historical disaster than the story of the watchers explained. Upon the destruction of the giants, their souls became evil spirits who further "lead astray, do violence, and make desolate (15:8, 11), desolation that will continue until the completion of the great judgment (16:1).

The indictment of the rebel watchers that Enoch receives in his vision provides a fuller revelation about the historical situation that the Book of Watchers addresses. The story of the watchers' generation of the giants explained the origin of imperial warfare and economic oppression. God's charge to Raphael, Gabriel, and Michael—to bind the watchers and destroy the giants—reassured "Enoch's" audience that the forces of destruction had been checked, pending God's final judgment. The disclosure in Enoch's prophetic vision, that the spirits of the destroyed giants have become evil spirits who continue the giant's devastation of human life and will do so until the final judgment, explains the current historical situation of the "Enoch" scribes who composed this text under Ptolemaic imperial rule. Several phrases in the description of the actions of the spirits of the giants (16:11) point to key aspects of that imperial domination sketched in chapter 1. The Ptolemaic imperial regime repeatedly fought wars against the rival empire of the Seleucids in Judea and surrounding territories ("violence, . . . attack"). The Ptolemies maximized their economic exploitation of the peoples they controlled ("make desolate"). Hellenistic imperial lifestyle and culture seduced Judean aristocrats to compromise the traditional Judean way of life ("lead astray"). All of these actions had debilitating effects on Judean social-economic and personal life ("hurt . . . and illness"). The spirits of the giants were causing the continuation of the destructive violence and exploitation that the giants began in the antediluvian time of Enoch.

Enoch's Journeys to the Northwest and East

Following the vision in which Enoch is commissioned to prophesy punishment to the watchers come two visionary journeys (*1 Enoch* 17-36). In these journeys, Enoch acquires knowledge of where and how the rebels, whose actions have brought violence and oppression upon the people, are now securely under the punitive control of the divine governance of the universe. These largely prose accounts are rooted in and draw upon long-standing astronomical, meteorological, and geographical "science" that was standard in Babylonian scribal circles, and to some degree among Judean scribal circles as well. Ben Sira clearly commands basic cosmological wisdom that he uses in hymns about the divine creation (16:24—17:24; 39:12-35; 42:15—43:33). Judging from the astronomical and meteorological wisdom in the oldest "Enoch" text, the Book of Luminaries, and its use in the later Animal Vision and the Epistle of Enoch, as well as in the Book of Watchers, the "Enoch" scribes were particularly interested in, perhaps specialists in, cosmological wisdom. Both of these "journeys" use this esoteric cosmological wisdom to shape the visions in which Enoch is shown the places where the rebel watchers have been securely confined.

In Enoch's visionary journey to the northwest (*1 Enoch* 17–19), the first two paragraphs establish his credibility: he clearly commands knowledge of "the place of the luminaries and the treasuries of the stars" and "the foundation of the earth . . . and the firmament of heaven" (17:1-7; 18:1-5). When he then sees the chasm of chaos beyond the firmaments of heaven and earth, the heavenly figure Uriel explains that this is where the rebel heavenly forces who had brought destruction on people are confined until the great judgment (18:6—19:3). A duplication appears to have occurred in the development of the text here, with the angels who brought destruction on people (18:6-11 + 19:1-2) standing parallel to the stars that transgressed the command of the Lord (18:12-16). What Enoch learns in this visionary journey provides yet another explanation for the violent destruction wrought by the dominant empires and offers another reassurance that God or the divine governance of the universe ultimately has them under control. That the rebel divine forces are now confined in the chaos beyond the divine order of the universe is a blatant irony for the imperial regimes that sought to impose order through military violence while appealing to the divine order of the universe for their own legitimation.

In Enoch's visionary eastward journey (*1 Enoch* 20–36), the closing paragraphs in particular (33:1-4; 34:1—36:4), along with what he sees at every stage of his cosmic travels, establish his credibility. In this wide-ranging journey, he has been shown virtually everything: the place of the luminaries, the treasuries of the stars, winds, lightning and thunder, the great mountains and rivers, the waters of the abyss, the regions of fire, the firmaments of heaven and earth, indeed the very foundations of the earth and the chaos beyond. Professional scribe that he is, moreover, he has it all written down. The narrative is prefaced by a list of the highest-ranking heavenly figures in charge of various jurisdictions in the universe (20:1-8). Enoch learns from each one in succession about what is under control in their particular area of jurisdiction. To understand the explanations by particular divine figures, it helps to keep in mind their particular area of responsibility. The narrative guides the reader by the repeated phrase "from there I traveled to another place" (21:1; 22:1; 23:1; et al.). At several points, the divine figures' explanations give fairly clear indications of the historical forces and relationships that the visions are intended to illuminate.

In 21:1-10, somewhat duplicating and probably dependent on 18:6—19:2, Uriel (again) explains that the chaos beyond the firmaments of heaven and earth is where the stars that transgressed the command of the Lord have been bound, virtually forever.

In 22:1-14, Raphael, who is in charge of the spirits of human beings, explains that the hollow places in the great high mountain are for the spirits of the souls of the dead. These are separated into the sinners, whose spirits are separated for torment, and the righteous and those "that make suit, who make disclosure about the destruction, when they were murdered in the days of the sinners" (22:12). "The destruction" usually refers to the violence wrought by the giants, who represent the great empires that made war on the people and expropriated their goods. But who are "the sinners" under whom ("in the days of") people "were murdered"? Is this a reference to a faction of the Jerusalem aristocracy who were collaborating with one of the Hellenistic imperial regimes? Were some of the dissident "Enoch" scribes assassinated or "disappeared" by the faction in command of the temple-state?

In 24:22—25:7, Michael, who has charge of "the good ones of the people," explains that the high mountain is "the seat where the Great Holy One will sit when he visits the earth in goodness," and the extremely fragrant tree which will bear food for "the chosen" will be "transplanted to the holy place by the house of God." This section makes clear that these visions of Enoch are concerned for "the chosen," "the good ones of the people," that is the Judeans who had remained faithful, "obedient" to God's commands while undergoing violence at the hands of the imperial regimes ("giants"), at the core of which the "Enoch" scribes surely included themselves.

In 26:1—27:5, Sariel explains that the cursed valley is "for those who are cursed forever," because they spoke hard things against the Lord (27:2). This could be a reference to imperial arrogance, which was much on the mind of Judean scribes, judging from the tales of Daniel. If the description of the cursed valley is an allusion to the valley of Hinnom outside Jerusalem, however, the reference would more likely be to the Jerusalem figures whom the "Enoch" scribes judge to have dishonored God in some way.

The purpose of the visionary journeys of Enoch, as of the rest of the Book of Watchers, is to explain the violence and destruction wrought by the Hellenistic imperial regimes and to offer reassurance that the heavenly forces that rebelled against the divine governance of the universe are (now) under God's control.[21] The visionary journey to the east also includes assurances that, when God finally "visits the earth in goodness," the "good among the people" will eventually be able to "live a long life on the earth" (25:3-6). Throughout Enoch's visionary travels, his elaborate esoteric cosmological wisdom is used to illuminate the historical experience of the destructive impact of the Hellenistic imperial regimes on life in Judea. The "Enoch" scribes are struggling to explain the origins of imperial violence and its containment by the heavenly governance of the universe.

Conclusion

Perhaps because the Book of Watchers is usually classified as Judean "apocalyptic" literature, interpreters often overplay the "eschatology" of the book.[22] While "the great judgment" (10:12; 16:1; 22:11) is anticipated, however, none of the sections of the book have any sense of urgency.[23] They have only what might be called an eschatological *perspective*. In the first visionary journeys, for example, the spirits of the rebel watchers will bring destruction on people "until the great judgment" (19:1). In the second journey, Enoch finds the spirits of the sinners separated for torment "until the great day of judgment" (22:11). At the judgment, finally, God will visit the earth in goodness (25:3-4). Nothing in either vision, however, suggests that God will act imminently to put an end to the destruction and to bring about a life of peace and plenty in a renewed creation. Reassurances that God is ultimately in control, that the rebel watchers are bound, and that demonic forces of destruction and exploitation will eventually be checked, are based in cosmological wisdom. The principal message revealed in this section, as in other sections of the Book of Watchers, is that knowledge of the universe, revealed by the highest-ranking officers of God's universal government, indicates that things are still ultimately under the control of the King of kings.

It is surely significant that the judgment of the watchers is separate from the future "great judgment" in the Book of Watchers. The imprisonment and immolation of the watchers has already been enacted (10:11; 18:14-16; 19:1; 21:5, 10; 23:4) and will continue at least until the day of judgment (10:12; 18:14). Similarly, the judgment of the giants generated by the watchers has already taken place, partly by a mutual war of destruction (10:9, 15), although now their spirits continue their desolation (15:1; 16:1). Also, the souls of the dead are already placed in the respective mountain hollows.

The blessings on the righteous and curses on the wicked, on the other hand, are still in the future. By comparison with the judgment of the watchers, the blessings and curses anticipated in the Book of Watchers are similar to expectations in late prophetic texts. The righteous will live long lives on an earth restored to productivity. The images of renewal of life on the earth in *1 Enoch* 5:5-9 and 10:18—11:2 are no more fantastic than those in Isaiah 65 or Jeremiah 31. The main message is of consolation, reassurance, and hope amid the circumstances of imperial rule. Yet there is no sense of urgency or imminence. That must have developed later when the empire became more "beastly" in its brutal attacks, and scribes were being martyred for mounting organized resistance to imperial attacks, as evident in Daniel 10–12 (see ch 5 below).

Whether or not we label it "apocalyptic," the Book of Watchers is a creative response to Hellenistic imperial domination that had become violently destructive. This is what the story of the rebel watchers explains, and this is the problem to which the visionary commissioning of Enoch, the oracle with which he is charged, and the revelation in his visionary journeys all respond: the destruction that has been wrought by the giants, which clearly represent Hellenistic imperial warfare and economic oppression.

Chapter 4

Wolves and Sheep, Eagles and Lambs: Enoch's Animal Vision and Other Historical Surveys

The bulk of the fourth book included in *1 Enoch* is an allegorical survey of the history of Israel under attack by foreign enemies that culminates in severe oppression by imperial regimes, with eventual resistance vindicated by divine judgment and deliverance (*1 Enoch* 85–90).[1] Another, much shorter survey of the history of Israel, framed by universal history, constitutes the first section of the Epistle of Enoch (*1 Enoch* 93:1-10 with 91:10-17). Interpreters have usually classified these historical surveys as "apocalyptic" texts, awarding them the now standard titles "The Animal Apocalypse" and "The Apocalypse of Weeks," respectively. In recent discussions of the *genre* of "apocalypse," these surveys are grouped with the visionary surveys of the escalating history of imperial violence and the divine deliverance of Judeans in Daniel 7–12.[2] These texts, it is argued, belong to a subcategory of "historical apocalypses" that come in visions, with an angel as interpreter. The early version of the *Testament of Moses*, which is also often included in discussions of "apocalyptic" literature, presents yet another, contemporary survey of Israel's history.*

---

* A new translation of the Animal Vision (1 Enoch 85-90) and "Enoch's" ten-week survey of history (1 Enoch 93:1–10 with 91:11–17) is now available in George W. E. Nickelsburg and James C. VanderKam, *1 Enoch: A New Translation* (Minneapolis: Fortress Press, 2004). The most accessible translation of the *Testament of Moses* is J. H. Charlesworth, ed., *Old Testament Pseudepigrapha* (2 vols; Garden City, NY: Doubleday, 1983–85), 1:919–34. I urge readers to read through each of these texts before they read the discussion in this chapter.

Getting Reoriented

The notion that these historical surveys are "apocalypses" is surely rooted in the traditional understanding of the book of Daniel as the prototypical "apocalyptic" text. Similarly, the related sense that the typical mode of revelation in these "historical apocalypses" is a "symbolic vision" stem from the images in the dream visions in Daniel 7 and 8. Further, the idea that these historical surveys usually involve an angel or other heavenly figure as interpreter also derive from the role of such figures in the texts in Daniel 7–12. But it is difficult to discern how the Animal Vision or Enoch's ten-week survey or the *Testament of Moses* could be classified as "historical apocalypses."

In the overall anthology of texts in *1 Enoch*, the ten-week survey of history (93:1-10 with 91:11-17) is introduced rather as a testament, a discourse from Enoch to his sons (93:1-2, 3). "Enoch" also says that he was shown a "heavenly vision." But he claims to have received his discourse through two other media as well: the oral communication of "the words of the watchers and holy ones," and the written medium of "the heavenly tablets." The parallelism of these three media suggests that they are interrelated. But the point of mentioning all three is to lend divine authority and credibility to his summary of future history. His survey of history, moreover, does not proceed as a vision, with the repeated cue, "And I saw." Although the narrative uses general terms of reference such as "a man" and "the righteous," without naming names, it does not involve special visionary imagery. Since the terms of reference are transparent to historical figures and groups, moreover, neither interpretation nor angelic interpreter is necessary.

The sustained survey of history in *1 Enoch* 85–90 is introduced as a vision (83:1-2; 85:1-2, 3) and proceeds as a vision, with the frequent cue "And again I saw" (86:1; 87:1; et al.). But it involves no interpreter since no interpretation is needed. The narrative proceeds in symbols, but it is patently allegorical. As is immediately obvious to an audience with any acquaintance with Israelite (Judean) culture, the story is only ostensibly about the predatory animals and birds, the sheep and their shepherd. These are signs transparent to the intended referents in universal international history centered on Israel (Judeans), their repeated experience of attacks by kings or empires, and the ups and downs of their relationship with God.

The anticipatory survey of history in the *Testament of Moses* is framed as a testament, matching its title. Like "Enoch's" surveys of history, that of "Moses" is delivered by a revered ancient figure, in this case the founding prophet of Israel and mediator of the covenant with God. But "Moses" does not derive his foreknowledge from a vision. With no symbolic images, no interpreter and interpretation are involved. Usually without mentioning names, "Moses" refers to historical events, peoples, and figures.

Since neither "Enoch's" ten-week survey, his Animal Vision, nor "Moses'" testamentary survey exhibits the features that supposedly constitute the scholarly subcategory of "historical apocalypse," it is unclear why they should be discussed in such terms. It makes more sense to focus on each text and its principal message as it addresses its historical context, while also looking for how it creatively adapts key forms and materials from the Judean cultural repertoire, and for features that it has in common with similar texts.

Scholarly attempts to delineate distinctive features of these texts as "historical apocalypses" see in them a "new departure" from prophetic tradition, not so much in literary form as in "the use of pseudonymity and extended *ex eventu* prophecy." Such features, it is claimed, express "a new worldview,"[3] one of "determinism." The prophetic segment as well as the Torah segment of the Judean cultural repertoire, however, had long included pseudonymous texts. The book of Deuteronomy claimed to be the covenantal teachings of Moses himself. The books of Amos, Hosea, and Micah came to include materials that originated long after those historical figures lived. Most frequently discussed is the book of Isaiah, which includes large blocks of "exilic" or Second Temple materials attributed to the prophet Isaiah. As for "prophecy after the event," it is not clear how the historical surveys of "Enoch" or "Daniel" differ from the attribution of the prophecies in Isaiah 26–29, 40–55, and 56–66 to Isaiah, or the prophecies of future restoration to Amos, Hosea, and Micah. It is difficult to see how these features make the foreknowledge of "Daniel" or "Enoch" or "Moses" any more deterministic than the oracles of Micaiah ben Imlah, Isaiah, or Zechariah, where historical events are already known in the heavenly council of Yahweh and declared as "the word of Yahweh," often as the judgment of Yahweh on oppressive rulers.

Each of these surveys of history has considerable narrative coherence as sustained sequences of events—especially in comparison with the loosely linked sections of the Book of the Watchers. The significance of particular episodes depends on their function in the overall story. The key questions of interpretation are what each survey presents as the main problem(s) or issue(s) in the history of Israel, how it portrays the origin of the problem(s), and what it presents as the resolution.

The Animal Vision

The extended allegory of the animals and birds attacking the sheep of the Lord in *1 Enoch* 85–90, recited as a vision that Enoch has already seen, is not just a history focused on Israel in the context of international politics. The allegory builds on the long-standing metaphor of Israel as "sheep" who belong to God as their "Lord" but who are under attack by predatory "animals" (see esp. Ezek 34). It focuses more particularly—strikingly—on the imperial rulers that had attacked Israel/Judeans militarily and oppressed them politically and economically.[4] The relative amount of attention that the survey gives to particular events or stages in humankind's or Israel's history is a key to the importance of the problem it portrays: the origin of empires and imperial violence, the origin of Israel in the struggle against imperial oppression, and the escalation of imperial violence and oppression—until some of the awakened Israelites mount a new struggle against it.

The first fifth of the narrative (85:3—89:8) is devoted to the origin of imperial regimes, the violence and oppression they perpetrate, and the measures taken by the divine governance of history to bring them under control. In the symbols of the vision, almost immediately after the origin of domestic animals (humankind), errant heavenly figures descend and propagate gigantic animals (empires) that "bite, . . . devour, and gore" the cattle (humans). To exert control, the stars are bound and thrown into an abyss, as the gigantic beasts destroy one another (imperial warfare), and the flood envelops the earthly stage of history, with only Noah and his family surviving. The second fifth of the narrative (89:9-38) is devoted to the origin of the sheep, their immediately being oppressed by the wolves, the glorious Lord of the sheep leading their escape, and the struggle of the sheep to follow the path shown them by the lead sheep and to cohere in or around a house. This transparently represents the origin of Israel in the exodus from oppression under the Egyptian Pharaoh and its struggle to form a covenant people.

Another several paragraphs (89:39-50; roughly a tenth of the narrative) deals with the attack by the Philistines and the struggle against them led by David, and the "house" becoming large and broad under Solomon. Only a brief paragraph (89:51-53) is devoted to the period of the monarchy when the "sheep" stray and kill the prophets sent to them. But a longer paragraph (89:54-58) portrays how the Lord of the sheep abandons them to predatory beasts such as lions, leopards, and hyenas, who "tear the sheep in pieces, . . . devour them, and carry them off."

Then, however, fully a third of the vision (89:59—90:19) is devoted to the escalation of imperial domination under a succession of empires, signified by the "seventy shepherds" and their "subordinates." The escalation of imperial violence and oppression is reflected in the escalation of images used to "explain" it. "Shepherds" had long been a standing metaphor for rulers; Jeremiah had referred to destructive Babylonian kings as shepherds (Jer 25:30-38). In the escalated imagery of Enoch's vision, the seventy shepherds represent superhuman heavenly figures that stand above and behind their "subordinates," the imperial regimes signified by the predatory beasts, such as lions and wild boars, and the predatory birds, such as eagles and vultures, who devour the sheep. The extremes of imperial domination eventually lead to the awakening of and resistance by the lambs who have their eyes opened, presumably the "Enoch" scribes.

The final section, about a sixth of the narrative (90:20-42), focuses on three steps in the resolution of the history of imperial violence and the oppression of Israel. The Lord of the sheep sits in judgment, again, of the errant stars who had propagated empires in the first place, the oppressive imperial shepherds, and the blinded sheep among the Judeans. The old house is folded up and the sheep brought into a new one that includes all the previously dispersed sheep, with the no longer predatory birds and beasts petitioning and obeying the sheep. Finally, in a short paragraph, all of the species, including the beasts and birds, morph into cattle (with which the vision began), a pastoral utopia.

In its version of antediluvian history, the allegorical vision explains the origin of violence not from acts of disobedience by humans, as does Genesis 2–3, but from superhuman heavenly forces that generated gigantic animals that "devoured" the domestic animals (86:1-6). This is a barely veiled repetition of the story of the rebel watchers' propagation of the giants who perpetrate imperial violence and destruction in the Book of Watchers (*1 Enoch* 6–11). "Stars," descending from heaven to mate with women, produce gigantic "elephants, camels, and asses" that attack and devour people (86:1-6). These predatory imperial regimes make war on one another and are supposedly destroyed in the flood (89:6). But they have unleashed violence and exploitation by powerful rulers.

Closely connected with the attacks by foreign kings is the relation between the sheep, Israel, and their Lord, particularly the blindness and straying of the sheep. The relation of Israel and its Lord cannot be taken in a narrowly religious way, since religion was inseparable from politics and economics in the ancient world. The relationship is focused on the symbol of the "house." The Hebrew or Aramaic term for "house" had various meanings, depending on the context: dwelling, household, lineage, dynasty, palace, and temple (the house of [a] god). From the various contexts in which it occurs in Enoch's allegorical vision, it is clear that the "house" of the sheep does not refer to the Temple in Jerusalem. The symbol for the Temple in Jerusalem could not be clearer: a "large and high tower built on the house for the Lord of the sheep" (89:50, 54, 56, 66).[5] The house must refer to the city of Jerusalem here, since the tower was built on the house (89:50) and the house is destroyed when the tower is burned (89:66).[6] Yet from other contexts, it is clear that "house" has a referent broader than the city.[7] It appears to signify the "house" of the people, of Israel. It was originally established by the sheep-become-a-man who signifies Moses (89:36). This house cannot signify the tabernacle, contrary to standard interpretation by biblical scholars, since the people stand in it (89:36), not the Lord (that is, the Temple, 89:50, which would correspond to the earlier tabernacle).[8]

That the house refers both to the people of Israel more broadly, and to Jerusalem from the time of David and Solomon onward, is grounded in the history and sociology of ancient Israel-Judea. In both historical and prophetic traditions, Jerusalem became the capital and symbolic center of Israel from the time of David and Solomon, and especially after the fall of the northern kingdom of Israel, Jerusalem/Zion became a symbol for the whole people (for example, in prophetic oracles such as Isa 40). The scribal producers of literature such as the animal vision, who were based in Jerusalem, moreover, would understandably think in just such terms: of Jerusalem as (representing) the people (of Israel).

The sheep recurrently alternate between opening their eyes and seeing and then becoming blind and straying—from the path or from their house. This signifies that the people were supposed to adhere to the path that Moses had shown them, as a disciplined obedient people (a further confirmation that the house represents the people, not just Jerusalem). The path that Moses showed the sheep and from which they stray later in the allegorical story must signify the Mosaic covenant, although the narrative makes no explicit reference to it in connection with the Lord's appearance at Sinai (89:28-32).[9] The "some from among the sheep" that the Lord sends to the sheep, who proceed to kill them, are clearly the Israelite prophets—and, as in the ten-week survey, Elijah escapes (89:51-53).[10] Numerous oracles of Amos, Micah, Isaiah, and Jeremiah indicate that the prophets were known to have repeatedly accused the kings of Israel and Judah of violating the covenantal commandments. And those same prophets declared that because of the rulers' violation of the Mosaic covenant, God was unleashing foreign imperial rulers to conquer them as punishment. This is clearly the referent of the sheep abandoning the house and the tower and the Lord abandoning the house and tower (89:54-58).

The vision of the animals and birds brings the superhuman origins of violence directly to bear on the relationship between God and Israel in its representation of the extreme violence and oppression to which Judeans were subjected under Babylonian, and especially Ptolemaic and Seleucid, imperial rule. The imperial violence under the Babylonians and Hellenistic regimes must have seemed far more destructive and inexplicable than did the oppression by the Egyptians and Philistines in earlier times. In its portrayal of the latter, the vision made no direct connection between the treatment of the sheep by the wolves and the dogs and the cruel offspring of the fallen stars in which violence originated. By contrast, however, it represents the Babylonian and Hellenistic imperial regimes' violence against Judeans as determined by an empirelike administration in the heavenly world. The imperial Lord of history abandoned his sheep (after they abandoned their house) and placed them under the domination of a sequence of seventy "shepherds" and their subordinates (89:59).[11] The vision thus attributes the extreme violence that Judeans experienced, especially under the Ptolemaic and Seleucid dominion, to superhuman heavenly forces that stand behind and give orders to the beastly imperial regimes. As Patrick Tiller notes, moreover, the allegorical vision here also "turns the imperial claims to divine descent on its head."[12] The imperial regimes do indeed have the support of heavenly forces, but the latter are heavenly powers who, in disobedience to God's command, become overly destructive of the people under their rule.

Thus, not only the powers of the heavenly world, but God himself, is ultimately behind the imperial violence, in punishment of Israel for its straying from the path and abandoning the house. The vision here represents God as a remote heavenly emperor who delegates punitive violence to his regional commanders, who in turn delegate to their subordinates (89:59). The vision represents "the Lord of the sheep" as having morphed from a divine shepherd directly involved in pasturing his sheep, appearing to them, and sending leaders, to a monarch elevated above the sheep in his tower, to an imperial king so remote that he is no longer directly in control of his empire. Though remote, however, the Lord of the sheep is ultimately in control, as signified by the heavenly figure that he charges as a secret informant who audits the extent to which the imperial satraps abuse and destroy his subjects and periodically shows him the heavenly ledger book (89:61-64, 68-71, 76-77).

In its account of the Persian period, the allegorical vision does not emphasize the imperial violence but focuses on the rebuilding of Judean society and the "tower." In contrast to the original tower, however, it is not "high" and the Lord is not standing on it. The narrative, moreover, states pointedly that the bread on the table before the tower "was polluted and not pure" and that the sheep were blind (89:73-74). The "Enoch" scribes thus make a serious indictment of the temple-state as problematic from the outset.

In a short paragraph but with strong images, the narrative portrays the Hellenistic empire of the Ptolemies as devastating for the subject Judeans. "The eagles and vultures . . . began to devour those sheep and peck out their eyes and devour their flesh . . . until only their bones remained" (90:2-4). In addition to the sequence of images and numbers of shepherds, the image of eagles indicates that these are the Ptolemies (many Ptolemaic coins display an eagle on one side).[13] The heavenly scribe charged with recording imperial overreach, however, does not step forward at this point to show the ledger of violent oppression to the Lord. When he finally does come forward, after resistance by the awakened sheep has begun, his book shows that the last twelve shepherds, those in charge of the Hellenistic empires (primarily the Ptolemies), "had destroyed more than those before them" (90:17). As we will see, this parallels the historical surveys of imperial violence and oppression in the visions of Daniel and the testament of "Moses."

The climactic historical crisis finally emerges under the Hellenistic empires. The allegorical narrative suddenly moves into more specific references to groups and struggles. Close examination of the duplication of certain terms and the apparent duplication of conflicts in the narrative (90:6-19) suggest that the text as we have it involves a secondary "updating" of the story, with 90:9b-10 and 90:12-16 having been inserted into an earlier version consisting of 90:6-9a, 11, 17-19.[14] The "great horn" that "sprouted on one of those sheep" and "the horn of that ram" (90:9b) are transparent references to Judas the Maccabee, who became the charismatic leader of the revolt. The predatory birds' battles against him that appear eventually to be successful (90:12-13, 16) are evidently the Seleucid armies' attempts to suppress the revolt he was leading.

Without this "updating," however, or prior to it, the narrative gives a coherent sequence of earlier opposition to Hellenistic imperial rule. "The lambs . . . who began to open their eyes and to see" are some Judeans who realized just how oppressive and intolerable Hellenistic imperial rule had become. Their "crying out to the sheep," who did not listen, represents their appeal to other Judeans, who are content to continue to acquiesce in the imperial order. But they have started a resistance sufficiently serious that the imperial birds of prey attack, seize the lambs, and dismember and devour others of the sheep. The emergence of horns on those lambs must be a reference to a more serious, organized, perhaps militant resistance. The ravens' casting down their horns must be further imperial attacks to suppress their opposition. And the escalated attacks by all the imperial birds of prey, flying upon the sheep and devouring them, point to expanded measures taken to suppress resistance.

The narrative flows easily from either of the two versions of the climactic crisis, in which Judeans mount resistance or rebellion against Hellenistic imperial rule that has become so violent, into the decisive joint victory of the imperial divine Lord, who finally intervenes on behalf of the sheep and a wider revolt by the sheep themselves (90:17-19). The images suddenly become more fantastic, suggesting that the narrative at this point moves from recent historical events to anticipated events in the near future. There might seem to be a tension between the decisive intervention by the Lord and the "large sword" wielded by the sheep. Yet not only does the Lord's action take place at a different "level" and "location" from the human action—the Lord finally asserts his sovereign control in the governance of the universe—but the vision here is yet another expression of the traditional Israelite understanding of the coordination of God's action with action by historical actors. The sheep wielding the large sword is the implementation of the Lord's final decisive reassertion of control in the divine governance of heaven and earth. The "Enoch" scribes here anticipate the action of God in support of their own resistance just when it seems hopeless, in a way that parallels the "Daniel" visions' anticipation of divine intervention at the low point, when the resisting maskilim are being martyred (Dan 11:33—12:3).

The resolution of the historical crisis, in God's judgment of the forces of empire and the renewal of Israel, indeed all peoples, comes in the final paragraphs (90:20-42). The list of those subject to the Lord's judgment is another indication of the Animal Vision's fundamental concerns. Judgment is executed first on the errant stars, in whose propagation of gigantic beasts the imperial violence and oppression had originated, and second on the seventy shepherds who had exercised overreaching imperial oppression of Israel through the Babylonian, Persian, and especially on the Hellenistic empires (90:20-25).

That the blinded sheep who had opposed the awakened lambs were also thrown into the abyss (90:26-27) indicates just how serious their actions had been in the eyes of the producers of the vision. Presumably the blinded sheep were (or included) the aristocratic faction in control of the Temple toward the end of Ptolemaic rule and the beginning of Seleucid rule. The "Enoch" scribes' opposition to and conflict with the rulers of the temple-state probably focused on their collaboration with Hellenistic imperial rule prior to and continuing into their leadership of the Hellenizing reform. But their criticism of the priestly aristocracy, or even of the temple-state itself, may have been of long standing (see again 89:72b-74).

The judgment clears the way for the fantastic restoration and revitalization of the people, centered on the symbol of the house. The new house, larger and higher than the first one (90:28-29), also includes Judeans (Israelites) who had been dispersed or destroyed by the brutal imperial regimes. The renewed house of Israel is erected on the site of the old house (presumably in Jerusalem, at the center of Judea/Israel). It is thus striking that it has no tower, that is, a temple. But of course the original house in which all the sheep were standing in the time when the Lord was directly involved in their life had no tower (89:28-36). The "high tower" had been built on the house by a ruler, apparently as a means of communication with the Lord, who stood on top of the high tower (89:50). The rebuilt temple was illegitimate ("polluted bread," 89:73). The new, enlarged, and higher house that the Lord erects at the end has no high tower. But since God was now directly involved in the restoration of the people (God is "present" in the house, 90:36), there was no need for a temple.[15] It may not be by accident that scribes who had come to oppose the temple-state as implicated in imperial domination were focused on the renewal of the people but not the restoration of the temple-state.

The envisaged renewal also includes the former attackers of Israel and the Judeans, although it may be that the beasts and birds now represent not so much the former enemies of Israel/Judeans, but all other peoples in general. The initial image is a reversal of the imperial relationship, as the former predators now "fall down and worship the sheep" (90:30). In the final images, however, the beasts and birds as well as the sheep are all transformed into white cattle, like the original inhabitants of the earth (90:38).

Clearly the narrative is especially interested in the lambs who began to open their eyes and cry out to the sheep—and thus precipitate the crisis (90:6). Insofar as the narrative identifies with these "lambs," who "cry out" to others, it seems likely that they represent dissident scribes. That the scribes who produced the Animal Vision make such good use of the story of the rebel watchers indicates that they stood in continuity with the "Enoch" scribes who produced the Book of the Watchers. It seems warranted to understand the narrative of the crisis (in 90:6-9b, 11) as a self-representation of the Enoch circle of scribes. They are portraying their own resistance to Hellenistic imperial rule. Yet it is difficult to discern precisely when, during the prolonged and escalating crisis in Judean society under the Hellenistic empires, their resistance fits.

One possibility is that the "Enoch" scribes did not simply express opposition to Hellenistic imperial rule in their production of texts (such as the Book of Watchers) but, as a circle of dissident scribes, stood in conflict with the dominant faction that controlled the Judean temple-state. Their "crying out" in protest and being rejected could well have evoked repression by the ruling faction in the aristocracy and/or their backers in the imperial court. And such a conflict could have happened well prior to the Hellenizing reform.[16] From what little we do know of how events unfolded in Jerusalem during the first three decades of the second century, the more serious resistance signified by the horns on the lambs would fit best as a reaction to the reform, which would, in this scenario, have been a rejection of the dissident "Enoch" scribes' appeal to return to the traditional Judean way of life.

Another possibility would be to take the narrative of the crisis as a reference to resistance by "Enoch" scribes and repression by Antiochus Epiphanes that began following the Hellenizing reform. The more serious resistance signified by the horns on the lambs would then refer to their joining the widening resistance in response to Antiochus's attacks on Jerusalem to bring resistance under control in 169–168 B.C.E. The escalation of attacks on the lambs in 90:12 would then be a reference to the escalating efforts by Antiochus to reestablish control of Jerusalem. And at that point, the narrative moves to the final intervention of the Lord of the sheep and the more fantastic images of "the staff of his wrath" and "a large sword given to those sheep." These could be references to wider revolt, but more likely represent the move from the present crisis to an eagerly anticipated divine deliverance. In any case, the earlier version of the crisis, in 90:6-9, 12, clearly pertains to events prior to the eruption of the wider revolt led by Judas Maccabeus.

The secondary insertion of the reference to Judas and that wider revolt (90:9b-10, 12-16) then served to bring the text up to date a few years later. And it suggests that the circle of "Enoch" scribes, who had been involved in some sort of opposition and resistance for years, joined in or otherwise supported the widespread revolt that began in 167.

History in Ten "Weeks"

In a much shorter survey (*1 Enoch* 93:1-10 with 91:11-17), "Enoch" discloses a prospective summary of the history of Israel/Judea framed by universal history in a sequence of ten "weeks." With no particular internal links to the sequence of woes and reassurances that comprise the bulk of the Epistle of Enoch in which it is embedded, however, it may well have been composed separately. One of the Aramaic fragments of Enoch literature found among the Dead Sea Scrolls confirms that 93:1-10 in the Ethiopic text was followed immediately by 91:11-17, as previous editors had concluded.[17] The ten-week historical survey is introduced as a vision in testamentary form by 91:1-2, but involves no heavenly figure as interpreter and no sequential "I saw. . . ."

The short survey of history in ten "weeks" focuses on the history of Israel without explicitly mentioning hostile and oppressive outside forces, in contrast to the Animal Vision (*1 Enoch* 85–90) and the *Testament of Moses,* in which the main problem is the origin, explanation, and termination of imperial violence against Israel. The ten-week survey does place Israel's history in the frame of universal history in the first two "weeks" and last two "weeks," however, and even includes judgment of the heavenly watchers, as in the Book of Watchers and the Animal Vision.

After the first week in which justice endured, "deceit and violence" will spring up in the second, at the end of which "a man" (Noah) will be saved and a law will be made for sinners. In contrast to other Enoch texts, the survey of "weeks" does not attribute the origin of violence to superhuman heavenly forces, although the judgment of the watchers in the tenth week suggests that they are implicated. At the conclusion of the third week, "a man" (Abraham) will be chosen, from whom "the plant of justice" will go forth into subsequent history. At the conclusion of the fourth week, with visions of the holy and righteous, "a covenant for all generations," along with a tabernacle, will be made (the only explicit mention of the Mosaic covenant in the early "Enoch" texts). "The house of glory and kingdom built forever"[18] in the fifth week suggests not so much the Temple as the people of Israel in their land around Jerusalem. In the sixth week, the people will become blind (as in the Animal Vision) and "stray from wisdom," although "a man" will ascend. That they stray from "wisdom" after "the covenant" was given suggests the scribal identification of the two, as in the Deuteronomic tradition and Ben Sira's instruction. The mention of the man who ascends here, as in the Animal Vision, indicates that Elijah was an important figure for the "Enoch" scribes as well as for Ben Sira (48:10). The burning of the house of the kingdom with fire at the end of the eventful sixth week seems to refer to the Babylonians' destruction of Jerusalem as a whole, and not just the Temple (as in 2 Kings 25:8-10), after which "the chosen" will be dispersed.

The seventh week is clearly the historical crisis that this survey of history addresses. The "perverse generation, . . . all [of whose] deeds will be perverse," evidently refers to the founders and heads of the temple-state generally (93:9-10; 91:11). That "all its deeds are perverse" is a blanket indictment of the Second Temple regime generally, parallel to the equally blunt condemnation of the Second Temple in the Animal Vision ("all the bread on [the table of the high tower]"; 89:73). The "perverse generation," whose deeds are also "perverse," applies more particularly to the dominant faction that had taken control in Jerusalem under the Ptolemies in the late-second century and finally instituted the Hellenizing "reform" program in 175 B.C.E. Those chosen at the conclusion of the seventh week "as witnesses of justice from the eternal plant of justice, to whom sevenfold wisdom will be given" must be the "Enoch" scribal circle (those who produced this and other early Enoch texts; 93:10).

That the chosen who receive the sevenfold wisdom "will uproot the foundations of violence and the structure of deceit in it to execute judgment" (91:11; a rather grandiose sense of their own historical role, as in the Animal Vision) suggests that the "Enoch" people had launched some sort of serious resistance. "The foundations of violence" appears to be a reference to the Hellenizing reform backed by Antiochus Epiphanes, which was doing violence to Judeans and their traditional way of life, and "the structure of deceit" appears to be a synonymous reference to the deceitful way that the Hellenizing aristocrats went about replacing the traditional "laws of the Judeans" with their new *politeia*. "The chosen" who receive "sevenfold wisdom" and "uproot . . ." (93:10; 91:11) then appears to be the "Enoch" scribes' reference to the active opposition they had begun to the reform.

This event at the "conclusion" of the seventh week is represented as the turning point in history. After all had strayed from wisdom under the monarchy in the sixth week, affairs became even worse with the "perverse generation" heading the temple-state, all of whose deeds were perverse. Just at that point of crisis, however, "the chosen" are "chosen" and, in response to the "sevenfold wisdom" they received (finally recognizing how desperate the situation had become and finally rededicating themselves to the covenant), began to "uproot" the Hellenizing reform. The portrayal of the turning point of history here in the seventh week thus parallels that in the Animal Vision where, just when the sheep are being most severely devoured by the predator dogs and eagles, "lambs" are born, begin to "open their eyes," and cry out to the sheep (90:6-7). In comparison with the Animal Vision's portrayal of scribal resistance to imperial domination, however, the ten-week summary of history seems confident that "the chosen" will be able to "uproot the foundations of violence." There is no hint of Antiochus's crackdown on the resistance in Jerusalem, in contrast to the Animal Vision where the ravens attack the lambs who have grown horns (90:8-9). "The chosen" in the seventh week appear to have begun active resistance before Antiochus's invasion of Jerusalem.

Judging from the scenario of the eighth week, moreover, the scribes behind the ten-week history are expecting that the uprooting they have begun will grow into a wider resistance. The revival of justice and wisdom and the execution of righteous judgment seem to continue directly from the seventh week into the eighth. The "sword given to all the righteous to execute judgment on all the wicked" anticipates a significant new development: a more widespread resistance, perhaps a revolt. That the wicked "will be delivered into their hands" suggests that such a wider revolt is anticipated imminently, or is at most barely under way. That the righteous will acquire possessions (households = livings) and "the house of the great King" be gloriously (re-)built[19] is a historical, and hardly fantastic, goal of the restoration of Judean society to what the "Enoch" scribes thought it ought to be. On the other hand, however, the building of the house of the kingdom for all eternity seems a bit more fantastic, more "unrealistically" off in the future, suggesting that the eighth week in Enoch's vision lies in the future, from the standpoint of the "Enoch" scribes.

In the ninth and tenth weeks, history will expand to universal horizons, with "all humankind" looking to the path of justice begun with Abraham and finally revived by the "Enoch" scribes in the present seventh week. The conclusion is clearly a fulfillment of history, with not a hint of some "cosmic catastrophe" followed by a literal new creation.[20] The "new heaven" that replaces the first consists in the restoration of divine governance to its proper functioning (to God's control?), with a judgment on the watchers, and all the heavenly powers (so central to the Enochic cosmological wisdom) shining with sevenfold brightness.

Throughout this review of history, "Enoch" makes no mention of God's agency, although it is implied in the passive verbs, such as "will be given" or "will be revealed" (by God). It is also striking in comparison with other Enoch texts that, except for the implication of judgment being executed on the watchers (they are presumed guilty of something), history is not subject to the control of heavenly figures other than God. The ten-week survey focuses on history, on human agency, for better or worse, and on political events and conflicts, particularly the political crisis in Judea under the Hellenistic empires. Like the Animal Vision, it indicates that the "Enoch" scribes were opposed to the Second Temple regime in general and engaged in active resistance to the Hellenizing reform in Jerusalem.

The Testament of Moses

The historical survey in the *Testament of Moses* is an "updating" of the prophecy of Moses at the end of the book of Deuteronomy (chs. 31–34). Anticipating his death, Moses commissions Joshua as his successor, gives commands to preserve the book of covenantal teaching, then narrates key events in Israel's history, including the people's breaking of the covenant and God's punishment, and finally announces how God will take vengeance on the people's enemies and deliver the people. Also evident in this survey is the pattern familiar, for example, from Deuteronomy 32 and the book of Judges, of Israel established in its land by God, falling away from the covenant and being punished by God, repenting and recommitting, and finally being delivered again by their gracious God. The survey's point of view is that of Judeans (presumably priests and/or Levites and/or scribes) firmly attached to the Second Temple as established by those "sent home to their own land" by a God-inspired emperor. "Moses'" survey uses the covenant (commandments) as criteria for Israel's history more explicitly and pointedly than "Enoch's" ten-week survey. Interpreters have long recognized that chapters 6 and 7 are later additions, updates under Roman rule after the Hasmonean dynasty and the kingship of Herod the Great (to be discussed in ch. 9 below).

The narrative moves quickly past the establishment of the people in their land[21] and the monarchy's violation of the covenant to focus on the history of the people under the succession of empires (the division into chapters 3, 4, and 5 correspond to key crises under the Babylonian, Persian, and Hellenistic empires, respectively). After the disastrous destruction of Jerusalem and the Temple by the (Babylonian) "king from the east," the exiled Judeans and Levites will take the lead in recognizing that they had broken God's commandments and will be servants (of the empire) for about seventy years (ch. 3). Under the Persian Empire, God "will inspire a king to send them home to their own land," where some will rebuild the walls (presumably of Jerusalem; ch. 4). In times of exposure under punishment by (Hellenistic) kings, the Judeans (and Levites) "will be divided as to the truth." That these kings "share their crimes" leads into the unprecedented iniquity, injustice, and pollution of those on the other side of that divide (those in control of the temple-state). In those times, "those who are their leaders, their teachers," and judges will abandon justice, pollute the temple and altar, and serve other gods (ch. 5).

The punishment and wrath perpetrated by "a king of the kings of the earth" (clearly Antiochus Epiphanes), however, falls on those who remain faithful (ch. 8). The characterization of the repressive imperial violence as unprecedented "from the creation till that time" is similar to that of the "time of tribulation/anguish" in the parallel review of history in Daniel 10–12 (12:1). The brutal repression even includes crucifixion and torture as well as imprisonment, forced blasphemy, and abominable polluting sacrifices on their altar. And the imperial measures of repression extend to those who compromise their faith, not just "those who confess their circumcision." "Moses'" review of history thus clearly comes from the high point of the extended crisis, when Antiochus Epiphanes had launched his program of forced abandonment of the traditional Judean covenantal commitment. Yet it addresses the situation prior to the revolt led by Judas the Maccabee.

This is evident in the sudden focus on "a man from the tribe of Levi whose name is Taxo and his sons" (ch. 9). The Latin text carries over the name *Taxon* ("staff," "orderer") from the Greek text, where it translated the Hebrew *mehoqeq*, "staff." The Damascus Document, also found among the Dead Sea Scrolls, takes "the staff" of Numbers 21:18 to signify "the expositor" of the law," the leader who instructs the movement (CD 6:3-12). "Taxo" must therefore be the scribal leader, or "orderer," of the "Moses" scribes who composed the *Testament of Moses*, and the "sons" his disciples.[22] The situation of Taxo and his sons resembles that of the Judeans portrayed in 1 Maccabees 2:29-38 who went out into the wilderness with their families, determined to remain steadfast in obedience to the covenant commandments, in resistance to the imperial decree. Taxo's and his sons' resistance (and presumed martyrdom)—"Let us die rather than transgress the commandments of the Lord of lords, the God of our fathers" (9:6)—parallels that of the maskilim in Daniel 10–12, as well as that of the people portrayed in 2 Maccabees 7. The sanction that Taxo cites as motivation for the impending martyrdom—"our blood will be avenged before the Lord" (9:7)—comes from "Moses" in Deuteronomy 32:43. He articulates the martyrs' anticipation of vindication by God.[23]

This appeal to the promise, in the Mosaic Torah, of God's vengeance on his and the people's enemies also sets up the concluding prophetic oracle of God's appearance to judge the oppressive empires and to renew Israel (ch. 10). The final establishment of the "kingdom" of God throughout the "whole creation" (10:1) parallels the similar reassertion of his active sovereignty and governance of the universe in both of "Enoch's" surveys of history (90:18, 20-26; 91:15). The end of "the devil" parallels the end of the errant or rebellious stars and shepherds and watchers in the Enoch surveys. The judgment and fulfillment also seem to involve a heavenly figure who watches out for Israel (10:2; cf. 4:1), parallel to the role of Michael in Daniel 10–12.

The appearance of "the Heavenly One" from his "kingly throne/holy habitation," with earthquake and solar eclipse and astronomical disarray (10:3-7), draws on and continues the long prophetic tradition of theophany, the coming of God to judge oppressive kings and to deliver the people (Mic 1:3-4; Jer 25), behind which was the traditional portrayal of the divine warrior coming forth to deliver his people (Deut 33:2; Judg 5:4-5).[24] Earlier interpretations of "apocalyptic" texts took the language derived from the traditional portrayals of theophany somewhat metaphysically as expressions of the end of the world in some sort of "cosmic catastrophe." But the purpose of the Heavenly One's coming forth from his heavenly habitation is explicitly and pointedly "to work vengeance on the nations" (10:7), that is, on Antiochus Epiphanes (or other imperial kings).

It is difficult to figure out how to construe the text (and formulate a translation) of 10:8. Considering the prominence of Deuteronomy 31–34 in the background of this review of history, it seems likely that "the wings of an eagle" alludes to the representation of God as an eagle that protects its young, spreading its wings and carrying them to secure heights of land where they are well nourished (Deut 32:11-13). The next lines have Israel carried by the divine wings to heavenly heights (10:9). The portrayal of Israel, or the martyrs to be vindicated by God, as being exalted in the midst of the heavenly bodies resembles the similar portrayal of the martyrs' vindication in Daniel (12:3) and the righteous in the Epistle of Enoch (104:2-6). Given the long tradition in the Israelite cultural repertoire of using fantastic language, full of metaphor and hyperbole, to portray the glorious fulfillment of history, particularly for Israel, it is doubtful that the language in 10:8-9 should be taken literally. The tone of vindication and vengeance of the exaltation of Israel over their now-condemned and suffering enemies resembles that of the Epistle of Enoch. The judgment and fulfillment in the *Testament of Moses* lacks the "universalism" evident at the end of both of "Enoch's" reviews of history.

In sum, the Animal Vision, the ten-week survey, and the *Testament of Moses* all see history as having come to a severe crisis in oppressive imperial rule and/or the "perversion" of the temple-state under Antiochus Epiphanes. They all see the turning point of history, moreover, in the recently begun resistance to the violence that has been directed against the people. This resistance has been mounted either by the scribes who are composing the texts or by their heroes (Taxo and sons). All of these texts also see the resistance as leading, in one way or another, to God's judgment of the oppressive rulers and the renewal of the people. In all three, while God's judgment and the renewal of the people are imagined in more or less fantastic or hyperbolic terms, they do not involve some sort of catastrophe of cosmic proportions, but a renewed earthly life and/or a renewed heavenly governance of the world. In the "Enoch" surveys, the renewal following the termination of imperial and/or Second Temple rule will be universal, as well as a restoration of the people of Israel/Judea. In composing these texts and reciting them to others, moreover, the "Enoch" scribes and the "Moses" scribes were encouraging and emboldening further resistance. These texts were an integral contribution to their resistance against oppressive imperial or priestly aristocratic rule.

Chapter 5
A Terrifying Fourth Beast: The Visions of Daniel

The book of Daniel, especially Daniel 7–12, was surely the most influential of Judean texts now classified as "apocalyptic. It quickly became influential among scribal circles in late second-temple Judea. As the one Judean text now thought of as "apocalyptic" that was included in the Hebrew Bible and Christian Old Testament, it had great influence both in Jewish communities and the Christian church. The visions and interpretations in Daniel 7–12 have also provided the paradigmatic texts for discussion of "apocalyptic" texts in modern biblical studies.*

Interpretations of Daniel are more likely to give attention to imperial rule than are discussions of other Judean "apocalyptic" texts. This is difficult to avoid, of course, since the interpretation sections in Daniel 7–12 and the summaries of history could not be more explicit in their focus on emperors. Since biblical studies treat ancient texts as concerned primarily with religion, however, interpreters frame the problem in Daniel as "(religious) persecution (of the Jews)."[1] In commentaries and handbooks, Antiochus Epiphanes and other Hellenistic emperors become "Gentiles," Antiochus's repressive military violence becomes "sin," and the struggle becomes a cultural conflict between "Jews and Greeks."[2]

It is clear in the visions and explicit in their interpretations that the focus is on the overwhelming political power of empires, on their escalating

---

* I urge readers to read through the visions and interpretations in Daniel 7, 8, and 10–12 in their Bibles and to consult the text regularly while working through this chapter. At points I offer alternative translations of key terms and phrases.

violence and destruction. Insofar as religion and politics are inseparable in antiquity, moreover, the violent measures that the imperial forces take to suppress religious practices are also attacks on a subject people's whole traditional way of life.

As with "Enoch's" surveys of history, we will look for the main concern in each of "Daniel's" visions and interpretations. In contrast to the tendency in biblical studies to focus on particular terms and motifs, we will attempt to discern the significance and function of images and statements in the overall visions and interpretive surveys of history.

Prophetic Visions and Interpretations

While the Animal Vision and the ten-week summary in *1 Enoch* are only introduced or thinly veiled as visions, the surveys of history in Daniel 8, 9, and 10–12 take the form of visions followed by interpretations. In Daniel 7 and 8, the accounts begin with dream visions (7:2-14, continued in vv. 19-22; 8:2-14) followed by the "interpretation" given by "one of the attendants" (in the heavenly court; 7:16-18, continued in vv. 23-27) or the divine messenger Gabriel (8:19-26). The survey of history in Daniel 10–12 begins with a "word" revealed to Daniel that is associated with his vision of a dazzling heavenly "man" (10:1, 5-9). The ensuing narrative, however, consists of "what is inscribed in the book of truth" revealed by Gabriel (10:21; 11:2—12:3).[3] The interpretation sections are all surveys of history, shorter in Daniel 7 and 8, longer in Daniel 10–12.

In contrast with the surveys of history in *1 Enoch*, however, the scope of the surveys in Daniel 7, 8, and 10–12 is confined to the Second Temple period. This more limited scope could simply be a function of attributing the visions to the figure of Daniel, the scribal hero of dream interpretation whom tradition placed in the Babylonian and Persian courts. Yet it might also mean that the scribes (maskilim) who looked to Daniel as the source of their revelation thought mainly in terms of the Judean people under one empire after another in Second Temple times. The visions and interpretations give no hint that the "Daniel" scribes were concerned with earlier Israelite history or tradition.

Recent discussion of the genre of "apocalypse" and its subtypes has found in these visions interpreted by a heavenly figure the prototypical "historical apocalypses."[4] Despite the classification of Daniel's visions as "historical apocalypses," however, and his portrayal as a wise scribe in the tales in Daniel 1–6, he was understood in antiquity as a prophet. The Gospels refer to prophecies of Daniel, often implicitly. Both Matthew (24:15) and a collection of prophecies among the Dead Sea Scrolls (4QFlor 2:4) refer to Daniel as "the prophet." For the Judean historian Josephus, he was "one of the greatest prophets," because he not only prophesied future deliverance, but also announced when the events would take place (*Ant.* 10.11.7, 266–68).[5]

The ancient Judean understanding of Daniel as a prophet should hardly be surprising, since the visions and their interpretations in Daniel 7, 8, and 10–12 present him in the role of a prophet. Like much in the Enoch texts (see chs. 3 and 4), the visions followed by interpretations given to Daniel are scribal developments of prophetic tradition. The prophet Amos had symbolic visions of locusts, a devouring fire, a plumb line, and a basket of summer fruit (7:1-9; 8:1-3).[6] While Amos has no need for a divine messenger as interpreter, since he dialogues directly with God, attendants in the heavenly court do play a role in Micaiah ben Imlah's and Isaiah's prophetic visions of the divine council (such as 1 Kings 22; Isa 6:1-6; 40:1-12). Ezekiel and Zechariah have more elaborate visions, with a heavenly messenger appearing to explain the significance of the images. Their visions and interpretations of future events, moreover, prefigure Daniel's in their political-religious focus. Ezekiel's vision of an idealized new temple focuses on the renewal of Judah (Ezek 40–48). Zechariah's basic message, in international perspective, is of God's care and protection of Judea still suffering from destruction by imperial armies (Zech 1:7-17; 2:1-4 [RSV 1:18-21]; and 6:1-8).

Other features of these visions and interpretations also arise from prophetic tradition. The vision of the throne of God and the divine court sitting in judgment (7:9-10, within the vision of 7:2-14) had become standard in prophetic tradition (1 Kings 22; Isa 40:1-12; Ezek 1). The "appearances" by heavenly interpreters (8:15-17; 9:21-23; 10:5-14) include features that are reminiscent of appearances of God's coming in judgment in prophetic oracles. The human appearance of the heavenly figures in Daniel's visions is prefigured in those of Ezekiel and Zechariah (Ezek 1; 8:2; 10:2; Zech 1:10-11; 2:5).

Another significant influence is evident, however, in the scribal shaping of prophetic tradition in Daniel's visions-and-interpretations. At the beginning and end of "Daniel's" accounts, he describes the circumstances in which he received the visions and how they disturbed him (7:1, 15, 28; 8:1-2, 27; 10:1-4, 15-17; 12:8). These features are missing in Zechariah's visions. But they appear in scribal reports of dreams in Mesopotamia from third-millennium Sumer to the Hellenistic period (and elsewhere in the ancient Near East). The conventional frame of these scribal accounts begins with the circumstances of the dream and concludes with the reaction of the dreamer and/or the fulfillment of the dream.[7] The interpretations of the visions in Daniel 7, 8, and 10–12, moreover, are predictions after the fact (*ex eventu* prophecies) of the rise and fall of kings and empires, usually in the stereotyped form "a king shall arise" (7:17, 23, 24; 8:23-25; 11:2, 3, 5, 14, 20, 21; 12:1). This form of "dynastic" or "regnal prophecy" is often found in collections of Akkadian prophecy. The *Dynastic Prophecy* is a near-contemporary example from Hellenistic Babylon.[8] The portrayal of Daniel, the prototypical scribal hero and specialist in visionary wisdom, as serving in the Babylonian court may reflect the background of the scribes who cultivated the tales and produced the visions of Daniel in Jerusalem. The latter may well have had "ancestors" who had worked in Babylon during the exile, where they were influenced by Babylonian scribal practice before being sent back to Jerusalem to staff the temple-state.

Judean scribal culture included some suspicions about revelation through dreams and visions. Both the Deuteronomic tradition and the Jeremiah collection were sharply critical (for example, Deut 13:2-6; Jer 27:9-10; 29:8-9). Ben Sira would not have been alone among those scribes nearly contemporary with the "Daniel" scribes in his skepticism about dream interpretation (for example, Sir 31:1-8).[9] A certain degree of this critical approach is also detectable in both the tales and the vision interpretation in Daniel. The understanding of visions comes not through the interpretation of the wise scribes, but only through interpretation by God-given wisdom or a heavenly figure.

While inclined to take "Daniel's" visions as scribal developments of the prophetic traditions with which they were thoroughly familiar, we should not exclude the possibility that visionary experiences underlie the accounts. The visionary description in Daniel 10, for example, has been influenced by Ezekiel's visions. Yet the mourning, fasting, and deep sleep, which do not stem from the tradition of Israelite prophecy, are similar to features of visionary experiences in other societies. Ethnographic studies have found that visionary experiences flourish among subject peoples whose traditional way of life is under attack by outside forces. Judean scribes who knew the prophetic tradition were faced with just this situation when Antiochus Epiphanes took forcible measures to suppress the traditional Judean way of life to which they were committed.

It has long been clear that the visions and interpretations in Daniel 7–12, couched as revelations given to the archetypal sage Daniel in the sixth century B.C.E., actually address a historical situation in the early-second century B.C.E. All of the visions and interpretations in Daniel 7–12 come to a climax with Antiochus Epiphanes's attacks on Jerusalem. This is their focus, what they are struggling to understand. The review of the previous empires places the escalation of imperial violence in perspective and helps explain the background, highlighting just how severe the crisis has become.

From the increasing detail that the surveys of history offer as they come to the height of the crisis they address, it is possible to locate the particular situations in which they were composed. The composers of the surveys in Daniel 10–12, moreover, have written themselves into the situation of crisis in the reference to "the wise (maskilim) among the people [who] give understanding to many [and who] fall by sword and flame . . ." (11:33-35; 12:3). Assuming that these maskilim are also responsible for Daniel 7 and 8, the visionary surveys of history in Daniel 7–12 provide several helpful clues about how this circle of scribes understood and responded to the escalating historical crisis under Hellenistic imperial domination.

A close examination of the detail toward the end of each of the surveys of historical events suggests that the sequence of the visions in Daniel 7–12 matches the escalation of Antiochus's attacks on Jerusalem and the corresponding response by the maskilim. The vision and interpretation in Daniel 7 is concerned with Antiochus's attempt "to change the sacred seasons and the law," but does not mention his attack on the temple sacrifices. This suggests that it was composed after Antiochus's attacks in 169 and 168, but before he launched a more systematic attempt to suppress temple operations. The interpretation offers a general message of hope that the Most High will destroy the kingship of Antiochus that has wrought such unprecedented violence and give sovereignty to the Judean people. The vision and interpretation in Daniel 8 are said to originate two years later (8:1), as is the interpretation of the seventy years (Daniel 9). Both evidently respond to the escalation of the crisis with Antiochus's suppression of the regular burnt offering and "the desolating abomination." The question now is "how long" the imperial violence will last (8:13-14, 25; 9:24-27). The climax of the survey of events in Daniel 11–12 focuses on the martyrdom of the maskilim who have offered resistance, as well as the abolition of the burnt offering and the desolating abomination (11:31, 32–35). The message of hope now focuses on the vindication of the martyred maskilim as well as the restoration of the Judean people (12:1-3).

The Devouring and Trampling Fourth Beast: Daniel 7

The account of Daniel's dream (7:2-14) is a powerful portrayal of an increasingly violent sequence of empires. After mentioning briefly, in one phrase, that the four beasts arose from the sea, the narrative gives an elaborate description of each of the beasts, with escalating emphasis on their ravenous appetite and destructive violence. The sequence of beasts climaxes in "the little horn." The portrayal of the fourth beast and its little horn (7:7-8) is double the length of the description of the previous three beasts and as long as the scene of their judgment (7:11-12), an indication of the dream's focus. In the continuation of the dream that expands on the destructive violence of the little horn, we come to the principal concern of the dream: the little horn was "making war against the holy ones and was prevailing over them" (7:19-21). Its "great iron teeth," along with "its claws of bronze," symbolized an insatiable appetite for violent destruction that was utterly out of control, "devouring, breaking in pieces, and stamping what was left with its feet" (7:7, 19, 29).[10]

The beasts clearly symbolize imperial political and military power. Monumental gates and buildings in ancient Assyria, Babylon, and Persia featured reliefs of beasts such as winged lions. The doorjambs of the palace of Darius at Persepolis were decorated with reliefs of the imperial hero battling a lion-monster.[11] The Israelite prophetic tradition in which "Daniel" was deeply rooted had long represented imperial kings as predatory beasts. The representation of Israel's imperial rulers as predatory animals in Ezekiel 34 had become standard. Such are presupposed in Hosea's portrayal of Yahweh, Israel's own king, threatening to step into the role of a ferocious lion, leopard, or bear (Hos 13:7-8). Jeremiah represents the Babylonian Empire as a lion that destroys peoples and lays waste their lands (Jer 4:5-8). His prophecies provide a striking precursor to the vision in Daniel 7, particularly insofar as God will punish the king of Babylon and restore the people of Israel (see esp. Jer 50:17-20). Horns, such as those on the extremely violent fourth beast in the vision of Daniel, were also symbols of imperial power. Images of the Seleucid kings wearing horned war helmets were stamped on their coins.[12] The same image was well known in Israelite prophetic tradition. In one vision, Zechariah focuses on four horns that had "scattered Judah, Israel, and Jerusalem" (2:1-4; ET 1:18-21).

These images of beasts and horns, standard in Israelite prophetic tradition as well as ancient Near Eastern culture generally, are fitting representations of imperial power and violence for the general scheme of four empires that provides the narrative pattern of the vision in Daniel 7, just as it did in the dream in Daniel 2. The four beasts in Daniel 7, however, have a different, more immediate application than those in Daniel 2. The point of the four-beast scheme in Daniel 2 was the succession of empires, which would be destroyed and succeeded by the rule of God. The beasts in Daniel 7 represent imperial power and rapacious violence that escalates dramatically with the fourth beast, which is "terrifying and dreadful and exceedingly strong."

An important recent scholarly interpretation of Daniel argues that "the basic character and significance of the beasts . . . is determined by the fact they rise from the sea." Thus "they are embodiments of the primeval power of chaos."[13] Since the dream has "assimilated a historical situation to a mythic pattern," its basic meaning is that "creation is threatened by the eruption of the beasts from the sea, but the threat will be overcome by the rider on the clouds."[14] This interpretation, which imposes a Canaanite myth onto Daniel's

A Terrifying Fourth Beast: The Visions of Daniel   87

dream, however, fits neither the account of the dream nor its interpretation. In fact, it conflicts with the explicitly political interpretation in 7:17-18, 23-27. It also seems to ignore the imagery and narrative of the dream. The sea is simply not the controlling image. The dominant images are those of the beasts as symbols of destructive empires whose dominion is taken away in a divine court of judgment (7:4-8, 10-12), not of primordial chaos that is destroyed by the Canaanite warrior hero called "rider on the clouds."[15] The one "coming with the clouds of heaven" (7:13-14) in the dream is not directly involved in destroying the beast(s).

If anything, the dream's imagery of the beasts (representing the great empires of the ancient Near East) arising out of the sea (that symbolizes chaos) is a symbolic "turning of the tables" on imperial mythic ideology. In the Canaanite myth of Lord Storm's battle with Sea, or the Babylonian myth of Marduk's battle with Sea (in Enuma Elish), the Storm-Warrior-King-god of the imperial city conquers and kills (establishes cosmic order over) Sea. In Daniel's dream, by contrast, the symbolic beasts of empire derive from and perpetuate the very chaos that they claim to have conquered. The predatory beasts in Daniel's dream, however, symbolize historical imperial domination and destruction, parallel to the giants in the Book of Watchers that symbolize imperial violence and destruction.

The account of the dream continues into the proceedings of the heavenly court of judgment and the destruction of the terribly rapacious and devastating fourth beast (7:9-12).[16] The throne portrayed in "Daniel's" dream has a different function from the otherwise similar throne of God in "Enoch's" visionary journey into the heavenly court. The throne at the center of the heavenly palace in *1 Enoch* 14 was where God sat when commissioning Enoch with his prophetic role and message (somewhat as in Isa 6; 40:1-11; and Ezek 1–3). The throne in Daniel 7:9-10 is for the Ancient One, seated in a court of judgment over the predatory beasts (somewhat as in 1 Kings 22).[17] The throne of God set up at the conclusion of the Animal Vision (*1 Enoch* 90:20-27) is the better parallel to the throne for the Ancient One in Daniel's dream. In both the Animal Vision and the vision in Daniel 7, the throne set in place signals that God is finally arriving in a court of judgment to sentence the oppressive imperial rulers.

The reference to books being opened points to the special role of numinous writing in heavenly books in scribal prophetic visions as well as in scribal culture generally.[18] Heavenly books preserved a permanent record of human obedience and disobedience to God commands. The appearance of the books in "Daniel's" vision parallels that in "Enoch's" Animal Vision (*1 Enoch* 89:61-64 et al.), where the Lord of the sheep ordered a scribal attendant in the heavenly court to keep a written record of the excessive violence and destruction of the shepherds charged with oversight of the sheep. As in the Animal Vision, the scope of the records kept in the heavenly books had been expanded from intra-Israelite social-economic relations to "international" political-economic relations between Judeans and their imperial rulers. The "books opened" in Daniel's vision clearly have a function and implication similar to those in the Animal Vision: the beasts' trampling and devouring had been recorded in heavenly books that were now testimony against them. Centuries of imperial oppression made history seem beyond the control of the heavenly Emperor. But scribal circles, who knew writing as an instrument by which rulers kept records that were used in controlling their peoples, projected numinous writing into the heavenly imperial court where God, while seemingly not in control of affairs on earth, was keeping records of imperial oppression that would eventually be used in judgment.

In the "logic" of the dream, which clearly symbolizes the violent treatment of Judeans by a succession of imperial rulers, the fourth beast has to be not just punished, but destroyed. Since it symbolizes the present Greek-Seleucid imperial regime, it still holds the people in its grip and must be killed to enable their deliverance. The other beasts, besides not having been so excessively violent, were also long since gone from the historical scene to which the dream images point, and had indeed been allowed to rule by the divine judge.

In the dream's final step (7:13-14), "one like a human being coming with the clouds of heaven" came before the Ancient One and was given "everlasting dominion." While not particularly pertinent to the beasts arising from the sea (Dan 7:2-8), the Canaanite myth centered on Lord Storm offers a telling contrast to the humanlike figure in Daniel's dream, despite the similarity of the image of "coming with the clouds of heaven" to "rider of the clouds." The "rider of the clouds" battles and slaughters Sea and threatens violent destruction to any who challenge the order he imposes. In "Daniel's" dream, by contrast, the "one like a human being" appears after, and in pointed contrast to, the predatory beasts who are the ones that resemble Lord Storm in their imposition of order by extreme violence. Similar to Lord Storm, the "one like a human being" is given everlasting dominion. In "Daniel's" dream, however, the humanlike one does not defeat and kill the fourth beast who arises from the sea. The Lord-Storm-like little horn of the fourth beast is put to death prior to the appearance of the "one like a human being" (7:11, 13). In fact, we might suspect that the "Daniel" scribes knew very well that the Canaanite Lord Storm stood behind the Syrian Ba'al Shamem (Lord of heaven)/Zeus Olympos, to whom the Seleucid emperors looked as their divine patron.[19]

A Terrifying Fourth Beast: The Visions of Daniel

The final step in the vision is thus the giving to the humanlike one the very "everlasting dominion" that Lord Storm/Ba'al Shamem/Zeus Olympos had claimed.

In the interpretation of the vision (Dan 7:17-18, 23-28), the heavenly "attendant" tells Daniel explicitly what was already abundantly clear from the dream images, that the four great beasts are the great empires that had ruled Judea and the ancient Near East. With regard to the main concern of the vision and interpretation, the attendant explains more fully that the highly destructive fourth beast represents (the ten kings of) the Hellenistic empire(s), more severe in oppressing subject peoples than the previous ones had been. The little horn, further, is the latest (and evidently the current) Hellenistic king who

> shall speak words against the Most High,
> and shall wear out the holy ones of the Most High,
> and shall attempt to change the sacred seasons and the law;
> and they shall be given into his power. (7:25)

Comparisons with the ensuing visions in Daniel and the accounts in 1 and 2 Maccabees make it clear that these lines refer to the Seleucid emperor Antiochus IV Epiphanes and his attack on the faithful adherents of the traditional Judean way of life centered in the temple-state in Jerusalem. His arrogant speech (7:25) surely refers to his attacks on Jerusalem, a city especially sacred to God, but probably also to his other treatment of gods and sacred institutions (cf. Dan 11:36-39). At the time of this first vision in Daniel, Antiochus had begun to threaten the Judean temple-state, its sacred festivals, and its law. But the explanation does not yet give any particulars, such as the attack on the sacrifices at the altar.

The most difficult part of the interpretation to explicate is that the "one like a human being" who is given dominion represents "the holy ones of the Most High" and then "the people of the holy ones of the Most High" (7:18, 27). Presumably, these are the same "holy ones" that the little horn attacks (7:21, 25) and that gain possession of the kingdom (7:22). Earlier interpreters often took "the holy ones of the Most High" as a reference to the faithful Judeans who were under attack. More recently, close attention to the use of the term "holy ones" in Daniel and other Judean texts, particularly in texts of the Qumran community found among the Dead Sea Scrolls, has complicated the issue. John Collins has made a carefully critical survey of key texts. Against the previously standard interpretation, he argues, in either/or terms, that in nearly all earlier and contemporary Judean texts, "the holy ones (of the Most High)" refers to celestial beings associated with God and faithful

Judeans.[20] Many of the passages he cites, however, can be used instead to illuminate the important role played by heavenly figures in God's governance of the universe, as well as the close relationship between the heavenly beings and faithful Judeans.

In early poetry and psalms, the "assembly of the gods" or "children of the gods" comprises a heavenly council of "holy ones" in which Yahweh stands preeminent (Deut 33:2; Ps 89:6-8). Prophetic texts represent Yahweh as leading a "host" when he comes to deliver or to punish Israel. These "holy ones" assist Yahweh in battle against would-be imperial conquerors in a late prophecy in Zechariah (14:5). Enoch texts place "the holy ones" parallel to or identical with "the watchers" who are charged with assisting God in the governing of the universe. Some have special assignments to protect Judeans, even to communicate wisdom to Enoch (*1 Enoch* 1:2; 93:2; 106:19; cf. Dan 4:14). "The holy ones of the Most High" appear to have a similar function in the vision and interpretation in Daniel 7. "The Most High" having become relatively remote in the imperial operations of the universe ("the Ancient One"), "the holy ones" were heavenly forces charged with caring for Judean society. They function as a heavenly counterpart of the Judeans.[21]

Antiochus's attack on the temple-state is thus seen as making war against "the holy ones" charged with protection of Judea in the divine governance. When, in the dream imagery, the Ancient One finally acts in judgment to destroy the empire of the little horn of the fourth beast and gives dominion to the "one like a human being," the divine governance has been restored, "the holy ones" have been given sovereignty (7:18, 22).[22] Insofar as they correspond to and represent Judean society, moreover, this means that sovereignty will be given to the (faithful) Judeans, as "*the people* of the holy ones of the Most High" (7:27).

As portrayed in Daniel 7, therefore, Antiochus's attack on the Judeans involves far more than religious persecution. The account of the vision portrays the attack in images of military violence, political domination, and the extreme devastation of human life and its material basis. Biblical interpreters have trouble discerning the political-economic aspects implicit in the references used in the interpretation (7:25). "Speaking words against the Most High" seems like mere "blasphemy," and "changing the times [NRSV: sacred seasons] and the law" seems to be "religious innovation," or "disruption of the cultic calendar."[23] Religious and political-economic dimensions, however, were inseparable in ancient Judean society. "Speaking words against the Most High" was, in effect, a declaration of war against the sacred symbol of the Judeans, their symbolic "head of state." This offense was all the more serious insofar as Judeans believed that the Most High God held sovereignty over international history as well as Judea. "Changing the times and the law" meant changing the very "constitution" of the temple-state. To "make war on" or "afflict [NRSV: 'wearing out'] the holy ones of the Most High" may be the most obvious indication that politics and religion were inseparable. Antiochus's attack on Jerusalem constituted war on the heavenly forces that represented the Judean people and were their guardians. Antiochus's blatant challenge to God's sovereignty is summed up in his arrogant assertion of "power over them [the Judeans]" (lit.: "they will be given into his hand"). The Judean people were thus no longer exclusively under the kingdom and power of their God, which was an impossible and intolerable situation.

The Most High God, however, would finally take the throne in judgment, terminate the reign of the devouring fourth beast, and give sovereignty to the holy ones, which meant a restoration to independence of the people of the holy ones.

The Fearful Destruction of a Bold King: Daniel 8

The vision and interpretation in Daniel 8, like that in Daniel 7, focuses on the overwhelming power of the empires that had dominated Judea, and particularly on the latest king's destructive attacks on Judean society. The vision is more of an allegory in which the principal images are transparent to the empires they represent. Since the language of Gabriel's interpretation is nearly as allusive as that of the vision, it makes sense to consider vision and interpretation together.

The two-horned ram and the goat (with a horn between its eyes) that dominate the first half of the vision (8:3-8), while less predatory than the beasts in Daniel 7, were also standard symbols of imperial military power. In "Enoch's" Animal Vision (*1 Enoch* 89:42-48), rams represent the kings of Israel. He-goats symbolized royal power in the Judean prophetic repertoire (Isa 14:9; Ezek 34:17; Zech 10:3). The succession of these particular symbols may have been influenced by the signs of the zodiac in Mesopotamian astrology, in which the ram corresponded to Persia and the he-goat to Syria, where the Hellenistic empire that ruled Judea was based at the time of the vision.[24] The two-horned ram charging westward, northward, and southward clearly signified the Medes and Persians, who conquered the whole Near East in the sixth century. The goat from the west with a single horn that struck the ram was even more clearly Alexander the Great, who defeated and replaced the Persian Empire in the 330s B.C.E. The four horns that replaced the broken single horn were obviously the Hellenistic imperial regimes that took control in sections of Alexander's empire when he died. Gabriel's interpretation (8:20-22) merely confirms what was already clear in the transparent images of imperial power.

With no influence evident from the four-empire scheme that structures the dreams in Daniel 2 and 7, the vision in Daniel 8 focuses on the empires that had dominated Judea for the previous four centuries. The vision narrative emphasizes first how the "charges" (military conquests) of the ram (Persia; in the interpretation, 8:20) overwhelmed all other beasts (peoples it conquered) and then mainly how the horn of the goat (Alexander the Great, 8:21) utterly overwhelmed the ram with its power (8:4, 5-7). The swift and complete conquest of Near Eastern kingdoms and peoples by the Greeks had been an event of huge proportions, one that left a lasting mark on the cultures of subjugated peoples such as the Judeans. Such peoples were left struggling to understand how and when the Hellenistic empire(s) might be ended, as in the four-empire scheme adapted in Daniel 2 and 7.

As in Daniel 7, the visionary narrative in Daniel 8 moves toward its climax in the little horn's attack on Jerusalem. The attack, however, now focuses on the profanation of the Temple and the removal of the burnt offering (8:9-13). This was far more than an attack on the temple cult, although it surely focused there. The narrative mentions, first, the arrogant military ambition of the little horn, including its invasion of "the beautiful land" (Judea) and its self-elevation to "the host of heaven" where it threw down and trampled some of the host and stars (8:9-10). The latter, like "the holy ones" in Daniel 7, referred to the heavenly forces that assisted God in the divine governance of the world, with special concern for Judea and the temple-state. Then the little horn became so completely out of control that, in blatant defiance of "the prince of the host" (God; cf. Josh 4:14), it "overthrew the place of his sanctuary" (the altar?) and suppressed the burnt offering (8:11-12). This was the central ritual of the political economy of the temple-state, as well as the central ceremony by which God was appropriately served by the priesthood in the Jerusalem Temple and God communicated with the people. Casting truth to the ground is probably a reference to the attempt to suppress the ancestral laws that were, in effect, the "constitution" of the temple-state.

The interpretation (8:19-25), like the vision, focuses on Antiochus's attack on Jerusalem, only now in even broader terms with emphasis on his arrogance and his violence against people and their protective heavenly forces more than on the Temple. That he is "adept in duplicity" (NRSV "skilled in intrigue," but literally "understands riddles"), a traditional attribute of kings in royal propaganda (as well as a skill of scribes such as Ben Sira and Daniel), is a mark of hubris (compare the king of Tyre in Ezek 28). He is scheming and deceitful. He has an exalted sense of his own greatness (8:23-25). Antiochus's attacks are directed mainly against people and the divine forces. "He will destroy many off guard" is probably a reference to his officer's slaughter of people in Jerusalem after feigning offers of peace (1 Macc 1:29-32). And he attacks "(the people of) the holy ones" and even presumes to rise against God ("the Prince of princes").

Like that in Daniel 7, the vision and interpretation in Daniel 8 has been shaped from many forms, motifs, and images previously cultivated in scribal circles. Again, many of those features, ranging from the primary structural components to the principal visionary images, derive from the prophetic tradition. The overall sequence of the vision and interpretation, including the epiphany of a heavenly messenger, is a development of prophetic tradition attested especially in Ezekiel and Zechariah.[25] Also derived from prophetic lore are the lament over the devastated condition of the people/Jerusalem ("how long?") and the representation of Antiochus Epiphanes as presumptuously exalting himself above the stars.[26]

Throughout the account, the vision and interpretation focus on historical events, the conquests and attacks by emperors and their armies. That the vision uses an image similar to "the myth of the Day Star" in one sentence is hardly a sufficient basis for claiming that it "transpos[es] the historical crisis of the Maccabean era to the supernatural plane," and thus "assimilat[es] the historical situation to timeless myth."[27] Even when he "grew as high as the host of heaven," and "threw down some of the host and stars," and acted against "the prince of the host," Antiochus was standing firmly on earth, specifically in Jerusalem. The vision specifies the attack against "the prince of the host" as Antiochus's attacks on the burnt offering and sanctuary, and the interpretation emphasizes his attacks on people that are symbolized as his attacks against the holy ones.

While the focus is clearly on Antiochus's attacks against the Judean people and their heavenly counterparts, the interpretation includes some phrases that indicate just how strongly it condemns imperial rule in general. The temporal phrase "in the latter time of the wrath" (NRSV: "period of wrath") refers to the prolonged period of time of imperial rule, and sees this as the time of (God's) wrath (like "the age of wrath" in CD 1:5; 1QH 3:28), in which Judeans are suffering oppression and tribulation at the hands of violent imperial agents.[28] It is only at the very end of that long period of tribulation under empire that Antiochus arises. He is the most violent and destructive in the succession of emperors, but imperial rule in general has been oppressive.

The interpretation finally declares that Antiochus "will be broken." This will happen "without human hands," but rather, by heavenly action (8:25e), since he has so arrogantly affronted the divine. That this is affirmed only in one line at the very end of the interpretation is striking by comparison with the more elaborate message of judgment in 7:9-14, 26-27. This suggests that the principal message of reassurance in Daniel 8 lies elsewhere. The message of deliverance surely appears in the exchange between the two holy ones with which the vision concludes (8:13-14, which corresponds structurally to 8:25e). The form of the question, a prayer of lament deeply rooted in the prophetic tradition (for example, Isa 6:11; Jer 12:4; and esp. Zech 1:12), focused on Antiochus's most heinous attack on God's authority, sets up the revelation. The "2,300 evenings and mornings" that means 1,150 days (since the burnt offering was made twice daily) is slightly less than the three and a half years of 7:25 (i.e., half of a "week of years," cf. 9:27). That is, the message of hope and reassurance in the vision in Daniel 8 is that Judeans are already through more than half of the period of the most violent oppression, at the end of their long time of tribulation under imperial rule.[29] The vagueness of the timing also indicates that this vision and interpretation were composed in and addressed to the situation of escalating repression by Antiochus Epiphanes, but prior to the wider Maccabean Revolt and the rededication of the temple.

They Shall Fall by Sword and Flame: Daniel 10–12

The survey of events in Daniel 11–12 focuses directly on the history of Hellenistic rule of Judea. The narrative of what is to happen to the Judean people in Daniel 10:1—12:3 is derived from a vision, but it is not presented as an interpretation of a vision that is also narrated. It is, rather, introduced by a theophany of and conversation with the heavenly revealer (10:2—11:1).[30] The survey of events (11:2—12:3) gives a far more detailed narrative than the visions and interpretations in Daniel 7 and 8, including a remarkably accurate sketch of the wars between the Ptolemies and the Seleucids.[31] Indicative of its principal concern, more than half of the survey focuses on Antiochus's attack on Jerusalem and the Temple. At the height of the crisis created by Antiochus's attacks on Jerusalem, the focus zeroes in on the Judeans who are resisting the imperial repression, especially the maskilim who presumably produced this survey and the previous visions and interpretations (11:31-35; 12:1-3).

The heavenly messenger who appears to Daniel (apparently Gabriel, as in 8:16; 9:21) explains that he and "Michael, one of the chief princes" were engaged in battle against "the prince of the kingdom of Persia" and would then fight against "the prince of Greece." This heavenly warfare was rooted in a view of reality that modern readers may have trouble understanding. But it was crucial in the scribal faith both that visionary revelation was trustworthy and that the divine forces would ultimately take action against the imperial forces that seemed to be out of control.[32] In the ancient

Near East, the gods of particular peoples or kingships, the heavenly powers that determined human affairs and historical life, were understood to protect and fight on behalf of their peoples or their earthly regents, the kings of those peoples. This is the assumption underlying the Assyrian emperor's taunt to the besieged Jerusalemites centuries earlier: "Who among all the gods of the countries have delivered their countries out of my hand, that Yahweh should deliver Jerusalem out of my hand" (2 Kings 17:35 = Isa 36:20). In the Israelite/Judean adaptation of this worldview, Yahweh/the Most High was understood as the preeminent heavenly power, the King of kings with sovereignty over the other gods or heavenly forces. Thus, in the Song of Moses, "the Most High . . . fixed the boundaries of the peoples according to the number of the gods" (Deut 32:8). This is the worldview presupposed in the narrative of second-temple history in Daniel 10–12, as well as in that of "Enoch's" Animal Vision.

Judean texts exhibit two variations on this standard worldview as it bears on Israel. One of the hymns in Sirach perpetuates the view in the Song of Moses (Deut 32:9): "He appointed a ruler for every nation, but Israel is the Lord's own portion" (Sir 17:17; cf. *Jub.* 15:31-32). The other variation, evident in the "Book of Watchers" (*1 Enoch* 1–36), has several (four or seven) of the highest-ranking heavenly officers or holy ones playing ad hoc roles or having general ongoing responsibilities in the governance of the universe (*1 Enoch* 9–10; 20). This is the worldview assumed in Daniel 10–12 as well, where Gabriel and Michael are fighting for the Judeans against the "princes" of Persia and Greece, who are the heavenly forces behind the ravages of the Persian and Greek imperial regimes.[33] Most significantly, in Daniel 10–12, God and/or Michael act against the violent imperial forces that have wrought destruction on the Judeans.

The survey moves quickly through the early wars between "the king of the south" (the Ptolemaic regime) and "the king of the north" (the Seleucid regime) to Antiochus III's attempts to take Syria-Palestine and Judea from the Ptolemies (11:14-19). The historical survey in Daniel 11 shifts the emphasis from the violence and destructiveness symbolized in the beasts of Daniel 7 to the overwhelming power of the imperial forces (for example, 11:15-16). The army of the scheming and deceitful Antiochus Epiphanes is utterly overwhelming (11:20-22). The narrative also reveals how imperial domination is economic as well as political-military. As we know from other sources, his treasury was drained by the indemnity imposed on the Seleucids by Rome and by his own military adventures. Antiochus, having plundered temples in some cities, made gifts to others to consolidate his hold on them (11:24).

The narrative of events further reveals that, in an escalating imperial interference in Judean politics, Antiochus's army invaded Jerusalem to bolster the aristocratic faction that mounted the Hellenizing coup d'état with his backing. The key clues are the connections in which "covenant" is mentioned.[34] That the "the chief [*nagid*] of the covenant" will be swept away (11:28) refers to the intrigue between the imperial regime and the "reform" party against the high priest, God's regent in Judea. "Those who forsake/violate the covenant" (11:30, 32; cf. "a small party," 11:23) are the Hellenizing "reformers" who cut the deal with Antiochus to depose Onias III as high priest and to transform Jerusalem into a city-state. Antiochus's own opposition to and action against the covenant (11:28, 30, 32) refers to his collaboration with the "reformers" and his military enforcement of the reform when serious opposition arose. That the covenant in Daniel texts may well include Mosaic teaching seems likely from the inclusion of the lengthy Deuteronomic prayer of covenant renewal in Daniel 9. But the narrative of Antiochus's collaboration with the reform party and his attacks on Jerusalem gives no reason to reduce covenant here to a reference only to Mosaic covenantal Torah. Judging from the connections in which it is portrayed in the narrative, it appears to refer to the constitution of Judean society and the temple-state broadly conceived: the bonds that hold the people together with God and each other and the temple-state.

In connection with Antiochus's escalating attacks against Jerusalem, the narrative mentions the crucial role of the dominant aristocratic faction that had schemed with Antiochus to take control in Jerusalem (11:30-35).[35] As just noted, "those who forsake the holy covenant" (11:30, 32) must refer to those who carried out the reform with the backing of Antiochus. The dominant reform party itself split when Menelaus outbid the original usurper, Jason, for the high priestly office. Since Antiochus had backed Menelaus's seizure of power and continuation of the reform, his control of Jerusalem now depended on the success of Menelaus and his faction in maintaining power. Thus, when he "pays heed" to "those who forsake the holy covenant" (11:30), it may be a reference to Menelaus and his supporters' appeal to Antiochus to help them maintain control of the city against Jason's attempt to retake the city, and/or others' resistance to their reform. Instead, or in addition, it could refer to Antiochus's repression of resistance by other groups (for example, "the sheep whose eyes were opened" in the Animal Vision, *1 Enoch* 90:6-9). Collaboration between the imperial regime and Menelaus's faction, moreover, would likely have involved some mutual manipulation ("seduce . . . with flattery," 11:32).

"Daniel's" most detailed account of the crisis in Jerusalem thus indicates raging internal political conflict in the temple-state, just as Antiochus took

A Terrifying Fourth Beast: The Visions of Daniel

more extreme steps to assert his own and his aristocratic allies' control. He attacked the Temple, which was fortified (hardly just a "religious" institution); discontinued the traditional cultivation of rituals in honor of God centered in the daily offerings; and set up the "desolating abomination," which was apparently an alien altar erected on the great altar of the Temple. The narrative, however, does not indicate the timing of these measures, which may have taken place over the better part of two years (168–167 B.C.E.).

The narrative sets "the people who know their God" against "those who violate the covenant" (11:32). This may refer specifically to the maskilim, but more likely signifies all of those who remained faithful to the traditional way of life. Judging from prophetic tradition, "knowing" refers to keeping the covenant with God (cf. Isa 1:2-3). "The people who know their God" would thus appear to be those who remained faithful to "the holy covenant." That they "stand firm and take action" clearly suggests that adherence to the covenant included resistance to Antiochus's repressive measures. This would not be a reference to the wider revolt led by Judas the Maccabee, which evidently had not started yet. The Hebrew verb behind "to stand firm" (NRSV) ranges in usage from "be strong/resolute" to "engage in battle" (1QM 10:6). The "action" that "those who know their God" were taking would thus appear to have been more "resolute" than passively waiting until some form of persecution came to them. Our reading of Enoch texts in chapters 4 suggests that at least one circle of dissident scribes had mounted serious resistance to the Hellenizing reform, perhaps ever earlier.

The "wise among the people" (maskilim, 11:33) are usually understood as those who composed the (visionary) surveys of history in Daniel 7–12. Assuming this is the case, they must have been a cohesive circle of learned scribes, only attached to the temple-state in Jerusalem and not serving in an imperial court, as their hero Daniel is represented in the tales (Daniel 1–6). That they would "impart understanding to the many" would thus be their own self-characterization. If these scribes were anything like those for whom Ben Sira speaks or those who produced the Epistle of Enoch, they would have seen their role as looking out for ordinary people. Yet if Ben Sira is a reliable guide, learned scribes communicated their wisdom mainly among other scribes or in the councils of the ruling aristocracy, and not to ordinary Jerusalemites. Given the crisis in which the dominant aristocratic faction had "abandoned the holy covenant," however, they may have been moved by their own visions to attempt to explain to others the divine revelation they had received about what was happening in the attacks by Antiochus Epiphanes.

It is unclear to whom the vague term "the many" refers. It seems unlikely to indicate the Judean peasants who lived in outlying villages, with whom scribes serving in the temple-state in Jerusalem would have had little contact.[36] More likely, "the many" referred to ordinary (nonscribal) Jerusalemites, such as artisans who would have been threatened by the transformation of Jerusalem into a Hellenistic polis, since their livelihood was connected with the Temple and high priesthood. In a small city such as Jerusalem, moreover, the scribes such as the maskilim would have known and been in frequent contact with other Jerusalemites.

That "they shall fall by sword and flame and captivity and plunder for some days" indicates that the resistance of the maskilim was persistent. The imperial soldiers were hunting them down and killing them. Steadfast in their resistance, at least some of them had been martyred (cf. 1 Macc 1:63). Modern interpreters have often taken "they shall receive a little help" (NRSV) in Daniel 11:34 as a reference to Judas the Maccabee. But there is nothing in the narrative to indicate that the revolt he led had started yet. A more precise translation of the clause in 11:34 would be that when the maskilim fall, "they will receive little help from anyone."[37] That makes more sense in parallel with the ensuing assertion that "many will join them insincerely." It would not be surprising that no one came to their aid. As a circle of wise scribes who had been engaged in service of the temple-state or, in the circumstances, perhaps a small faction of the aristocracy, they would not already have had a network of relations with Jerusalemites of lesser status, much less with peasants in outlying villages.[38]

Whatever their motives and differences in intentions, many others apparently were engaged in resistance of some sort. As noted in chapter 4, "Enoch" scribes (the "lambs who began to open their eyes") had begun their resistance before Antiochus's attacks on Jerusalem. And the (scribes among the) Hasidim, who later joined forces with the Maccabean Revolt, had probably also begun their resistance (1 Macc 2:42; 7:12-13; 2 Macc 14:6). The focus throughout this summary of imperial repression and Judean resistance is clearly on the maskilim themselves. And the martyrdom of those who fell had an important effect: refining and purifying them, and making them white.

The narrative returns to the utter arrogance and depredations of Antiochus Epiphanes. It charges that his attacks against Jerusalem and the temple are paralleled by his more general disrespect for and replacement of his own and others' ancestral gods (11:36-37). That he honored "the gods of the strongholds" and acted on behalf of "those who fortify strongholds" (11:38) probably refers to his sending a military colony to maintain control over the city (1 Macc 1:33-40). The imperial project of imposing a new political form and new way of life in Judea having evoked mounting resistance, he resorted to coercive military force. In establishing the military colony in Jerusalem, however, Antiochus also established an accompanying religious cult, including sacrifices to their god(s). This would have exacerbated the situation of the maskilim and other Judeans, for now they had hated Syrian troops watching over them and even occupying what had previously been their land, and defiling the altar of their God.

Antiochus's "honoring people of a strange god who rule over the common people and divide the land as their wages" points up again the political-economic dimension of imperial domination that went together with the political-religious measures. Imperial rule, in this case enforced brutally by military force, was a pyramid of relations in which those who acknowledged the claims of the holder of imperial power and thus enhanced it were enriched and empowered as subordinate rulers who controlled the produce of the land. It usually worked more subtly. But Antiochus was now imposing it by blatant military force. At "the time of the end," the narrative anticipates, when the wrath represented by Antiochus comes to its end, the arrogance of the emperor will come to a final crescendo of military violence. At the end, however, he will have no one to help him (11:40-45).

Coming after a long and detailed account of imperial domination and invasion, the portrayal of judgment in Daniel 12:1-3 is as anticlimactic as the judgment scene in the vision in Daniel 7 is climactic. After all his intervention, invasion, and repressive violence, Antiochus Epiphanes just seems to fade away (11:45). And no judgment is pronounced on "the prince of Persia," and especially on "the prince of Greece" with whom Gabriel had been battling (10:20). It could simply be that God's judgment of Antiochus is already presupposed, insofar as the survey of events in Daniel 11–12 is positioned after the elaborate portrayal of his judgment in Daniel 7. The survey of events in Daniel 11 turned its focus toward the end to the martyrdom of the maskilim who were resisting the imperial invasion, in 11:33–35, and the focus returns to them in its final step, the brief reference to the judgment.

The judgment has both a general focus (12:1) and a particular focus (12:2-3). The judgment begins with the deliverance of the people of Judea (12:1). The heavenly guardian of Judea has seemingly been busy throughout the narrative doing battle on behalf of the people against the prince of Persia and the prince of Greece (10:20-21). Now Michael shall finally "arise" (12:1), step forward in the divine court of judgment as advocate for the Judean people (and/or as the one who executes the divine judgment).[39] "Your people will be delivered," while far less evocative than the new "house" in "Enoch's" Animal Vision and ten-week survey of history (*1 En*och 90:28-36; 91:13), is an anticipatory declaration of the restoration of Judean society—or at least those who have faithfully adhered to the traditional way of life, whose names will be "found written in the book." As with "the people of the holy ones" finally receiving sovereignty in Daniel 7 and the new "house" in the Enoch surveys, so too the "deliverance of your people" in Daniel 12:1 is imagined as a historical renewal of Israel or Judean society.

The renewal of the people was precisely what the maskilim had been fighting for in their opposition to the Hellenizing reform and Antiochus's attacks on "the holy covenant" in his attempts to stamp out resistance. Precisely because of their stalwart defense of the covenant holding the people together in loyalty to their God, "giving understanding to many," however, they were being martyred by the imperial soldiers. In the logic of the covenant (blessings for adherence), however, it would have been utterly baffling that the scribes who were being martyred for faithfulness would not be included in the renewal of the people. The maskilim were looking to God's judgment to vindicate the death of their colleagues for having been martyred for the covenant people.

The vindication of the martyred maskilim is thus the more particular focus of the judgment. Daniel 12:2-3 has habitually been cited as a proof text for a supposedly general Palestinian Jewish concept of "the resurrection." Like other standard concepts used in interpretation of Daniel and *1 Enoch*, such as "apocalyptic," "resurrection" is a synthetic theological construct whose features are derived from a variety of texts that span several centuries, languages, and cultures.[40] It does not appear to be applicable to the images in Daniel 12:2-3, and may simply obscure the text's focus on the vindication of the martyrs.

The narrative of the judgment in Daniel 12:2-3 portrays the vindication of the martyrs in two basic images, both of which should be understood in the context of the restoration of the people as announced in 12:1. The one is "awakening" from sleep, that is, resuscitation to life for the judgment—some to "everlasting life," others to "shame and everlasting contempt." Taking the "awakening" image as a reference to "resurrection," interpreters appealed to prophetic texts such as Isaiah 26–29 ("Your dead shall live, their corpses shall rise," 26:19) and Ezekiel 37 ("the valley of the dead bones") as earlier examples of such belief. These late prophetic texts, however, speak of the restoration of the people of Israel, the broader focus of the judgment in Daniel 12:1-3. Interpreters have also taken "everlasting life" (NRSV) as explicit language of resurrection. The expression so translated, however, a vague term that occurs only here in the Hebrew Bible,[41] is a vague term of uncertain meaning, probably meaning something more like "long life." More germane to the two-pronged judgment in Daniel 12:2 is that some will be vindicated with long life (presumably the maskilim) while others will be shamed with lasting contempt (presumably those who abandoned the covenant).

The second image comes in the parallel phrases "those who are wise (maskilim) shall shine like the brightness of the sky, and those who make many righteous like the stars forever and ever" (12:3). That is, the wise whose dedication to righteousness has resulted in their death at the hands of the imperial forces will be vindicated at the judgment by being exalted so that they will shine *like* the heavenly bodies.[42] A modern literalistic reading would be inappropriate. The language is metaphorical, with similes that are also hyperbole. The thought-world is the same one we have encountered before in Daniel's visions and interpretations and the prophetic tradition in which they are rooted: in a heavenly vision or audition, a prophet hears voices of heavenly beings in the divine court; heavenly forces, "the holy ones of the Most High," have a special protective responsibility in interactive relationship with "the people of the holy ones" (Dan 7:15-27; 8:9-14). The learned scribes who cultivated the Israelite prophetic repertoire were steeped in a culture in which there was an affinity and close interaction between the heavenly forces and the people of Judea, especially the prophets and wise scribes. A few generations after the maskilim, the scribal-priestly community at Qumran understood themselves as involved in a closely interactive relationship with heavenly beings (see further ch. 7 below). Closer to the time of the maskilim, the "Enoch" scribes insisted that in the judgment, the oppressed righteous "will shine like the luminaries of heaven; . . . will have great joy like the messengers of heaven; . . . you will be companions of the host of heaven" (*1 Enoch* 104:1-6). Learned scribes such as the maskilim had a special relationship with "the holy ones" of the heavenly world from whom they received their wisdom and revelation. In their vindication for having died in their steadfast loyalty to God, their glory would be like that of the heavenly luminaries of, and from which, they have their wisdom.

In imagining their vindication for faithful resistance to abuse by imperial rulers, moreover, the maskilim were almost certainly influenced by the servant of Yahweh in Isaiah 52–53. That they were "making the many righteous" in 12:3 seems like a fairly clear allusion (cf. Isa 53:11).[43] If we look more broadly at the two texts, however, we can discern in Isaiah 52:13—53:12 a whole pattern evident in the narrative of Daniel 11–12. In the earlier "servant song," the servant (that is, Israel), who has steadfastly pursued justice, is vindicated in the divine judgment over against the (foreign) kings who have violently attacked him. The survey of imperial domination in Daniel 11–12, which stands in the same prophetic tradition, having already pronounced the deliverance of the people, concludes with the vindication of the steadfastly faithful maskilim who have suffered martyrdom at the hands of the most violent of kings. Their vindication, however, is a special component of the broader deliverance of the Judean people from their oppression by the Seleucid Empire.

Conclusion: Opposition to Empire in Daniel's Surveys of History

The three surveys of history in Daniel 7, 8, and 10–12 all focus on Antiochus's attacks on Jerusalem and the Temple in support of the transformation of the temple-state into a Hellenistic *polis*. The crisis was far more than a religious persecution or a conflict between the cultures of "Judaism" and "Hellenism." It involved military attack and military colonization, evidently to enforce the change of the constitution of the temple-state into a Hellenistic city-state, in which only the elite would enjoy the rights of citizenship, and the traditional Judean way of life would be relativized or abandoned (the "change of times and seasons" and the "abandonment of the covenant"). Since the religious and political-economic dimensions were inseparable, attacks on the altar and sacrifices were political as well as religious; attacks on the city and its people were also attacks on God and "the holy ones" who were their heavenly representatives and protectors.

"Daniel's" surveys of Second-Temple history, moreover, locate Antiochus's attacks to enforce the Hellenizing reform in the context of the succession of empires that had ruled Judea. Antiochus's attack on Jerusalem is only the most extreme and severe since the Babylonian conquest. The dream images of the fearsome beasts in Daniel 7 and 8 clearly represent the destructive empires that dominated the Judean people, with the Hellenistic empire the most destructive and devouring of all. The more detailed survey in Daniel 11 recounts the imperial wars between the Seleucids and Ptolemies for control of Judea and nearby peoples. The destructive violence of the sequence of empires provides the context out of which emerges the extreme violence of Antiochus's attack on the central institutions of Judean society: the covenant and the Temple.

In longer or shorter portrayals, all three surveys also anticipate the ending of the historical crisis in God's judgment. The other empires will be terminated and Antiochus Epiphanes destroyed, and the Judean people ("the people of the holy ones of the Most High") will be renewed and given the "dominion." In both Daniel 7 and 10–12, it is clear that this renewal of the people is not the end of the world or earthly life, but a restoration to an independent historical life under the rule of God.

God's sovereignty in the broader political-economic-religious sense is in fact the overarching issue in all of the surveys of history, "Daniel's" as well as those of "Enoch" and "Moses." In Israelite-Judean tradition, the overarching sovereignty or kingdom belonged to the Most High God, and the people were to live directly under God and maintain exclusive loyalty. Imperial rule interposed another, often competing, sovereignty between God and the people.

A Terrifying Fourth Beast: The Visions of Daniel

In carrying out the Hellenizing reform, the dominant faction of the priestly aristocracy had shifted its loyalty to the sovereignty of the Hellenistic empire, its political form *(polis)* and its political culture. Antiochus and his predecessors carried out violent attacks to impose and enforce their own sovereignty. And, according to the logic of the scribes' faith, when an utterly arrogant emperor was so blatantly challenging God's sovereignty, surely God would act to restore the divine sovereignty over history generally and over the Judean people in particular.

If they were to maintain their loyalty to God's sovereignty, the kingship of the Most High, then the maskilim and other scribes had no choice but to resist. The transformation of Jerusalem into a Hellenistic city-state not only posed a threat to the traditional Judean way of life, of which scribes were the professional guardians, but also undermined their professional role in the temple-state. So it may not be surprising that the maskilim included their own efforts to resist the Hellenizing reform and Antiochus's attacks in the more detailed account of events in Daniel 11. Their opposition now paralleled that of the "Enoch" scribes (the "lambs with their eyes opened") which had evidently begun prior to Antiochus's attacks. In opposition to the dominant aristocratic faction who had abandoned the covenant, they sought to bolster "the people who are loyal to their God" with leadership. Their opposition to the Hellenizing reform must have constituted an irreconcilable break with their former patrons. Presumably, it was their active opposition to reform that brought Antiochus's actions down on their heads, resulting in the martyrdom of some. And through the thick of the resistance and repression, they sought to "give understanding to many." While the "Enoch" scribes appear to have joined the wider Maccabean Revolt, judging from the revision of the description of their continuing resistance, the account in Daniel 11 gives no hint of the activities of the maskilim after their steadfast resistance that evoked Antiochus's repressive measures.

While the maskilim indicate their concern to maintain the covenant that bonded the society together, they give little hint of their attitude toward the Temple. They seem to be concerned about the termination of the burnt offering and "the abomination that makes desolate" (Dan 8:1; 11:29-35), which we would only expect of scribes whose role was to advise on ceremonial as well as other aspects of the temple operations. Yet their (albeit brief) portrayal of the renewal of the people does not include a restoration of the Temple or offerings or a priesthood. Perhaps, like the "Enoch" scribes, their concern was the renewal of the people. Yet there is no indication in Daniel 7–12 of any criticism of the second Temple that matches the pointed rejection in the Animal Vision.

One line in what looks like an editorial conclusion or epilogue to the book of Daniel may offer a clue that the Daniel scribes understood their own resistance as at least a temporary substitute for a key function of the Temple. A principal transaction performed at the altar had been sacrifices of atonement. By the time the accounts in Daniel 8 and 10–12 were composed, however, the altar had been profaned, and the offerings suppressed and replaced with polluted ones. Yet the conclusion to the book of Daniel includes the statement that "many shall be purified, cleansed, and refined" (12:10). "Many" appears to refer back to the martyrdom of some of the maskilim (11:33-35). The implication is that the atonement that was transacted in the temple offerings is now happening in the steadfast resistance and martyrdom of the maskilim.

Part II

Scribal Resistance to Roman Imperial Rule

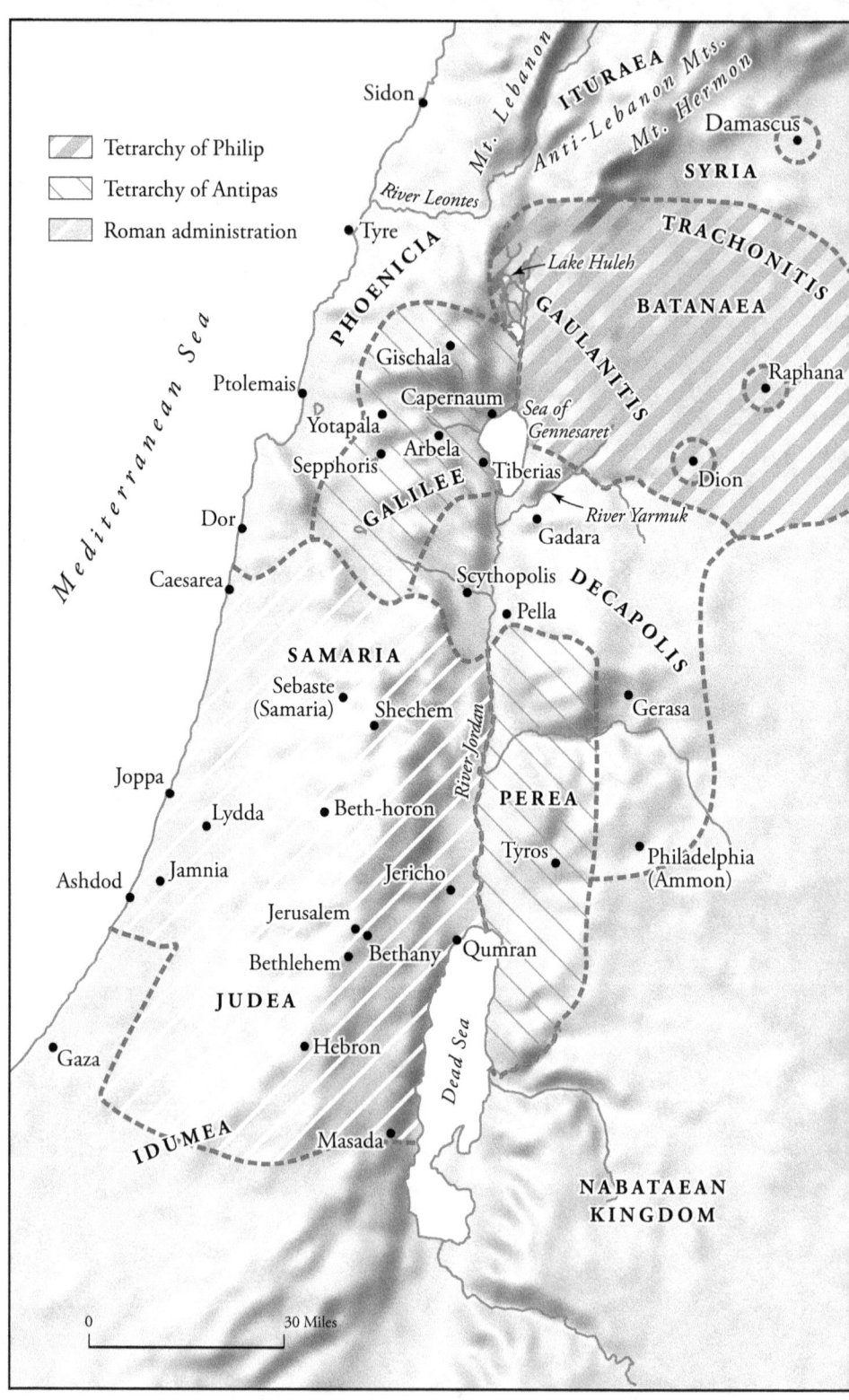

Map of Palestine after the Death of Herod the Great

Chapter 6
Roman Conquest and Roman Rule

The Maccabean Revolt against the Seleucid Empire has always been understood as a great watershed in Judean history. It resulted in the rededication of the Temple, considerable independence for the Judean temple-state under the Hasmonean dynasty, and the emergence of what the Judean historian Josephus calls the "philosophies" or "parties" of the Judeans: the Pharisees, Sadducees, and Essenes. Yet little or no change took place in the basic political-economic-religious structure of Judean society. Under the restored high priesthood scribes served the temple-state, with the Pharisees and Sadducees quickly emerging as the largest and most influential factions. In protest against the Hasmonean consolidation of power, a group of dissident scribes and priests, the Essenes, withdrew from Jerusalem into the wilderness by the Dead Sea. In a time when the weakened Seleucid regime could no longer control Palestine, however, the Hasmonean high priests carved out their own mini-empire in a succession of wars of expansion. Before long, the Romans conquered the eastern Mediterranean and again made the temple-state into a local extension of imperial rule. Roman conquest and Roman rule of Judea were far more invasive and had a more profound impact on Judeans than the Hellenistic empires did.

Hasmonean Expansion and Roman Conquest

Measured by images of God's judgment of imperial rulers and restoration of the Judean people in the texts of "Enoch," "Daniel," and "Moses," the results of the Maccabean Revolt in which the Seleucid armies were fought to a standstill must have been sorely disappointing to the scribal circles that produced them.

A number of scribal circles had engaged in some sort of resistance to the repressive measures of Antiochus Epiphanes, many having been martyred for their loyalty to God. The "lambs" who began to "have their eyes opened" and "sprouted horns" were attacked by "the ravens," as the other "sheep" were "torn in pieces by the eagles and vultures" (Animal Vision, *1 Enoch* 90:6-11). Some of those "lambs" updated the Animal Vision to include the wider rebellion led by "the great horn," Judas (90:9-10, 12-16). The resistance of the maskilim was sufficiently threatening to the Seleucid forces that they came after them "by sword and flame . . . for some days," and captured and killed at least some of them (Dan 11:33). The Levite Taxo and his seven sons, heroes of the "Moses" scribes, died at the hands of the imperial soldiers rather than transgress the commandments (*T. Mos.* 9). And the *hasidim*, a large circle of scribes who left no text that survives, joined forces with the popular revolt led by Judas to fight back against the imperial forces sent to suppress the traditional Judean way of life.

The scribes who resisted the escalating imperial encroachment on their traditional way of life were motivated by the conviction that God would act to end imperial domination and to renew the people in a new era of peace and abundance. Many of their images focused on the restoration and renewal of the Judean people in a "larger and higher," "broad and very full" new "house," with no "tower with polluted bread" (*1 Enoch* 90:28-36; of cf. 89:73). "The people of the holy ones of the Most High" would be given the sovereignty (Dan 7:13-14, 27; cf. *1 Enoch* 90:30). Some of their images of renewal were wider in scope, with "all the earth [being] tilled in righteousness . . . cleansed from all lawlessness and all sin," and the blessings of heaven "descending upon the works and the labor of the sons of men" (*1 Enoch* 10:18—11:2), or with "righteous law revealed to the whole earth" (*1 Enoch* 91:14). Many of the maskilim, "Enoch" scribes, and heroes of the "Moses" scribes went to their death anticipating the vengeance of God on the imperial kings, the renewal of the people, and their own vindication as martyrs. Some "Enoch" scribes, as well as the hasidim, evidently joined in the wider revolt led by Judas "the hammer" ("Maccabee," hence "the Maccabean Revolt") in 167.

What the revolt accomplished, however, fell far short of the anticipations articulated by the circles of scribes in their visions and interpretations. In a series of brilliant guerrilla battles against the imperial armies and their war elephants, "the Maccabees" did fight the Seleucid regime to a standoff.[1] But the Hellenizing aristocrats and a garrison of Seleucid troops remained in Jerusalem, often holed up in the citadel. While the scribes behind the Animal

Roman Conquest and Roman Rule

Vision yearned for a "new house" without a "tower" with polluted bread on its altar, the rebels led by Judas took control of the Temple and the priests rededicated it in 164 (1 Macc 4:42-58). After the death of Judas, his brother Jonathan resumed the struggle against Seleucid attempts to bring Judea again under their control (1 Macc 9:23—12:53; Jos., *Ant.* 13.1–212). Contrary to the preferred agenda of the several scribal circles that composed surveys of history, however, Jonathan maneuvered between rivals to the imperial throne to negotiate the restoration of the high priesthood in Jerusalem with himself as high priest (1 Macc 10:18-21; 11:27). When he was treacherously killed by the Seleucids, his brother Simon negotiated the high priesthood for himself and in effect made Judea an independent temple-state (1 Macc 13:1—16:17; esp. 13:41-42). And contrary to the hopes of the "Enoch" scribes that the sword given to the "sheep" would be laid down (*1 Enoch* 90:36), Jonathan and Simon built up their army and refortified Jerusalem. They thus gradually consolidated power in the Hasmonean family, as Simon handed on the high priesthood to his son John Hyrcanus.[2]

With Seleucid imperial power now severely weakened by repeated wars and rivalry, John Hyrcanus began two generations of expansion of Hasmonean rule over other districts and cities in Palestine—in increasing imitation of imperial patterns. To buy off the next Seleucid king, Antiochus Sidetes, John Hyrcanus opened the tomb of David and took three thousand talents. He then used much of the spoil to hire mercenary troops, an unprecedented step, according to Josephus (*War* 1.61; *Ant.* 13.249). With such a professional army, he conquered the Idumeans to the south, forcing them to submit to "the laws of the Judeans," and Samaria to the north, razing Samaria and the temple at Gerizim to the ground and enslaving the inhabitants (*War* 1.62–66; *Ant.* 13.255–58, 280). His eldest son and first successor (104–103 B.C.E.) claimed the title of king, the first Judean ruler to do so. He had his favorite brother murdered and imprisoned the others, along with his mother. Attacking the Itureans to the north, he took over much of their territory, including Galilee, and the Galileans were also subjected to "the laws of the Judeans" (*War* 1.70–84; *Ant.* 13.301–10, 318–19). After Aristobulus's death, his wife Salome Alexandra appointed his brother Alexander Yannai as king (103–6 B.C.E.; *Ant.* 13.320). He was engaged in virtual constant warfare, with his army of mercenaries, against rival rulers in the wider area or in conquests of neighboring cities and territories (*War* 1.85–106; *Ant.* 13.320–406).

Such "successes" of Hyrcanus and his sons, says Josephus, led the Judeans to oppose them. A break occurred between Hyrcanus and the Pharisees. Josephus's account (*Ant.* 13.288–98), a parallel of which was told about "King

Yannai" in rabbinic circles (*b Qid.* 66a), suggests that the break involved a struggle between the Pharisees and the Sadducees for influence in the ruling of Judea. The Sadducee Jonathan, one of Hyrcanus's intimate advisers, prevailed on the high priest to join the Sadducees. The Pharisees thus lost their influential position in the administration of the temple-state, as Hyrcanus "abrogated the regulations (derived from the succession of ancestors) that they had established for the people, and [threatened] to punish those who observed them" (*Ant.* 13.296).

Far more serious and sustained opposition emerged against Alexander Yannai. At the festival of Tabernacles, the people pelted him with citrons. "Enraged . . . he killed six thousand of them" (*Ant.* 13.372–73). When the people attacked him after a military defeat, "he made war on them and within six years slew no fewer than fifty thousand Judeans" (*War* 1.91; *Ant.* 13.376; even if we reduce Josephus's exaggerated number, the scale is nevertheless jarring). Again a large number of Judeans fought against Yannai and were defeated, with many taken prisoner. "He had eight hundred of his captives crucified . . . and their wives and children butchered before their eyes, while he looked on, drinking, with his concubines reclining beside him (*War* 1.96–98; *Ant.* 13.379–83). With this brutal repression, Yannai evidently broke the back of the resistance, as "the following night eight thousand of the hostile faction fled Judea." Although Josephus does not mention them in his accounts, Pharisees may have been active in the opposition to Yannai and among those torturously executed. This seems likely in the light of ensuing events and from a passage in the *pesher* (interpretation) of Nahum (2:12) found among the Dead Sea Scrolls, for which "seekers of smooth things" was a code word for the Pharisees.[3]

> Interpreted, this concerns the furious young lion [who executes revenge] on those who seek smooth things and hangs men alive [a thing never done] formerly in Israel. (4QpNah 1:6-7, trans. Vermes)

Yannai's wife and successor, "Queen" Salome Alexandra, succeeded him as ruler of the "kingdom" (76–67 B.C.E.; *War* 1.107–16; *Ant.* 13.405–18). She placed her elder son Hyrcanus II in the office of high priest and placed the feistier younger son, Aristobulus, in a military role at a distance from the center of power in Jerusalem. Whatever her motivation, she reinstated the Pharisees to positions of power in the administration of the kingdom/temple-state, and also restored their regulations, derived from the tradition of the ancestors, to their previous status as an integral part of state law (*War* 1.110–12; *Ant.* 13.405-8). As Josephus tells it, they attempted to defuse the popular anger over Yannai's treatment of his subjects, freeing the political prisoners and recalling those who had gone into exile. They also persuaded Alexandra to execute "the powerful ones" who had urged Yannai to kill the eight hundred opponents. We may suspect that at least some of those "powerful ones" may have been Sadducees highly placed in Yannai's administration. Alexandra, however, placed some of these "powerful ones" in charge of the outlying fortresses, in command of military forces, like Aristobulus, with whom they were closely allied.

As his mother lay dying, Aristobulus seized the fortresses, Hyrcanus's troops deserted him, and Aristobulus took power as king and high priest (*War* 1.117–22; *Ant.* 13:422–29; 14.4–7, 41, 97). Antipater, the ambitious (Idumean) governor of Idumea, persuaded Hyrcanus to induce the Arab king Aretas to help him retake power in Jerusalem (*Ant.* 14.8–18). In their attack on the city, the Jerusalemites joined Hyrcanus's side, "while only the priests remained loyal to Aristobulus" (14:19–20). Josephus makes no mention of Sadducees and Pharisees in his accounts of these events. But we may detect hints that the Pharisees, who had advocated the execution of "the powerful" allied with Aristobulus, continued as partisans of Hyrcanus, and that the priests who remained loyal to Aristobulus included priestly aristocrats who were Sadducees. For well over a generation, from late in the reign of John Hyrcanus until Pompey's conquest in 63 B.C.E., there had been intense, often violent struggles for power within the Hasmonean regime that ruled Judea and the territories it had conquered. One large group of scribes and priests (the Essenes) had long since withdrawn to form a utopian *yahad* in the wilderness at Qumran (see next chapter). The Pharisees surely, and probably other circles of scribes trained to serve the temple-state, were in the thick of those struggles in Jerusalem, sometimes in alliance with and sometimes opposed to the Hasmonean in power.

At this point, Pompey, leading the Roman legions then steadily taking control of the eastern Mediterranean areas, intervened. Roman troops lifted the siege of Jerusalem.[4] Both Aristobulus and Hyrcanus pleaded their case to Pompey in Damascus (*War* 1.127–32; *Ant.* 14.29–40). "The people," however, says Josephus, "were against them both, and asked not to be ruled by a king, saying that it was their ancestral custom to obey the priests of God" (*Ant.* 14.41). Impatient at Pompey's indecision, Aristobulus headed for Jerusalem to prepare for war but was persuaded to surrender and admit Pompey to the city. His partisans, however, refused to allow Pompey's troops to take over the city and took refuge in the Temple. The party of Hyrcanus handed over the city and the palace to Pompey, who then laid siege to the Temple. Taking advantage of the Judean law prohibiting fighting back against enemies not actively attacking, the Romans filled in the deep ravine to the north of the

Temple and erected siege works with *ballistae* (catapults hurling stones) to weaken the walls and towers (*War* 1.133–47; *Ant.* 14.46–63).

When the walls were finally breached, the Roman soldiers rushed into the Temple where they slaughtered large numbers of people, butchering priests at the altar where they continued to pour libations and offer incense. Pompey himself and his officers even profaned the sanctuary, the Holy of Holies, which before that time had never been entered by any except the high priests, and beheld "the candelabrum and lamps, the table, the vessels for libation and censers, all of solid gold, an accumulation of spices and the store of sacred money amounting to two thousand talents," but touched none of these nor any of the other sacred treasures (*War* 1.148–53; *Ant.* 14.66–72; Cicero, *Orations: Pro Flacco*, 28.670). Pompey then ordered the Temple to be cleansed, restored the high priesthood to Hyrcanus, and beheaded those who had led the resistance to his advance on Jerusalem. He took Aristobulus and his family off with him to Rome for his triumph (victory procession), as "Pompey the Great." The Judeans, having thus lost their freedom, were laid under tribute (*War* 1.153–54; *Ant.* 14.73–79).

Warlord Brutality and Herodian Tyranny

Judeans quickly found out how brutal and exploitative Roman rule could be. Three purposes drove the escalating conquests of Roman warlords such as Pompey and Julius Caesar in the mid-first century.[5] One was the Roman Senate's drive to control their expanding *oikoumene* (= "empire") to keep supply lines open for goods that satisfied the patricians' passion for a luxurious lifestyle and mollified the growing urban mob displaced by the patricians' foreclosure on the land of the indebted peasant-soldiers. The second was the warlords' own passion for the greater glory that would accrue from great conquests followed by a triumphal procession in Rome. The third was greed: for plunder for the warlords themselves, for revenues from conquered peoples that would underwrite the expense of maintaining the military, and for slaves that would provide labor for the burgeoning estates of Roman patricians. In the first two decades of Roman domination, Judeans were repeatedly subjected to the brutality of warfare led by rival Roman warlords and extraordinary economic exploitation.

Pompey may have mitigated the worst slaughter in the initial conquest of Jerusalem, but other Roman warlords soon came to the East in quest of glorious conquests (*War* 1.159–202; *Ant.* 14.80–157). Crassus marched his legions through the countryside, with the usual decimation of land and crops, on his way to conquer the Parthians, only to lose a whole Roman army across the Euphrates. Galileans bore the brunt of the frustration of his surviving officer and successor, Cassius, who carried out a massacre in Magdala (Tarichaeae), where he enslaved thousands (*War* 1.179–80; *Ant.* 14.105–06, 119–20). The rival Hasmonean pretender Aristobulus, and his sons Alexander and Antigonus, repeatedly played one warlord off against another and easily recruited Judeans opposed to Roman rule, provoking the rival warlords into wars of reconquest that decimated the countryside (*War* 1.183–285). The empire-wide civil war between Roman warlords that resulted from the assassination of Julius Caesar had its counterpart in Judea. Thus, for the first quarter century of Roman rule, Judeans suffered the effects of chronic warfare, mainly between rival Roman warlords and the related rivalry of Hasmonean forces.

Immediately upon conquering Jerusalem, Pompey had laid Judea under tribute (*War* 1.154; *Ant.* 14.74–79, 202–03). As under previous empires, the imperial tribute came on top of the dues already owed to rulers in Jerusalem, the taxes, tithes, and offerings to the Hasmonean regime, Temple, and priesthood. To fund their armies of conquest, moreover, Roman warlords plundered the Temple and imposed special levies of taxes on subject peoples. Crassus "stripped the Temple of all its gold, his plunder including the two thousand talents left untouched by Pompey" (*War* 1.179; *Ant.* 14.105) to underwrite his disastrous invasion across the Euphrates. Toward the beginning of the Roman civil war, Cassius imposed an extraordinary levy of tribute, beyond the ability of subject peoples to pay, to support his legions in Syria. The young military strong man Herod brought in his quota from Galilee. But when district towns in Judea were slow to pay, Cassius simply had the inhabitants sold into slavery (*War* 1.219–22; *Ant.* 14.272–76).

Meanwhile, the Romans were tinkering with the arrangements by which they would keep Judea and related territories under their control. They had already reduced the power of the high priesthood, which was itself again an instrument of imperial rule. They had also removed from Jerusalem rule the cities that had been conquered by the Hasmoneans. While Hyrcanus II continued as high priest under the Romans, his principal minister, the Idumean Antipater, was the prime mover who maneuvered between Roman warlords, consolidating his own power in Judea (summary of these events in *War* 1.183–285). In the 40s B.C.E., Antipater appointed his sons as military governors, setting the young Herod over Galilee. By his vigorous suppression of banditry along the Syrian frontier, which evoked a considerable outcry from Galileans, and his efficiency in the collection of the extra levy of tribute, Herod caught the attention of Roman warlords such as Cassius and Antony who appreciated the ruthless use of brutality to control subject peoples. Desperately needing such military strongmen to maintain local control wherever possible amid the chronic Roman civil war, the leading warlords Octavian and Antony jointly sponsored the Senate's appointment of Herod as "king of the Judeans" in 40 B.C.E. (*War* 1.285; *Ant.* 14.385–89). And the Romans provided him with military forces as needed to conquer his realm.

Herod was already hated at every level of Judean society, and not just in Galilee. Delegations of high-ranking Judeans ("the [most] powerful," "those in office," *War* 1.242–45; *Ant.* 14.324–27—which points to ranking priests and scribes) had protested to Antony a year or so earlier about Herod's effective seizure and abuse of power. And when he arrived to claim his kingdom, he was opposed in every major district and had indeed to conquer his subjects. Once he gained control, his rule was tyrannical and repressive. He maintained an elaborate network of fortresses and another of informers (*Ant.* 15.366–68). And he required that the people take oaths of loyalty to Caesar and to himself. The Pharisees' refusal to take the loyalty oath (*Ant.* 15.368–70; 17:41–42) likely indicates at least reluctance on the part of other Judeans as well. Herod was "king of the Judeans" by the might of Rome, not the recognition of the Judeans.[6]

Herod became a model Roman client-king, apparently Caesar's favorite, probably because of his massive building projects in honor of Augustus.[7] He constructed two cities in honor of his imperial Lord and named for him, Sebaste ("Augustus") in Samaria, and his new seaport on the Mediterranean coast, Caesarea. In these, he built temples to Augustus and Roma, the temple and huge statue of Caesar in Caesarea dominating the harbor and city center. He built another temple to Caesar in Panias near the grottoes dedicated to the god Pan. In Jerusalem itself, as well as in other cities, Herod built theaters, amphitheaters, and hippodromes, standard institutions of the dominant imperial Hellenistic Roman culture (see, for example, *War* 2:44; *Ant.* 15.268; 17.255). He also made lavish gifts to various cities in the eastern empire, as well as to Augustus and other members of the imperial family. A key marker of his orientation to and imitation of imperial Roman culture was the construction of his own family mausoleum in Jerusalem on the same pattern used in Augustus's mausoleum in Rome. Herod's massive and extensive building projects were concrete manifestations of the ways in which he was the face of Roman rule in Judea. As Josephus observed, "One can mention no suitable site within his realm which he left destitute of some mark of homage to Caesar" (*War* 1.407).

Some historians have emphasized that in not building temples in honor of Caesar Augustus in Jerusalem or elsewhere in Judea itself, Herod was being sensitive to the religious sensitivities of the Judeans. The Judean historian Josephus, however, our principal historical source for the practices of Augustus's favorite client-king, pointedly presents just the opposite picture. As scion of a wealthy priestly family and, when he composed his histories, a beneficiary of Flavian's imperial patronage, Josephus appreciated the hegemonic function of traditional religious customs—that is, keeping the masses under control. More than once he explains that Herod "departed from ancestral customs and through foreign practices gradually corrupted the ancient way of life which had previously been inviolable" (*Ant.* 15.267). Among these, he focuses on "the athletic contests [that Herod] established every fifth year in honor of Caesar, the theater in Jerusalem, . . . and the very large amphitheater in the plain, both spectacularly lavish but foreign to Judean customs" (17.268). Not only were these imperial institutions, they embodied the imperial presence just as the temples and shrines dedicated to Caesar did in the Greek cities.[8]

> All round the theater were inscriptions concerning Caesar and trophies of the [subjected] peoples that he had won in war, all of them made for Herod of pure gold and silver. . . . There was also a supply of wild beasts. . . . It seemed a glaring impiety to throw men to wild beasts for the pleasure of other men as spectators, and it seemed a further impiety to change their established ways for foreign practices. But more than all else it was the trophies that irked them [as] against their ancestral customs. (15.272-76)

A military strongman whose father was an Idumean and imposed as king on the Judeans by the warlords of the Roman Senate, Herod lacked legitimacy in Judean lineage and tradition. Presumably to gain at least a modicum of acceptance and appreciation, Herod took measures to memorialize the heroes of Israelite-Judean tradition. Many of the lavish monuments he built focused on the patriarchs and matriarchs of Israel at the legendary sites of their memorable moments.[9] He built an impressive monument over the caves at Machpelah, the legendary burial place of Sarah, Abraham, and Isaac (Gen 23; 25:9-10; 35:27-29), a building that was a virtual prototype of Herod's rebuilding of the temple in Jerusalem. He built another memorial at ("the oaks of") Mamre, where God had appeared to Abraham to announce the birth of Isaac (Gen 18). In the town of Hebron, he built a memorial for Abraham and Sarah, Isaac and Rebecca, and Jacob and Leah. Hebron, of course, was also the town where David had been made "messiah" (that is, anointed) as king of Judah and reigned before being anointed as king of all Israel. Presumably to associate himself with King David, the prototypical messiah, Herod erected a memorial to David at the entrance to his tomb (*Ant.* 16.179-84). Sensitivity to Judean memorial sensibilities, however, did not prevent him from plundering David's tomb when he was desperate for funds to meet the huge expenses of his largely pro-Roman building projects and diplomatic largesse in the Roman imperial world.

One of Herod's principal measures was to make the Temple and high priesthood a tool of his own rule. Although one of his wives was a Hasmonean princess, he quickly eliminated the last Hasmonean qualified to serve as high priest. He then set a succession of his own appointments into the office, some from outside of Judea, and their families gradually formed a new priestly aristocracy beholden to Herod and Roman rule.[10] Insofar as Herod was now the ruler, and the temple apparatus now subordinate to him, the others who served the temple-state, such as the Pharisees and other scribes, were in effect demoted, no longer having their previous influence in the operations of the society.

Most noticeable externally would have been Herod's massive rebuilding of the Temple edifice on a grand scale inevitably influenced by the Hellenistic patterns dominant in the eastern empire. This may well have become a source of pride for many personnel who served in the temple apparatus, but it would also have meant departures from Judean tradition in numerous respects. Two features of the Temple and its sacrifices under Roman and Herodian rule were particularly controversial and eventually sources of open conflict. Among the ceremonies conducted at the altar were regular sacrifices on behalf of Rome and Caesar. Judging from how adamant the priests were in refusing to continue these sacrifices in the heady time at the beginning of the great revolt against Roman rule in 66 (*War* 2.409, 417), they must have been conducting these sacrifices reluctantly for decades. The other controversial feature of Herod's temple was the golden Roman eagle erected over the great gate (*War* 1.650), a constant visible reminder of Judeans' subjection to Rome. This became the target of a protest demonstration by Jerusalem sages and their students toward the end of Herod's reign (*War* 1.648–53; *Ant.* 17.149–59), to be discussed in chapter 11 below. "Herod's" Temple became a prominent feature in the face of Roman rule in Judea.

To fund his many massive building projects and munificence to the imperial family and Hellenistic cities, Herod taxed his subjects heavily. Villagers fell ever more heavily into debt, unable to support their families as well as render up taxes, tithes, and offerings, and still support themselves without loans. Archaeological explorations in Jerusalem and the hill country of Judea suggest that during Herod's reign, his high officers and the high priestly families became increasingly wealthy, with increasingly large mansions in the city and landed estates in the hill country. Unsparing in repressive measures, he kept tight rein on the people at every level. When he died, however, the

Roman Conquest and Roman Rule

people of Jerusalem clamored for justice and reform and the people erupted in widespread revolt. That the revolt in every major district of Herod's realm, Galilee, Perea, and Judea, took the form of movements led by popularly acclaimed "kings" (according to Josephus's accounts, *War* 2.55–65; *Ant.* 17.271–85)—that is, popular "messiahs"—suggests how deep the opposition had been to Herod as the Roman-imposed king.[11]

Roman Reconquest and Direct Rule

Judeans and the other Israelite peoples subjected to Rome's client-king quickly asserted their independence from Herodian and Roman rule (*War* 2.55–65; *Ant.* 17.269–85). In Galilee and Perea, the rebels attacked the royal fortresses to "take back" the goods that had been taken and stored there. In Judea, the peasant uprising targeted Romans and Herodians and even attacked a Roman supply train bringing grain and weapons to the army. Under the leadership of the (David-like) shepherd Athronges and his brothers, the popular messianic movement in Judea managed to maintain its independence in the hill country for three years. To reassert their control of Judea and Galilee, the Romans had to mount a reconquest (*War* 2.68–75; *Ant.* 17.286–96).

The Romans became particularly brutal when they had to reconquer subject peoples who had revolted. Their practices of extreme devastation of the countryside, slaughter and enslavement of the people, and crucifixion of rebel leaders for the "demonstration effect" on the rest of the populace, were designed to terrorize the newly conquered people into submission. Under the leadership of Varus, a large army of Roman legions and auxiliary troops first attacked in western Galilee, destroyed Sepphoris, at the center of the area of the revolt there, and enslaved its inhabitants. He then advanced through Judea, destroying villages as he went. "The whole district became a scene of fire and blood" (*War* 2.70). Varus had the town of Emmaus burned to the ground in vengeance for the attack on the Roman supply train. Sending his soldiers to scour the hill-country for the leaders of the insurrection, he had two thousand of them crucified, and left a legion in Jerusalem as a garrison to maintain control of the country.

Following the Roman reconquest, Augustus placed Judea and Samaria under Herod's son Archelaus, with Galilee together with Perea under another son, Antipas. After Archelaus's rule proved unsatisfactory, however, the Romans brought Judea under direct Roman rule. A Roman governor, based in Caesarea on the coast, with a contingent of troops, was in charge. The governor in turn entrusted control of affairs in Judea to the high-priestly aristocracy of the families that Herod had appointed to the high-priestly office. The Roman governor exercised control of the high priesthood by his power to appoint and depose high priests. And the Romans again laid the Judeans under tribute, which was collected by the priestly aristocracy in charge of the country.

This restoration of a weakened Jerusalem temple-state as the local representative of imperial rule set up a conflictual situation with Pharisees and other scribes "caught in the middle." With the Herodian royal administration no longer running affairs in Jerusalem, the Pharisees and other scribes who served as advisers and representatives of the priestly aristocracy in charge of the Temple now presumably regained a certain degree of authority and influence in public affairs. While the high priests now again headed a temple-state, however, they presided in Herod's Temple, still under construction, and had the sacrifices in honor of Rome and Caesar regularly performed. The high-priestly families who held their position because Herod's previous appointments to the high priesthood, and the succession of high priests appointed by Roman governors would thus have had at least questionable legitimacy among the regular priests, traditionalist scribes, and Judean people. At every point when the Roman governors took some action that offended or provoked the Judean people, moreover, the high-priestly families did little or nothing to protest or to represent the people's interest.[12] And the high-priestly families used their positions of power to enhance their lives of privilege, steadily expanding their wealth and building ever more lavish mansions in the New City of Jerusalem, to the east of the temple. The high-priestly families that the scribes and Pharisees served thus regularly acted against the interest of the Judean people and in violation of the principles of Judean sacred tradition, both of which scribes had traditionally defended. The Herodian high-priestly aristocracy presiding in Herod's Temple became increasingly the face of Roman imperial rule in Judea.[13]

The imposition of direct Roman rule also brought the fundamental conflict between imperial domination and the very core of Judean tradition to the fore in periodic Roman provocations and Judean protests. Rome had become master of the world. Caesar was the Lord and Savior who had established Peace and Security. Caesar demanded tribute and viewed the failure to render the tribute in timely fashion as tantamount to revolt, inviting vengeful reconquest. According to Israel's foundational story, however, God had delivered the people from oppressive foreign rule in the exodus from bondage under Pharaoh. According to Israel's covenant with God on Sinai, God was the exclusive King of the people; they could not "bow down and serve" any other lord and master. According to the prophets, God was also the Lord of all peoples and held overall dominion over history.[14]

The most vivid illustration of this fundamental conflict was surely the annual celebration of Passover, the weeklong festival commemorating the people's exodus from the oppressive rule of Pharaoh. Because it was such a potentially volatile time, the Roman governors made a regular practice of bringing Roman troops up to Jerusalem and posting them on the porticoes of the temple to watch over the crowds gathered for the celebration. But this only exacerbated the tension. At Passover one year the crowd celebrating the people's liberation took offense at an obscene gesture by one of the Roman soldiers and challenged the governor, Cumanus, who sent out his soldiers to suppress the demonstration (*War* 2.223–27; *Ant.* 20.105–12).

Although the Romans prided themselves on tolerating subject people's customs, the Roman governors of Judea repeatedly took actions that brought the fundamental conflict between Roman imperial rule and Judean traditions to the fore in overt conflict. Two of the many provocations were by Pontius Pilate, who was hardly the governor easily manipulated by the Judean chief priests portrayed in the Christian Gospels. Shortly after being sent to Judea as governor, he brought Roman troops into Jerusalem with images of Caesar on their military standards, violations of the covenantal laws against images, according to Josephus's lengthy accounts (*War* 2.169–74; *Ant.* 18.55–59). The severity of the offense is indicated by the intensity of the Judeans' reaction. Large numbers followed Pilate back to Caesarea where they continued their protest for several days. In another action to which Judeans took exception, Pilate used Temple funds for the construction of an aqueduct to bring water to Jerusalem. "Indignant, the populace formed a ring round Pilate's tribunal in Jerusalem, and besieged him with angry clamor" (*War* 2.175–77; *Ant.* 18.60). This time, Pilate did not back down, but turned his troops against the protesters.

The most serious Roman provocation in the fundamental conflict between imperial rule and Judeans' commitment to their sacred tradition came from the emperor Gaius (37–41 c.e.). Piqued at the refusal of Jews in Alexandria to honor his imperial person as divine, Gaius ordered that a statue of Zeus with his own features be erected in the Temple in Jerusalem. It was standard in most cities of the empire for the statue of the emperor to be displayed along with the statue of the god in that god's temple. He further ordered Petronius to advance into Judea from Syria with a large army and, if the Judeans resisted, to subdue them by force. According to the accounts of Josephus (*War* 2.184–203; *Ant.* 18.261–88), as supplemented by the rhetorical embellishment of the events by the Alexandrian Jewish philosopher Philo (*Leg.* 222–32), thousands came to Petronius when he marched into Galilee to petition that he "not use force to make them transgress their ancestral code" (*Ant.* 18.261–63). Petronius could see that enforcing Gaius's order would result in great slaughter. The people adamantly continued their protest for weeks, neglecting their fields just at planting time. Petronius and the local Herodian client rulers advising him could see that if he proceeded with force against the people, the result would be "a harvest of banditry," since if the fields remained unsown—that is, with no crops—there would be no tribute for the Romans, but only many bands of social brigands that would result from yet another Roman military devastation of the land and people (*Ant.* 18.269–74). Another Roman conquest of Judea was avoided only by the assassination of Gaius in January, 41. But Gaius's order to install his likeness in the Temple had brought the rule of Caesar into direct confrontation with the ultimate rule of God.

Provocations by Roman governors continued, along with periodic violent suppressions of social banditry, as Judean peasants unable to meet payments for taxes, tithes, tribute, and interest, and still feed their families, fled to the hills. The high-priestly families and Herodian families, expanding their wealth and control of fields at the expense of indebted peasants, far from representing the people's interest to Roman officials, collaborated ever more closely in imperial rule. As social turmoil escalated, prominent high-priestly figures and Herodians became increasingly predatory on the people. They even sent their private gangs of thugs out to the threshing floors at harvest time to expropriate the tithes that rightfully belonged to the ordinary priests, and plundered people's goods generally, according to Josephus's accounts (*Ant.* 20.181, 206–7, 214).

The last three Roman governors exacerbated the growing social unrest with sharp repressive measures against banditry and extraordinary taxes, again following Josephus's accounts (*War* 2.271–73). The actions of the final governor, Florus, particularly outraged the Judeans, who appealed to the governor of Syria (*War* 2.277–83). His move to extract seventeen talents from the Temple treasury evoked protest, to which he responded by marching on Jerusalem with an army. The governor's provocations and the Jerusalemites' responses escalated, with brutal attacks on the people that only evoked more intense outcries. Florus's sharp escalation of repressive violence, including the crucifixion of protesters, led to the outbreak of revolt in Jerusalem in the summer of 66 C.E., as the people managed to drive the Roman forces from the city. Resistance in Jerusalem sparked an eruption of widespread revolt in the countryside. The Judeans and Galileans managed to reassert their independence of imperial rule.

Rome, however, was not about to allow a subject people to assert their independence for long. A year later, a huge Roman army under Vespasian again devastated villages, slaughtered and enslaved the people, and regained control of Galilee and northwestern Judea. When, at the death of Nero, Vespasian hastened to Rome, where he successfully claimed the imperial throne, Judeans had a respite before the Romans' renewed onslaught. A "provisional government" of some high priests and "leading Pharisees" attempted to maintain

Roman Conquest and Roman Rule

a modicum of control over the territory and to negotiate with the Romans, but were overwhelmed by a coalition of newly organized resistance forces from different parts of Judea that took refuge in Jerusalem.[15] After a severe devastation of Judean villages and a prolonged siege of Jerusalem, the huge Roman army eventually took the city, killed the defenders, and destroyed city and Temple alike. The fundamental conflict between Roman imperial rule and the Judeans' commitment to their sacred traditions had resulted in the Roman destruction of the Temple and temple-state. The temple-state was no longer a viable option for Roman imperial control of Judea, since the high-priestly aristocracy had lost control of the people. And with the end of the Jerusalem Temple and temple-state, there was no longer any clear role for the Pharisees and other scribes. And at this point, we lose track of what happened to the scribes historically.

Chapter 7

The War against the "Kittim": The Covenant Community at Qumran

The scribes and priests at Qumran who left behind the Dead Sea Scrolls present a unique case of a scribal-priestly community living in separation from the rest of Judean society. They and the texts they composed are similar in many ways to the circles of scribes and their texts examined in previous chapters. Yet they are also different in significant respects. They were the only scribal (priestly) group, so far as we know, to withdraw to the wilderness and form their own tightly disciplined residential community. And they were the only scribal (priestly) group that anticipated engaging the dominant imperial forces in battle.*

Virtually none of the many texts they produced is classified as an "apocalypse" by scholarly interpreters. Yet many of the motifs and themes in their texts have seemed so similar to those in "apocalyptic" literature that the people living at Qumran have been called an "apocalyptic community." Indeed, one of the principal impacts of the discovery of the Dead Sea Scrolls was the resurgence of interpretation of Jesus's followers as an "apocalyptic" movement, suddenly more credible because of the apparent discovery of another Jewish community living in intense anticipation of "the end-time."

---

* I am working primarily from the translation of the Dead Sea Scrolls by Geza Vermes, *The Complete Dead Sea Scrolls in English* (London: Penguin, 1997), at points adjusting Vermes' translation somewhat. Readers should consult this or another translation of the Community Rule, the Damascus Document, the Pesher to Habakkuk, and the War Scroll in connection with the discussion in this chapter.

From the many texts they left, we know a great deal about their community life and its regulations. Yet few of the texts they produced include references to contemporary persons, events, or institutions, and those scattered references are allusive, often in codelike terms, rather than specific. It is necessary to consider the many allusive references in Qumran texts critically in comparison with other sources to identify the historical context and the community's attitudes and actions.[1] Texts from Qumran have been interpreted by scholars trained in biblical studies who bring Christian and Jewish theological interests and concepts over from the standard approaches and discourse of their fields. As in the reconsideration of Judean texts classified as "apocalyptic," it will be important not to allow modern theological concepts and concerns to obscure what may have been the inseparable political and religious concerns expressed in the texts. And it is important, as one of the basic steps in critical investigation, to consider how the literary patterns and community concerns of the texts determine meaning, and not to lift motifs and terms out of their literary context for anachronistic systematization in modern intellectual constructs.

The Movement and Communities

What was distinctive about the scribes and priests who left the Dead Sea Scrolls was that they formed a community in the wilderness, or perhaps a main community at Qumran and other, smaller "camps" in various towns and villages of Judea. Josephus puts the number of the Essenes at four thousand. Since he almost always exaggerates numbers, we should probably cut that estimate at least by half. Archaeological excavations had indicated the settlement at Qumran could have accommodated little more than 200, suggesting that the community there could not have been large.[2]

The two principal "charters" of the community(ies) found in multiple copies among the Scrolls—the Community Rule (1QS and variant versions), and the Damascus Document (CD and copies found at Qumran)—are for somewhat different yet evidently related groups.[3]

The Community Rule is intended for an ascetic "community" or "assembly" of priests and laity (Aaron and Israel) in the wilderness that was likened to later monastic communities by early interpreters.[4] The members were to "eat in common and bless in common and deliberate in common" (1QS 6:3–4). In complete obedience to what was commanded by Moses and the prophets, they were to love one another and to share their "knowledge, powers, and possessions" (1QS 1:2–3, 11–12). Entrance into full membership required a probationary period of two or three years for the candidates, after which their property was amalgamated with the others' (1QS 6:14–22).

To support themselves, they evidently farmed and made their own pots and other goods—and cured hides to make the parchment on which they copied texts. Having rejected and abandoned the Temple as having been profaned by the incumbent priests, the Qumranites carried out their own ceremonies, purity observances, and communal discipline. Their rigorous purity regulations involved ritual bathing. Their central ceremony was the common meal at which they observed strict procedure by rank (1QS 6:4–5). And wherever ten were present, they would "watch for a third of every night of the year, to recite the book and to search the justice-ruling(s) and to bless in common" (1QS 6:6–8, author's trans.).

Leadership of the community was provided by "the council of the community," consisting of "twelve men and three priests perfectly versed in all that is revealed of the Torah," who would "preserve faith in the land . . . thus atoning for sin by practice of justice and by suffering the sorrows of affliction" (8:1–4). The most important "officer" was evidently the "guardian" (mebaqqer), who may have been the same as the "master" (maskil), who combined the role of master-teacher and spiritual adviser-examiner to the members with that of administrator of the common life and property (6:11–22).

The Damascus Document applies to a movement that (at least) includes people who "live in camps, . . . marrying, begetting children" (CD 7:7–8; 12:19, 23; 13:7–22).[5] The members of the movement addressed by the Damascus Rule have also rejected and abandoned the Temple and its sacrifices, although they may have sent burnt offerings to the altar (11:16–17). "None of those brought into the Covenant shall enter the Temple to light His altar in vain. . . . They shall separate from the sons of the pit and shall keep away from the unclean riches of wickedness acquired . . . from the Temple treasure" (CD 6:11–12). Members of the "camps" evidently lived in Judean towns and villages but remained separated from other locals. Members of the camps did not have property in common, like members of the community at Qumran. But they were required to give two days' earnings per month into the hands of the guardian and the judges for the support of orphans, the poor, and the sickly (14:13–16). As in the Community Rule, so also in the Damascus Document, community members were to love one another, to succor the poor, and "to act according to the exact formulations of the Torah during the age of wickedness" (6:14–15, 19–21; 16:2). The individual discipline can be seen, for example, in the rules for strict observance of Sabbath (10:14–11:18). The particular concern for purity that the Damascus Rule shares with the Community Rule can be seen in the requirement of ritual bathing (10:12–14).

While looking to priests for local leadership, wherever ten men are gathered in the camps (13:1–2), the Damascus Document also vests leadership primarily in the guardians of the camps and a principal guardian for all the camps, who meet in assembly. The roles of the guardian(s) resemble those described in the Community Rule, as teacher(s), spiritual adviser(s)-examiner(s), and administrator(s) of common funds (13:7–13, 20–23; 14:9, 13–16). While the Damascus Document does not mention the council of the community, it does have provision for courts and judges, who were elected for a definite term (10:5–11).

Considering the many close similarities between the Community Rule and the Damascus Document, and the fact that ten copies of the latter were found at Qumran, it appears that they attest to a single movement of priests and scribes, with a main community in the wilderness at Qumran and "camps" resident in various Judean towns and villages. The Damascus Rule appears to address both the wilderness community and the camps. And it may be that the guardian of the community at Qumran was also the guardian of all the camps.[6]

The movement addressed in the Community Rule, the Damascus Document, and many of the other texts found at Qumran, also appears to have been more or less identical with the Essenes described in previously known ancient sources by Josephus, Philo, and Pliny the Elder.[7]

A number of the features of the Qumran community and wider movement addressed in the Community Rule and Damascus Document, as noted just above, indicate that the membership and orientation were scribal as well as priestly. This should be clear simply from the extensive composition and copying of texts attested by the large "library" of documents found in the caves near Qumran, that is, "the Dead Sea Scrolls" left behind by the community when it was destroyed.[8] The scribal character of the community should also be evident in the nightly "watches" in which they recited the book (of Torah), searched the ruling(s of righteousness), and blessed in common (1QS 6:6–8). But it comes to the fore particularly in the titles, requirements, roles, and responsibilities of its leaders. The "master" was primarily a teacher, as indicated by his title in Hebrew, *maskil*, which means "enlightener." His most prominent function clearly required the acquisition of great wisdom, so that he could "instruct all the sons of light and teach them the nature of all the children of men . . . the signs identifying their worlds during their lifetime, their visitation for chastisement, and the time of their reward" (1QS 3:13–15, as exemplified in the ensuing "instruction," 3:15—4:27). That fourfold knowledge covers much of the traditional repertoire of a learned scribe, as indicated in the book of Sirach and the texts of Enoch (see the introduction and chs. 3–4 above). The "teacher of righteousness," who evidently had led the movement to establish the community at Qumran, was not only the movement's great instructor in the Torah, but had special training and insight to "all (the mysteries of) the words of the prophets" (1QpHab 2:7–9; 7:3–5), adept in the full range of the Judean scribal repertoire (Sir 38:24–39:4). At Qumran as in Jerusalem, many priests were also trained as scribes. The priest who was appointed to head the congregation was to be "learned in the book of Hagu [Torah, or perhaps meditation] and in all the judgments of the Torah so as to pronounce them correctly" (CD 14:6–9). One of the two principal roles of the Guardian was to teach the members of the community. In that connection, the Guardian of all the camps was to have "mastered all the secrets of men and the languages of all their clans" (CD 14:9–10).

Covenant Community and Driving Spirits

What is most striking about the community in both the Community Rule and the Damascus Document is not that it is "apocalyptic," but that it is the *community* (and broader movement) of the *new covenant*. This is a striking contrast with texts usually classified as "apocalyptic." The Mosaic covenant was supposedly central to the life of Judean society as well as in scribal knowledge and commitment. In the instructional speeches of Ben Sira, obedience to the covenant is central not only in scribal training and practice in the service of the temple-state, but also in scribes' efforts to mitigate the worst effects of their priestly patrons' exploitation of the poor. This is confirmed in the Epistle of Enoch's use of covenantal criteria in indictment of the priestly rulers for their oppression of the righteous, although without being drawn out explicitly. The survey of history in Daniel 10–12 accuses the Judean allies of Antiochus Epiphanes of having abandoned the covenant, but makes no mention of its restoration or renewal. The covenant and covenantal themes are, if anything, conspicuous by their absence in the key texts of Enoch and Daniel that are usually classified as "apocalyptic." Of the texts discussed in earlier chapters, only the Testament of Moses worked explicitly with Mosaic covenantal criteria in its survey of Israel's history up to the crisis of Antiochus's invasion of Jerusalem.

It is all the more striking, therefore, that the charters of the Qumran community (and its satellite camps) not only condemn the priestly rulers in Jerusalem for abandoning the covenant, but are both explicitly covenants for covenantal communities. Both documents are covenantal in form and covenantal in substance and refer to covenantal ceremonies by which the remnant of Israel is constituted. The covenant was made by God with the ancestors, but it was disobeyed again and again. Thus it was necessary for God to make a (new) covenant with the remnant of Israel who have formed the community in the wilderness. The covenant is thus, depending on the context, the pact made historically between God and Israel and/or the community of the remnant in Israel and/or the enacted covenant by which the members enter that community (e.g., 1QS 1:6–7, 17–18; 5:8–12; CD 1:5, 20; 2:2–3; 3:13–14; 6:12). The understanding of the Qumran community and its satellite camps as (new/renewed) covenant and covenantal thinking about Israel, its history and its destiny, are thus dominant in the two major "charters" of the movement.

This covenantal thinking at Qumran, however, shows a significant difference from the covenantal thinking in earlier Judean texts with regard to the motivation of obedience and disobedience of Israelites/Judeans. In earlier covenant (renewal) ceremonies (such as Josh 24), the people chose to serve the god who had delivered them and, in the face of the blessings that would result from obedience and the curses that would ensue from disobedience, to observe the covenantal laws and regulations. The Deuteronomic history saw, in retrospect, a pattern of the people's disobedience that brought God's punishment, which in turn induced the people's repentance and God's new deliverance and the people's renewed commitment (for example, Judg 2). In the Damascus Document and the Community Rule, the people's obedience or disobedience and repentance and recommitment are still involved. But superhuman forces are now also involved in obedience to or violation of covenantal laws and their social-political effects.

In the Damascus Document, the disobedience of rebellious Israelites is what leads to punitive judgment by God, and repentance by the remnant leads to God's new acts of deliverance (CD 1:2–4; 3:7–13; and repeatedly). While not as prominent as the people's own disobedience in the crises of Israel's covenantal history, however, superhuman forces are also involved. The Damascus Document mentions the fall of "the heavenly watchers" in passing (2:18). In contrast with the watchers' rebellion as the cosmological explanation for imperial violence in the Book of Watchers (*1 Enoch* 1–36), however, the watchers' fall is merely one among several illustrations from the (scriptural) traditions of Israel of the failure to "keep the commandments of God," by following the "guilty inclination" and the "eyes of lust," still a matter of following "one's own will" (2:14—3:9). That "Belial was unleashed against Israel" during the years when "the converts of Israel" had "departed from the land of Judah" turns out to be the consequence of the "three nets of Belial," which are "fornication, . . . riches, . . . and profanation of the Temple" (CD 4:13–18), again motivational forces in disobedience of covenantal principles. "Belial" had figured already "in ancient times," having "raised up Jannes and his brother when Israel was first delivered," as the counterpart of "the prince of light," by whose hand Moses and Aaron arose (5:18–19). And "Belial" also turns up as another of God's agents of destruction (8:2–3), which had previously figured in scribal portrayals of judgment (as in Enoch texts).

In the Community Rule, more ominously, superhuman forces have virtually come to control people's actions. The time in which the Qumran community lives is under "the dominion of Belial," and the community is struggling against its opponents who are of "the lot of Belial" (1:23; 2:5; 2:19). By far the most striking change in covenantal thinking comes in the now-famous exposition of the "two spirits" (1QS 3:15–4:26). In his "whole design" for humankind, God has appointed two spirits, of truth and injustice, in which people will walk. "All the children of righteousness are ruled by the prince/officer of light and walk in the ways of light, but all the children of injustice are ruled by the messenger of darkness and walk in the ways of darkness" (3:18–22). While the messenger of darkness leads all the children of righteousness astray, and their sin and unrighteous deeds are caused by his dominion, the God of Israel and his messenger of truth will succor all the children of light. For it is God "who created the spirits of light and darkness . . . and established every deed [upon] their [ways]" (3:24–26). He loves the one and loathes the other. Yet the two groups of people do not correspond strictly with the two spirits. All people "have a portion of their divisions and walk in (both) their ways." And their reward for their deeds shall be "according to whether each person's portion in their two divisions is great or small" (4:15–17). "Until now the spirits of truth and injustice struggle in the hearts of people and they walk in both wisdom and folly" (4:23–24).

The dominion of Belial, and especially the determination of human action by the struggle between the two spirits, have been taken as explanations of "the origin of evil" and expressions of a "cosmic dualism," which are often also understood as marks of the "apocalypticism" of the Qumran community. Since Qumran texts are not among the scripturally authoritative texts for Jewish or Christian doctrine, however, it is unclear why we should apply later theological or philosophical concepts such as "(the origins of) evil" to them. While the "whole design" of the two spirits is indeed schematic, it also seems inappropriate to systematize the phrases and forces spoken of here in the Community Rule with those elsewhere in the Rule itself or in other Qumran texts such as the War Rule, which have different concerns. There is also no warrant for reading this or other passages in Qumran texts as if they were expounding a metaphysics, as was often done in earlier theological constructions of "apocalypticism."

The two spirits are indeed superhuman forces. Yet in contrast to some of the heavenly figures in the Book of Watchers (Shemihazah, Raphael), there does not appear to be any basis in the text for the personification and reification of the spirits as suggested by the capitalization of their "names" in various translations, such as "the Prince of Light" and "the Angel of Darkness."

The text uses a variety of phrases in reference to the two spirits ("officer/prince of light," "messenger of truth," "spirit of light," and "messenger of darkness," "spirit of darkness," and sometimes just "the spirits")—so it seems inappropriate to collapse these multiple phrases into a capitalized title for each one. The two spirits are not cosmic forces, again in contrast to several of the forces in the Book of Watchers that have the names of heavenly bodies.[9] They are, rather, superhuman ethical or social-economic-political forces that influence human action. They have their determining effect on historical affairs through human action. The whole passage and scheme of two spirits is concerned to explain the long-standing struggle between the movement that has remained faithful and righteous, on the one hand, and their opponents on the other, evidently those who control the Temple in Jerusalem. Finally, while the struggle between the spirits is fierce (4:17–18), there is no battle between the two spirits that results in the destruction of the spirit of darkness. Rather, God has ordained "an end for injustice," at which point God will "root out all spirit of injustice" from humankind and "cleanse humans of all wicked deeds with the spirit of holiness" (4:21–22).

It seems doubtful that "Belial" in the phrase "during the dominion of Belial" in the covenantal ceremony (1:23; 2:19) and "Belial" in the Damascus Document should be identified with a (personified reified) messenger of darkness in the struggle between the two spirits (1QS 3:15–4:26). "During the dominion of Belial" refers to the time of the struggle of the Qumran community against its opponents in Jerusalem, who are "the men of the lot of Belial" (2:5). In the Damascus Document, "Belial" was active also in ancient times, as a counterpart of the "officer of lights" (5:18–19). But "Belial" acts as an agent provocateur, seducer, or an agent of destruction, and not a more determining force of unrighteousness as a counterpart of a force of righteousness. It is also unclear whether either text presents "Belial" as a personified figure, as often assumed. "Belial" seems more like the force of wickedness, which is what the term means in Hebrew texts, often in the form of "men of wickedness," who usually stand in opposition ("scoundrels"). In fact, the term could easily be translated "wickedness" in all occurrences in both charter texts: "during the dominion of wickedness" (1QS 1:23; 2:19); "the three nets of wickedness" (fornication, and so on; CD 4:13–19).

In both the Community Rule and the Damascus Document, the superhuman forces help explain the keeping or breaking of the covenant. The struggle between the two spirits may be dualistic thinking, but it is a struggle between ethical-historical forces, not cosmic forces or even heavenly powers. In the Community Rule, the teaching that the two spirits determine human action serves to explain the intense struggle in which the Qumran community was engaged with their opponents, the incumbent rulers of the Temple.

The War against the "Kittim"

When Josephus explains the Essenes in the Greek philosophical terms that his readers would understand, he states that they believe that human actions are determined by fate, not free will. The explanation in the Community Rule, however, was more complex, subtle, nuanced, and political-ethical than Greek philosophical thinking about fate and free will.

Against Empire: the Motives of Withdrawal from the Temple-State in Protest

So why did a large number of priests and scribes abandon life in Jerusalem centered on the Temple, for which they had been trained, and withdraw to form rigorous covenantal communities in the wilderness or in the towns of Judea? We can piece together a sketchy picture of the covenant community's origins and its motives for abandoning the Temple and rejecting its ruling priesthood by matching the scattered and allusive references to contemporary events and figures in Qumran texts with what is known of the history of second-century Judea from Josephus and other sources.

The opening of the Damascus Document provides the most important clues about the origin of the movement/community.

> And in the age of wrath, three hundred and ninety years after He had given them into the hand of king Nebuchadnezzar of Babylon, He visited them, and He caused a plant root to spring from Israel and Aaron to inherit His land and to prosper on the good things of His earth. And they perceived their iniquity and recognized that they were guilty men, yet for twenty years they were like blind men groping for the way. And God observed their deeds, that they sought Him with a whole heart, and He raised for them a righteous teacher to guide them in the way of his heart. (CD 1:5–11)

Other key clues about a crisis that may have led to the "founding" of a community in the wilderness can be derived from references to *the righteous teacher* and *the wicked priest* in the "interpretations" *(pesharim)* unique to the Qumran community. They believed that while the prophets, such as Habakkuk, had not known the application of the words that God had told them to write down, God had now revealed to the righteous teacher how particular names, words, and phrases applied to their own historical circumstances (1QpHab 7:1–5).

> (Ps 37:32-33) Interpreted, this concerns *the wicked* [priest] who [watched the teacher of righteousness] that he might put him to death [because of the ordinance] and the law which he sent to him . . . But [God] will pay him his reward by delivering him into the hand of the violent of the nations, that they may execute upon him [judgment]. (4Q 171 4:5–12)

> (Hab 2:5-6) Interpreted, this concerns *the wicked priest,* who was called by the name of truth when he first arose. But when he ruled over Israel his heart became proud, and he forsook God and betrayed the precepts for the sake of riches. He robbed and amassed the riches of the men of violence who rebelled against God, and he took the wealth of the peoples. (1QpHab 8:4–14)
>
> (Hab 2:8b) Interpreted, this concerns *the wicked priest,* whom God delivered into the hands of his enemies because of the iniquity committed against *the righteous teacher* and the men of his council, that he might be humbled by means of a destroying scourge, in bitterness of soul, because he had done wickedly to His elect. (1QpHab 9:7–12)
>
> (Hab 2:15) Interpreted, this concerns *the wicked priest,* who pursued *the righteous teacher* to the house of his exile that he might swallow him with his venomous fury. And at the time appointed for rest, for the Day of Atonement, he appeared before them to swallow them, and to cause them to stumble on the Day of Fasting, their Sabbath of repose. (1QpHab 11:2–8)

Ezekiel had prophesied 390 years as the time of punishment for Israel after the destruction of Jerusalem by the Babylonians armies in 587 B.C.E. Even if the composers of the Damascus Document took Ezekiel's number of years literally, they lacked accurate chronology of the years since the destruction of Jerusalem. As a rough number for the long period since the Babylonian destruction of Jerusalem, however, the figure would bring us into the early second century B.C.E. And as indicated in the texts examined in chapters 4 and 5 above, this was a time of crisis for priests and scribes in Jerusalem, with the Hellenizing reform, resistance by several circles of scribes, and Antiochus's repressive measures to enforce the reform. If the twenty years of groping refer to the period of scribal resistance, Antiochus's invasion, the prolonged Maccabean Revolt, and the uneasy time of turmoil after the rededication of the Temple in 164, we come to mid-second century.

At that time, the obvious referent of the "wicked priest" who was hostile to the righteous teacher and his movement, even pursuing him to his place of exile, but was himself killed by "the violent of the nations" (4Q 171 4:5–12; 1QpHab 9:7–12; 11:2–8), would have been the Hasmonean Jonathan.[10] As explained in 1 Maccabees, after finagling appointment as high priest by the Seleucid king Alexander Balas in 152 B.C.E., who desperately needed his military support, Jonathan gradually consolidated his power in Jerusalem (1 Macc 10:15–67). This included launching some rebuilding projects, such as the fortifications of the city and Temple. Almost certainly he would also have confiscated the property of the families involved in the reform ("the riches of the men of violence who rebelled against God") and that of their foreign military supporters whom Antiochus Epiphanes had brought into Jerusalem ("the wealth of the peoples," 1QpHab 8:4–14). After maneuvering skillfully between rival Seleucid pretenders competing for control of the empire, however, Jonathan was eventually captured and killed by one of them ("a destroying scourge" by "the violent of the nations," "his enemies" 4Q 171 4:5–12; 1QpHab 9:7–12; cf. 1 Macc 12:35—13:30).

The movement that had been "groping" for twenty years would thus have begun in reaction to the Hellenizing "reform" in Jerusalem launched in 175, parallel to the circles of scribes that had produced the visions in Daniel 7–10, "Enoch's" surveys of history, and the *Testament of Moses*. It has been suggested that the righteous teacher who provided the leadership that consolidated the movement and led it into exile in the wilderness of "Damascus" may have been a prominent figure in the priesthood in Jerusalem prior to Jonathan's negotiation of an official imperial appointment in 152 (he is identified as a priest in 1QpHab 3:15–16). Whatever his status in Jerusalem, he may well have criticized Jonathan ("the law which he sent to him") when he "betrayed the precepts for the sake of riches" (4Q 171 4:5–12; 1QpHab 84–14). Even after the righteous teacher and his followers withdrew from Jerusalem to found the community in the wilderness ("the house of his exile"), Jonathan, eager to eliminate an opponent of his consolidation of power, "pursued [him] to swallow [kill] him with venomous fury" (1QpHab 11:2–8). He craftily took advantage of the exiled community's fasting and rest on the Day of Atonement, which they observed on a solar calendar that differed from the official lunar calendar of the newly dominant Jerusalem priesthood.

It has been suggested that the epithets "the scoffer," "the liar," and "the spouter of lies" all refer to the same figure as the wicked priest.[11] But the connections in which those epithets are used fit Jason, the usurping high priest who led the Hellenizing reform, much better.[12] Jason, the usurping brother of the high priest Onias, not Jonathan the brother of the leader of the Maccabean Revolt, would have been the "scoffer" who misled Israel in "abolishing the ways of righteousness and removing the boundary with which the forefathers had marked out their inheritance, . . . transgressing the Covenant" (CD 1:13–2:1; cf. 5:20–21). Jason in the 170s B.C.E., rather than Jonathan in the 150s, would have been "the spouter of lies who led many astray that he might build his city of vanity with blood and raise a congregation of deceit" (1QpHab 10:7–12; cf. "the liar'" in 2:1–2). The Damascus Document has nothing like the grand scenario of God's judgment upon Jason and the others who abandoned the covenant that appears in Enoch's Animal Vision, perhaps because it was composed in retrospect. But it views the apostates' abolition of the covenant as having brought the covenantal curses down upon themselves when they were given up to the sword, as the chief of the kings of Greece wrought vengeance on them (CD 7:22–8:1; 8:10–11).

Assuming that the movement had been "groping for twenty years" before the righteous teacher provided more definitive guidance in the 150s, it seems likely that it began as a protest against the Hellenizing reform led by Jason and sponsored by the Seleucid emperor Antiochus Epiphanes. In its origins, therefore, the movement that formed a covenantal community at Qumran and covenant camps in Judean towns was parallel to other circles of scribes (and priests?) who mounted protests against their priestly aristocrats' attempt to transform Jerusalem into a Hellenistic polis, more in tune with the dominant imperial culture. And the righteous teacher himself parallels the "Enoch" scribes, who stepped into the role of the prophets whose prophecies they had long cultivated to address the crisis of imperial encroachment and their own aristocracy's collaboration with the imperial regime and assimilation to its culture. The teacher "interpreted the words of the prophets through whom [God] foretold all that would happen to his people," interpretations that were rejected by "the men of violence and breakers of the Covenant" (1QpHab 2:5–9; CD 1:11–13).

Recognizing the origins of the movement in the anti-imperial struggle of the 170s and 160s, moreover, helps us discern what may have been a prime motive of the movement's exile into the wilderness of "Damascus." The outcome of the Maccabean Revolt, fifteen years after it had begun, must have been a sore disappointment for the teacher and his followers. Jonathan and his brothers had led the popular revolt against the Hellenizing reform in battles against the imperial armies. When Jonathan then turned around and negotiated an official imperial appointment as high priest, the local representative of the imperial regime, it would have seemed like an utter betrayal of the anti-imperial resistance in which scribal circles such as the righteous teacher's had been struggling. "The wicked priest has defiled the Temple of God" (1QpHab 12:7–8).

Given the heavy emphasis on purity and ritual regulations in Qumran texts, many specialists focus only on such issues as the basis for the Qumran community's rejection of the wicked priest and abandonment of the Temple. A closer reading of the Damascus Document indicates that their concerns were far broader, including political and economic relations. Those who had abandoned the covenant had "wallowed in the ways of wicked wealth . . . for the sake of riches and gain" (CD 8:5–7; 4:16–19). The covenanters who withdrew saw this happening again with "the wicked priest." This evidently went beyond Jonathan's confiscations of the wealth of the previous covenant breakers. The new high priesthood was again amassing "the unclean riches of wickedness acquired by vow or anathema or from the temple treasure," and robbery of the poor, widows, and orphans (CD 6:15–17). The covenanters at Qumran condemned the even more imperial later Hasmoneans, "the last priests of Jerusalem," for "amassing money and wealth by plundering the peoples (1QpHab 9:5–6). Since the Temple had thus again been corrupted, therefore, "none of those brought into the covenant shall enter the Temple to light His altar in vain . . . [and] they shall separate from the sons of the pit" (CD 6:12–15).

While the Qumranites hoped eventually to take over the operation of the Temple in Jerusalem, they meanwhile strove to embody the covenantal commitments that they condemned the Hellenizing reformers and the Hasmonean rulers for violating, in their collaboration with or pretentions to imperial rule. Consistent with Ben Sira's instruction to an earlier generation of scribes (Sir 4:1-10), the covenantal community exiled to "Damascus" were to "succor the poor, the needy, and the stranger," and in keeping the "golden rule," to seek one another's well-being (CD 6:20–21). They even explicitly prohibited one of the devices by which resources needed for support of families locally were siphoned off for support of the Temple, an issue that crops up later in Jesus of Nazareth's disputes with the scribes and Pharisees who had come down from Jerusalem to Galilee (Mark 7:1-13). "No one shall *consecrate* the food of his household to God, for it is as he said, 'Each hunts his brother with a net (or votive offering: Micah 7:2). Let no one *consecrate* . . . And if he has *consecrated to God* some of his own field . . . he who has made the vow shall be punished" (CD 16:14–17).

Anticipating the Battle against the Roman Imperial Armies

In addition to sustaining a covenantal community/movement as an alternative social order to the increasingly imperial Hasmonean temple-state, the Qumranites opposed Roman imperial rule that replaced that of the declining Seleucids. They sharply condemned the later Hasmonean rulers, "the last priests of Jerusalem," for their pretentious imperial practices of "amassing money by plundering the peoples," prophesying that "their riches and booty shall be delivered into the hands of the army of the Kittim" (1QpHab 9:4–7). But they were far more concerned about those "Kittim," the fast-rising empire from the West. It is clear from one of the many references to them that "the Kittim" was the code term for the Romans: "They sacrifice to their standards and worship their weapons of war" (1QpHab 6:5–6).[13] The repeated deciphering of the words and phrases of Habakkuk in the "interpretation" of the prophet's book as references to the Kittim gives eloquent expression to the Qumranites' concern about imperial violence and exploitation. It has been claimed that the portrayal of the Kittim in the *pesher* on Habakkuk, as God's "instruments to punish the ungodly priests of Jerusalem" is "neutral."[14] A fuller reading of the extensive portrayal of the Kittim, however, reveals an ominous tone resembling that found in Enoch texts and Daniel visions, even though the Qumran text does not repeat their particular images.

> "For behold, I rouse the Chaldeans, that [bitter and hasty] nation" (Hab 1:6a). Interpreted, this concerns the Kittim [who are] quick and valiant in war, causing many to perish. [All the world shall fall] under the dominion of the Kittim, and the [wicked . . .] they shall not believe in the laws of [God]. (1QpHab 2:10–14)
>
> (Hab 1:6b) They shall march across the plain, smiting and plundering the cities of the earth. For it is as He said, "To take possession of dwellings which are not their own" (1:6b). "They are fearsome and terrible; their justice and grandeur proceed from themselves" (1:7). Interpreted, this concerns the Kittim, who inspire all the nations with fear [and dread]. All their evil plotting is done with intention and they deal with all the nations in cunning and guile. (1QpHab 2:15–3:6)
>
> "They fly from afar like an eagle avid to devour. All of them come for violence" (Hab 1:8-9a). [Interpreted, this] concerns the Kittim, who trample the earth with their horses and beasts. They come "from afar," from the islands of the sea, to "devour" all the peoples like "an eagle" which cannot be satisfied, and they address [all the peoples] with anger and [wrath and fury] and indignation. (1QpHab 3:7–13)
>
> (Hab 1:14-16) . . . the Kittim. And they shall gather in their riches, together with all their booty, "like the fish of the sea. . . . For through them their portion is far and their sustenance is rich" Interpreted, this means that they divide their yoke and their tribute—"their sustenance"—over all the peoples year by year, ravaging many lands. "Their sword is ever drawn to massacre nations mercilessly" (1:17). Interpreted, this concerns the Kittim who cause many to perish by the sword—youths, grown men, the aged, women and children—and who take no pity on the fruit of the womb. (1QpHab 5:12—6:12)

While these applications of the words of Habakkuk to the Roman warlords does not repeat the particular images used in earlier Judean texts, the actions of the Romans they condemn are much the same as those of earlier empires condemned in Enoch texts and Daniel: the devastating violence of military conquest, domination of other peoples and their land, economic exploitation of subject peoples, and the pretentious arrogance with which they lorded their power over the conquered. This ominous portrayal of the powerful Kittim bears the marks of the recent experience of the Roman conquest of Jerusalem and continuing Roman military brutality aimed at "pacifying"

The War against the "Kittim"

Judea, as well as the collaboration of the Hasmonean high priesthood as client rulers.

> The commanders of the Kittim ... despise the fortresses of the peoples.... To capture them, they encircle them with a mighty host, and out of fear and terror they deliver themselves into their hands.... On the counsel of [the] house of guilt, the commanders of the Kittim pass one in front of the other; one after another [their] commanders come to lay waste the earth. (1QpHab 4:1–12)

The Qumran covenanters, however, were not only concerned about Roman imperial rule, but also eagerly anticipated the time when they would join in the war that would end Roman domination. Among the scrolls found at Qumran, the one that was most striking to many is the War Rule. This is also the text that led many early interpreters to believe that the Qumran community was caught up in an intense "apocalypticism" focused on the "eschatological" war between God and the forces of evil.[15] Some interpreters, juxtaposing the War Scroll with the two spirits discussed in the Community Rule, find in it a dualism, even a "cosmic dualism," of the "Prince of Evil (Darkness)" and the "Prince of Light" as opposing primordial powers locked in combat.[16] The text of the War Rule itself, however, on a more careful reading, does not portray the war it anticipates as the great "eschatological" battle, or as a war against "evil." The anticipated battle for which the Qumranites were preparing is rather focused on the Kittim, the Romans.

While the War Scroll (1QM) appears to be a composite of different sections, there are significant links between them. Column 1 gives a brief outline of the same seven-stage war of which columns 15–19 offer a fuller description. Columns 3–9 offer instruction for the ritual organization of trumpets and banners by which the priests are to lead the battle and the ritual formations of the army that are put into practice in columns 15–19. Columns 10–14 give instructions for the priestly exhortation of the soldiers and psalms of praise and victory that the priests put into practice in columns 15–19. Only column 2, a brief outline of the hierarchical organization of the people and of the remaining thirty-three years of war (placed in a forty-year scheme), does not have a substantive link with other sections. The most extensive of the many parallel manuscripts from cave 4 (4Q496) has material that overlaps with columns 5–7, 9, 12–14, 15–17, and 19. Insofar as 1QM was dated on paleographical grounds to the second half of the first century B.C.E., and 4Q496 was dated to mid-first century, the text must have taken shape soon after the Roman conquest of Jerusalem in 63 B.C.E.[17]

The ritual organization and priestly leadership of the army draws heavily upon scriptural traditions of holy war. The priestly leadership in ritual preparation and battle prescribed in columns 7–9, 10, 13, and 15–17 was derived from the instructions for holy war in Deuteronomy 20, which were simply incorporated into the instruction for the priests (10:1-4) and exemplified in the similarly ritualistic battle of Jericho in Joshua 7. The priestly blasts on the trumpets in columns 3, 8, and 16–17 are rooted in the use of trumpets to summon the people for festivals and battles in Numbers 1:1-20. The organization of the people in terms of thousands, hundreds, fifties, and tens, similar to the schematic organization of the covenant community in their charter texts (1QS 2:21–22; CD 13:1–2), is rooted in Jethro's instruction to Moses in Exodus 18. The prominent use of banners finds its scriptural warrant in Numbers 2:2 and 17:2-3. But it may also reflect the influence of the Roman army, which prominently displayed banners and emblems on their standards. The instructions for military formations (columns 5–6 and elsewhere), on the other hand, have far more significant parallels with Roman practice than with any Judean precedent, including the recent descriptions of Maccabean formations.[18] This suggests that the covenanters in the wilderness were strongly influenced also by the armies against which they were preparing to do battle.

In order to appreciate the Qumran community's adamant opposition to Roman imperial rule, it is necessary to look closely at the text of the War Rule and to recognize how several interrelated interpretive generalizations have obscured its focus on an anticipated historical battle against the "Kittim."

(1) The War Scroll refers not to an "eschatological war" but to an anticipated historical war that "the sons of Levi, Judah, and Benjamin," who had become exiles in the wilderness, would fight against the Kittim (the Romans). The text makes no suggestion that the battle terminates or transcends history, but states simply that it would mean "salvation for the people of God" as "the domination of the Kittim would come to an end" (1:4–6).[19] In the victory song at the end, the historical tables have been turned so that Israel now has dominion and the kings of the peoples serve Zion/Judah. The long opening statement has "the sons of light" attacking the "sons of darkness," who are also "the army of wickedness (Belial)." The latter consist of nearby historical enemies such as the Philistines and the current imperial rulers, "the Kittim," along with "their allies, the ungodly of the covenant." In the outline of the war (col. 1), "the sons of light," the exiles in the desert, are also "the people/company of God," opposite "the company of wickedness" who are the Kittim and, in other code names, Assyria and "the sons of Japheth." The longer description of the war (cols. 15–19), while highly ritualistic, has the same historical combatants, except that the reference to "sons of light" and "sons of darkness" disappears.

The warriors of "the company of God" camp before "the king of the Kittim and the host of wickedness (Belial)." Three times the priests and warriors, "the saints of God's people," attack the Kittim and, when the hand of God finally takes direct action, they defeat the Kittim. The anticipated outcome in the concluding song of the Hero is not some "eschatological" transformation of the world, but an overturning of the tables of history, so that Israel has dominion and the previously oppressive kings serve them (12:10–17 = 19:3–9).

(2) The repeated references to God and other divine forces fighting for His people and against their enemies, far from indicating an "apocalyptic" or "eschatological" battle, draws on the long Israelite scriptural tradition of Yahweh and the heavenly hosts fighting for the people and defeating the historical enemies that were oppressing them. As stated in the instruction to the priests to exhort the people not to fear, quoted from Deuteronomy 20:2-4, "For your God goes with you to fight for you against your enemies that He may deliver you." The reassurance that "You will fight with them from heaven" (11:16–17) is almost an idiom from scriptural tradition. "The holy ones" and "the host of the [heavenly] messengers" (11:1–2) are standard Judean scribal terms for the heavenly beings that assisted in the divine governance, a development of the "sons/children of the gods" in earlier Israelite tradition (as noted in the discussion of Daniel 7 in ch. 6). Reassurance that God will fight for the poor in the anticipated battle against the Kittim is drawn from historical examples such as the defeat of the Philistines and Pharaoh's chariot forces and from scriptural prophecies (11:1–16).

Participation of God and other divine forces, moreover, is ancillary to the battle between the exiled covenanters and the Kittim. Except for the direct intervention of the hand of God in the seventh lot, the aid of God and other heavenly powers does not play a role in the battle itself, but is mentioned in the priests' exhortation to the warriors to embolden them for battle in the first and third lots (15:9–16:2; 17:1–9). It also forms part of the parallel psalms and prayers that comprise columns 10–14 (esp. 11:1–12:9; 13; 14:4–18). The priests and the warriors are the ones who fight against the Kittim (and God fights through them, as in 16:1–2). Only in the seventh lot of the battle does God raise his hand directly against [the force of] wickedness, yet it is still the warriors in their formations who destroy the Kittim (18:1–5). Except for the key role of God's hand in the seventh lot, the War Rule does not portray the holy ones or spirits or Michael as engaged in battle on behalf of or parallel to the priests and warriors, or fighting against the force(s) of darkness. Only in one of the psalms of reassurance of divine aid is it stated that "the congregation of the holy ones is among us, . . . the host of His spirits is with our foot-soldiers and horsemen" (12:6–9).[20] And there as elsewhere, the thrust of the reassurance is to embolden the warriors to fearless action: "[thus] we will despise kings, we will mock and scorn the mighty, for the Lord is with us together with the holy ones."

(3) The framework of the War Rule is the narrative of the anticipated seven-lot battle between the exiled covenanters and the Kittim. This is obscured by interpreters' projection of a metaphysical dualism between primordial powers, the "Prince of Evil" in battle with the "Prince of Light." This dualism is constructed by reading selected passages of the War Scroll through a reification of the two spirits of 1QS 3:18–23. But not only is "Prince of Evil" a foreign term and concept to the War Rule, the two spirits play no role in the War Rule, and are certainly not portrayed as engaged in battle. With the various phrases it uses in referring to people and superhuman forces, the War Rule, like the Community Rule, is far more subtle and nuanced than its modern interpreters who are looking for schematic thinking in them. The superhuman divine forces, ancillary to both sides of the battle, were multiple and not reducible to two opposed reified figures, "the Prince of Light" and "the Prince of Darkness." The framework of the War Rule is not a cosmic dualism but a narrative of an anticipated historical battle between (the remnant of) Israel and the Kittim (the Romans).

A closer reading of the War Rule, less obscured by inappropriate interpretive concepts, thus reveals that the Qumran community was anticipating a battle in which they would attack the Roman forces that had recently conquered and dominated Judea, and reestablished the incumbent Hasmonean high-priestly aristocracy as client rulers. Just as their God, the Lord of the heavenly armies, had fought to free their ancestors from Pharaoh and the Philistines, so God and the holy ones protecting Israel would come to their aid against the Romans. In preparation for the great battle, the community evidently held drills of ritual warfare, for which the War Rule must have served as a "handbook." Their ritual rehearsals for the battle adapted the holy war ideology and instructions in the Judean scriptures about banners and trumpets and priestly leadership. For the formations in which the warriors would advance and fight, however, they adapted what they knew of the formations of the very Roman troops that they anticipated attacking.

The Community Rule instructs the master (maskil) to have "everlasting hatred in a spirit of secrecy for the men of perdition" (1QS 9:22–23) and, in the following psalm, the speaker says, "I will not grapple with the men of perdition until the day of revenge" (10:17–19). Archaeological excavations indicate that the settlement at Qumran was among the many destroyed by the Roman military in its brutal suppression of the widespread popular revolt of 66–70.

The War against the "Kittim"

The site was also evidently defended. We probably cannot know whether the exiled "sons of light" thought that the day of revenge had finally arrived and went out to fight the king of the Kittim and his forces. If so, they must have been slaughtered by the Roman troops. Mixed into all of the prescribed rituals of their preparation, they at least had knowledge of Roman military maneuvers. But that hardly sufficed against the military might of the Kittim.

Chapter 8

The Arrogance of the Dragon: Roman Conquest in the *Psalms of Solomon*

Having the *Psalms of Solomon* enables us to grasp the range of scribal reactions to Roman rule. The scribal composers and collectors of the *Psalms*, like the scribes and priests at Qumran, sharply opposed Roman violence and rapacity. Their psalms, however, illustrate that visionary surveys of history were not the only kind of text in which opposition to empire was articulated. This makes them useful for comparison and contrast with texts classified as "apocalyptic" as vehicles for expression of resistance to imperial rule.*

The *Psalms of Solomon* are a collection of eighteen psalms produced in the mid- or late first century B.C.E. Composed originally in Hebrew, they now exist in Greek and Syriac translations.[1] The *Psalms of Solomon* have often been included among Judean texts considered to be "apocalyptic," as previous interpreters referenced lines from the *Psalms* among their proof texts for particular themes and motifs of "apocalypticism." Like other texts produced in late Second Temple Judea, the *Psalms of Solomon* are usually interpreted primarily as expressions of religion. And they do exhibit a strong devotion to God and dedication to a life of righteousness. Several of the psalms in the collection, however, express shock at the (recent) conquest of Jerusalem by Roman armies, along with condemnation of the Hasmonean kings and high priests. However, these psalms' response to imperial rule display some significant differences from, as well as similarities to, the response in earlier Judean "apocalyptic" texts.

---

* I am working with the translation of the *Psalms of Solomon* in J. H. Charlesworth, ed., *Old Testament Pseudepigrapha* (2 vols; Garden City, NY: Doubleday, 1983–85), 2.639–70. Readers are encouraged to read the appropriate psalms while working through the discussion here.

Scribal Piety under Persecution

Although there was no good evidence behind the earlier view that the *Psalms of Solomon* were produced by the Pharisees,[2] previous interpreters' instincts were right to associate the psalms with such a circle of scribes. Psalms, which were sung from memory, not read from cumbersome scrolls, could have been composed by nonliterate ordinary people. The songs now included in Luke 1–2, for example, which speak of bringing "the powerful down from their thrones" and "lifting up the lowly," appear to have been popular compositions that were only later written down and included in the Gospel. There are many features in the *Psalms of Solomon*, however, that signal their scribal origins and viewpoint.[3]

The *Psalms* are oriented to Jerusalem and the Temple, where the priests presided and scribes served as retainers in the temple-state (see especially psalms 1, 2, 8, 11, 17). The Judean tradition out of which the psalms work goes back through the Jerusalem elite who were exiled to Babylon and then were restored to power in Jerusalem under the Persians (9:1). Like rulers and their scribal elite before them, the producers of these psalms look to God's covenant with Abraham and his descendants as the source of their legitimacy as authority figures in Jerusalem (for example, 9:9-10; 18:3). As carriers of the cultural traditions of Judea, the composers of the psalms were well prepared to ponder "the judgments of God since the creation of heaven and earth" in an attempt to justify God's acts of judgment in events of their own time (8:7).[4] They accused others of "deceitfully quoting the law" (4:8), about which they claimed to be the experts. Scribes would presumably have been the only people in Judean society who possessed astronomical knowledge, to which psalm 18 appeals at the end. Reminiscent of the earlier Jerusalem scribe, Jesus Ben Sira, theirs was a moderate life in the capital city, neither struggling for subsistence nor wielding wealth and power. "Happy is (the person) whom God remembers with a moderate sufficiency; for if one is excessively rich, he sins. Moderate (living) is adequate—with righteousness; for with this comes the Lord's blessing; to be (more than) satisfied with righteousness" (5:16-17).

As suggested by the "beatitude" just cited, moreover, these psalms give expression to a kind of personal pietism of those who understand themselves as the faithful righteous at the center of the people of Israel. As articulated in psalm 14, those who love the Lord "live in the righteousness of his commandments, in the Law, which he has commanded for our life." The life of the devout appears to be an unquestioning commitment to a "Deuteronomic" faith in a "cause-and-effect" relation between one's behavior and the way one will be rewarded by God in earthly life. "The Lord's judgments are according to the individual and the household" (9:9). But God "will cleanse from sins the soul in confessing, . . . when they repent" (9:6-7). Devotion is thus expressed in a life of prayer (psalm 6). The life of the righteous is almost penitential, in accepting adversity as "discipline," "proving the Lord's judgments right," removing unintentional sins, and making atonement by fasting (psalm 3:3-8; of course, there is always the backup reward of "eternal life in the Lord's light," 3:12). "Happy the man whom the Lord remembers with rebuking, . . . cleansed from sin. The Lord is good to those "who endure discipline," as in "the Law of the eternal covenant" (10:1-4).

This life of strict devotion to God and acceptance of whatever comes as the Lord's discipline appears to be closely related to the persecution about which several of these psalms complain. The pious reassure themselves that God, "the shelter of the poor," will surely care for them, as he does for other people and creatures, so that they can appeal for help "when [they] are persecuted" (5:5). One aspect of the persecution seems to be the slander that more influential people are spreading about the devout, which are threatening to bring their households to ruin (psalm 12). This is so serious, moreover, that the pious, righteous one petitions God for the restraint not to retaliate in anger and for the strength not to grumble and sink into despair (16:7, 10-15).

In recent decades, biblical interpreters have tended to posit the existence of particular communities or movements behind particular texts. The anachronistic projection of the concept "sect," which was developed in study of the various splinter movements and "churches" during the Reformation, probably reinforced this tendency. So also did the recent recognition that a scribal-priestly community at Qumran had used and, in many cases, composed texts found among the Dead Sea Scrolls. There is nothing in the *Psalms of Solomon*, however, that suggests a community of the "devout" separate from the rest of the people of Jerusalem and Judea.[5]

A brief review of the political-economic-religious structure of Judean society under imperial rule may help clarify the context that the *Psalms* address. Judean society consisted of hundreds of village communities ruled by the priestly aristocracy (and sometimes a king as well) based in the Temple in Jerusalem. The ruling aristocracy/kingship was served by scribal retainers, artisans, traders, and sometimes military forces also resident in Jerusalem.[6] "Councils" of aristocrats and possibly leading scribal advisers were convened, probably on an ad hoc basis, to consider matters of importance, and more rarely, public assemblies were held in Jerusalem. These were the aristocracy's devices to control the city and the society more widely. Village communities were semi-self-governing, running their own affairs, with representatives of the temple-state intervening mainly to collect tithes and taxes. The social form of community governance and cohesion in the villages was the local assembly, called *knesset* in Hebrew and Aramaic, *synagōgē* in Greek. These local assemblies evidently met regularly. As archaeological excavations have made clear, however, until late antiquity there were few buildings in which the local synagogues (assemblies) could meet.[7]

It seems likely that in addition to occasional public assemblies in the courtyard of the Temple, there were smaller gatherings (*synagōgai*/assemblies) in Jerusalem as well, perhaps on the basis of neighborhood, kinship, or groups of artisans. The book of Acts mentions "the *synagōgē* (assembly) of the freedpersons (as it was called)," composed of previously enslaved diaspora Jews from particular cities who were now resident in Jerusalem (Acts 6:9). Conceptually, there was always a certain overlap between the Hebrew terms *yahad* and *edah*, and the Greek terms used (often interchangeably) to translate them, *ekklēsia* and *synagōgē*. "The assembly of Israel" was a virtual synonym for "the people of Israel," and "the assembly of Israel" was, practically speaking (since they lived in separate villages), embodied in the "synagogues of Israel."

While many of the *Psalms of Solomon* focus primarily on personal piety and discipline, the "righteous/devout" are always part of the larger people of Israel. The psalms express confidence that God "will have compassion on the people of Israel/house of Jacob" (7:8-10; 11:8), although God regularly "judges Israel in discipline" (8:26), just as he subjects "devout" individuals and households. The devout who live in the Law can have confidence in the Lord, "for Israel is the portion and inheritance of God" (14:5). And while the devout have their own personal piety of prayer and repentance, they "shall give thanks in the assembly of the people, . . . [as] "the synagogues of Israel glorify the Lord's name" (10:6-8).[8] That is, the devout scribes who produced and used these psalms were active members of Israel, participating in the assembly/synagogues of the people as they gave thanks and glorified God. Similarly, the anointed son of David is expected to "judge the people [tribes] in their assemblies, . . . bring [good fortune] to pass in the assembly of the tribes." Considering this close relationship between "the devout," Israel, and "the synagogues of Israel" that runs through many of the psalms, "the assemblies of the devout" from which "those who loved [them] fled" (17:16) evidently refers to the local assemblies in which the people of Israel was embodied.

"The council of the devout" (4:1), on the other hand, seems to refer to a governing council of the temple-state, judging from the context. It is the council in which sits the "profaner," a lawbreaker and tyrannical judge, evidently the Hasmonean pretender Aristobulus, who displaced his older brother Hyrcanus as high priest and king in a military coup a short time after the death of Alexandra Salome (see ch. 7 above). Some of the scribal circle that produced these psalms, who saw themselves as (the leaders of) the devout, were evidently members of this council, scandalized at the arrogant behavior of the usurping Hasmonean.

Those who produced the *Psalms of Solomon* thus appear to have been a circle of scribes in Jerusalem, custodians of the Torah and other traditions of Israel, and exemplary devout Judeans who were attempting to explain the judgment of God in recent affairs of the temple-state. As in the collection of psalms that later became part of the Hebrew Bible, so in these eighteen psalms, many are oriented to the piety of the individual. It is difficult to find any expressions that suggest orientation to a particular group. Certainly their statements that the judgments of God are meted out by individual and household do not suggest a group orientation. Instead, the *Psalms of Solomon* move easily back and forth from the pious individual to the people of Israel as a whole.

The Roman Conquest and God's Judgment of the Hasmonean Kings

Judging from the clear historical references in several of the *Psalms of Solomon*, the principal issue that the devout scribes who produced the psalms were dealing with, in their struggles to justify the judgments of God, was the Roman conquest of Jerusalem.[9] This is the concern particularly of psalms 2, 8, and 17, and appears also in psalms 7, 13, 15, and the opening psalm. In order to avoid slipping into the "proof-texting" procedure pursued in some treatments of such texts, we will proceed psalm by psalm, attempting to respect the hymnic integrity of each.

Psalm 1, the only one without a heading, appears to have been composed as an introduction to the collection. If so, it provides the whole series of psalms with a setting in the early decades of Roman imperial domination. The speaker, evidently a personified Jerusalem, cries to the Lord as war comes upon her, confident that God will hear her, since she is full of righteousness (1–3). The description of imperial wealth, glory, arrogance, and lawlessness that follows surely pertains to the Romans. The Roman warlord Pompey "profaned the sanctuary of the Lord" (in 63 B.C.E.), as had Antiochus Epiphanes before him (in 168–167 B.C.E.). But extending their wealth and glory "to the ends of the earth" fits the imperial reality as well as the ideology of the Romans, not that of the Seleucids. Judean scribes knew firsthand about Roman imperial expansion in the East. Judging from Josephus's accounts of the repeated military invasions and special levies of tribute, the charge that "their lawless actions surpassed the nations before them" (7) seems to fit Roman actions in Judea from Pompey to Herod and their suppression of the revolts following Herod's death in 4 B.C.E.

Some of the psalms in the collection appear to have been composed prior to the Roman conquest led by Pompey. Psalm 7 even seems to be anticipating Pompey's invasion, pleading with God not to allow "those who hate us without cause [to] attack us, . . . to trample your holy inheritance, . . . not to turn (us) over to the nations (7:1-3). Psalm 7, like several others in the collection and like many of the psalms and prophetic oracles in the Judean cultural repertoire, expresses confidence that God can take an active role in historical events, allowing or blocking the actions of "the nations."

Psalm 2 unfolds in seven steps. The short opening section on the sinner's/foreign nations' attack on Jerusalem and the Temple (2:1-2) leads to a long explanation of the reason: that the sons of Jerusalem have defiled the sanctuary of the Lord (2:3-10). This is supplemented with a further list of their lawless actions (2:11-14). The middle section (2:15-21) declares that the nations' trampling of Jerusalem is God's just judgment on the wicked actions of the sinners. The psalm then appeals to the Lord to take action against the nations for attacking Jerusalem so viciously (2:22-25), which leads to the declaration that the Lord is King over the heavens, judging even kings and rulers, as illustrated in the satisfying death of the sinner for his arrogant pretense of becoming lord of land and sea (2:26-32). The psalm ends with praise of God for his mercy on the righteous and punishment of the sinners (sons of Jerusalem) and the arrogant sinner (2:33-37).

Several concerns are interwoven through psalm 2. Some of these focus on the recent conquest of Jerusalem by Pompey and the Roman army. Briefly but in strong language, the psalm expresses horror that the arrogant sinner, who can only be the Roman general Pompey, had breached the fortified walls with a battering ram and then trampled the very altar of the Temple (2:1-2, 19). The psalm also expresses horror at the vicious rage and plunder of the imperial attack, imploring that Jerusalem has suffered enough, and appealing to God to repay the invaders with punishment (2:22-25). The reference to Pompey as the "arrogant dragon" (25) is a comparison to King Nebuchadnezzar of Babylon, who had "devoured" Jerusalem like a monster in the Babylonian destruction of the city and the Temple centuries earlier, a disastrous event that loomed prominently, indeed formatively, in the historical awareness of Judean culture (Jer 51:34; cf. Ezek 29:3; 32:2). The psalm thus takes great satisfaction when "God showed me his [Pompey's] insolence pierced on the mountains of Egypt" (26).

Closely related to the horror of the destructive attack on the fortified Temple and the trampling of the sacred altar is the shock at the utter arrogance of the world-conquering Roman general Pompey. After sounding the theme of the arrogance of the warlord and his army in the opening lines, the psalm expands on this concern about Pompey's overweening superhuman ambition for several lines (26–29). This sixth step forms the resolution of the psalm's struggle with the crisis of conquest that also posed a serious crisis of faith. Pompey is mocked for his ambition to become "the lord of land and sea." *Psalms of Solomon* 2 has this condemnation of imperial rulers in common with earlier prophetic oracles against imperial kings (Isa 10; 14; Ezek 28; 31–32) and the tales in Daniel 1–6. Psalm 2, however, does not represent Pompey as mounting a direct attack on the heavenly governance of the world or God himself, as the visions and interpretations in Daniel 7–12 do in their portrayal of Antiochus Epiphanes. Psalm 2 focuses rather on the stark contrast of the seemingly invincible warlord and conqueror, Pompey "the Great," suddenly "pierced on the mountains of Egypt," the juxtaposition of the one who aspired to become "lord of land and sea" with "his body carried about on the waves in much shame" (26–29). The tone of the criticism of the warlord's overweening arrogance is more politically and theologically pointed than Latin texts' use of Pompey's assassination as an illustration of the commonplace of reversal of fortune and in admonition against excessive pride (see, for example, Seneca, *Marcia*, 16).[10]

Pompey's downfall and dishonor could not have provided a better basis on which the psalm can proclaim, with earlier prophetic oracles and the tales of Daniel, that "it is God who is great" (versus "Pompey the Great"). "He is king over the heavens, judging even kings and rulers" (2:29-30). The great warlord's ignominious assassination enables the psalm to call, with a certain bravado, upon the officials of the earth to acknowledge that God is the great heavenly King who judges earthly kings and rulers (32). And Pompey's death enabled the psalm to articulate the resolution to the crisis of faith posed by the Roman conquest of Jerusalem. Events had proven that God was the divine King who would judge imperial warlords.

Despite the concern about the vicious rage of Pompey and the Romans, psalm 2 in effect blames the Hasmoneans for the Roman conquest of Jerusalem and the trampling of the Temple. God did not intervene (2:1). The conquest was the just judgment of God. The Roman conquest was God's punishment of the "the sons of Jerusalem" for their sinful actions (2:3-10). If length of coverage is any guide, this is the principal concern of the song, for the psalm then elaborates on the lawless actions of "the sons of Jerusalem" (2:11-14) and repeats the charge that the Romans' trampling of Jerusalem is God's rewarding of the sinners according to their sins (2:15-21). The "sins" of "the sons of Jerusalem" are stated only generally: they "defiled the sanctuary of the Lord, they profaned the offerings of God with lawless acts" (2:3). That "her glorious beauty was despised before God" (5) suggests that these "sons of Jerusalem" were the priests in charge of the sanctuary and offerings, who because of their "lawless acts" were rejected by God.[11] That "they sinned by not listening" might refer to their not listening to criticism from certain scribal circles, possibly from those who produced these psalms. The most sustained charge is that "the sons of Jerusalem" had turned Jerusalem into a "prostitute, . . . available to all" (13). Given the long tradition of sexual promiscuity as a metaphor for compromises with foreign, often imperial, rulers and their gods and culture, these lines may be indicting the rulers of Jerusalem for having transformed the temple-state into a Hellenistic kingdom, with a lavish lifestyle at court and mercenary troops.

Judging from the punishments mentioned, "the sons of Jerusalem" appears to refer primarily to Aristobulus, his family, and supporters. That "the sons and daughters" were taken "into harsh captivity, their neck in a seal, a spectacle among the nations" (2:6) accords particularly well with Josephus's accounts that Pompey carried off Aristobulus and his sons and daughters as prisoners to be displayed in his triumphal procession in Rome (*War* 1.157; *Ant.* 14.79).[12] One suspects that the "defilement of the sanctuary and profaning of the offerings" may refer more generally to the Hasmonean actions as high priests and kings, reaching back at least as far as Alexander Yannai. Among the known acts of the Hasmonean high priests, only Yannai's crucifixion of his opponents and slaughter of their wives and children before their eyes would seem to qualify for the description that "no one on earth had done what they did" (2:9).

It is striking how easily the psalm moves, toward the end, from praise of God as the divine King who judges kings and rulers (30–32) to exhortation to those who fear the Lord to praise God because he punishes sinners and has mercy on the righteous (2:34-35, 36-37). But this is a theme running through many of the psalms in the collection. And it clearly reflects the sharp and ongoing conflict between the dissident scribal circles, such as those who produced these psalms, and the Hasmonean rulers in Jerusalem.

Psalm 8 proceeds in three major steps, framed by the opening references to the sound of war and the closing praise of God (1–5, 33–34). A listing of the sins, evidently of the priests presiding in the Temple, is intended to prove that the judgments of God are just (6–13). Then comes a fairly detailed description of Pompey's attack on Jerusalem and the Temple as God's punitive judgment (14–22). God being thus justified in his condemnation, the final step is a plea for God's mercy and deliverance of Israel (23–32).

Like psalm 2, psalm 8 is deeply distressed at the "slaughter and destruction" during the recent Roman conquest of Jerusalem (1–2). It does not mince

The Arrogance of the Dragon

any words about the horrifying violence against fellow Jerusalemites, including "everyone wise in counsel," whose blood was "poured out like dirty water" (20). It is unmistakably clear from the particulars that the psalm is describing Pompey's attack on Jerusalem in 63 B.C.E. "The leaders of the country met him with joy" (16) must refer to the partisans of Hyrcanus having admitted him to the city, whereupon he "captured the fortified towers and the wall of Jerusalem" (19), as in both accounts by Josephus (*War* 1.142–51; *Ant.* 14.57–70).

Even more bluntly than psalm 2, however, psalm 8 presents the Roman conquest of Jerusalem as ultimately the action of God in just judgment against those who sinned. "God . . . brought someone from the end of the earth, one who attacks in strength; he declared war against Jerusalem and her land" (15). That the Roman destruction and slaughter were God's judgment was difficult to accept, and one of the concerns of the psalm is to review the historical judgments of God and to "prove God right" (7) in the punitive conquest of the holy city.

Psalm 8 presents a more specific set of sins by the priests who preside over the operations of the temple that have brought God's judgment upon the city. These include adultery, stealing from the sanctuary of God, walking on the place of sacrifice with uncleanness, and defiling the sacrifices as if they were common meat (10–12). These are the same general areas of sinning (the three "nets of Belial") with which the Damascus Document, now also known from Qumran manuscripts, charges the illegitimate Hasmonean priests: "fornication," "riches," and "the profanation of the Temple" (CD 4:15–17).[13] Maintenance of purity codes was important to scribes trained to interpret them, as well as to the priests who performed the sacrifices in the Temple. The high priest and other key members of the priestly aristocracy had custody over the resources of the Temple, including those intended for the poor, orphans, and widows. The use and abuse of those resources was yet another concern of scribes, as we know from the instructional speeches of Ben Sira. Since scribal circles had no real power to prevent abuses, it is not surprising that they developed standard charges against the incumbents, in this case the Hasmoneans who had drawn wide opposition among the people as well as by scribal circles such as the Pharisees.

In a third step, psalm 8 turns to the situation of Israel's again being subject to imperial rule, concern that "the nations" would simply "devour" the people (30), and appeals to God to have mercy and deliver them. The scope now broadens from a focus on the plight of the recently attacked Jerusalem and slaughtered Jerusalemites to "the dispersed of Israel," who had long been languishing under imperial rule (28). The closing lines of the psalm, however, "we will not be troubled at the end of time" (33), while evidently using a concept familiar from "apocalyptic" texts, indicate no sense of "eschatological" urgency.

Psalm 13 and 15 may also refer to Pompey's conquest of Jerusalem. Psalm 13 sounds more specific than psalm15. Both refer in horror to "the sword, famine, and death," standard terms for the experience of military attacks and their effect (13:2; 15:7). Psalm 13 refers to an attack that has already happened: "Wild animals attacked them viciously, . . . the destruction of the sinner is terrible" (13:3, 6). "The godless person [who is] terrified lest he be taken along with the sinners" may well be a reference to Aristobulus, who was taken with his family as prisoners to Rome. Psalm 15, which refers to the sword and death overtaking the sinners in the future, was perhaps composed in anticipation of the Romans' attack on Jerusalem, rather than after the fact. "The day of the Lord's judgment" (15:12) would thus appear to refer to the anticipated attack by the Romans, which would agree with the understanding of God's role in historical events in both psalms 2 and 8. Also similar to psalms 2 and 8, both psalms 13 and 15 represent the attack as God's judgment on the sinners, while the righteous will avoid the sword, famine, and death, and only be admonished and disciplined by the Lord (13:2-3, 7, 9-10; 15:7-8, 10-12). If these psalms do have reference to Pompey's conquest of Jerusalem, then "the righteous" would appear to be the partisans of Hyrcanus, or at least not the partisans of Aristobulus, who took refuge in the Temple and were slaughtered by the Roman soldiers once they broke through the walls.

In Psalm 17, the first half describes the utterly desperate situation of the people under harsh foreign rule, setting the stage for the announcement of how the anticipated anointed king, the son of David, will restore Israel on the land. Like psalms 2 and 8, psalm 17 expresses sharp condemnation of the Hasmonean kingship. Appealing to God's covenant of kingship with David and his descendants, the psalm insists that the Hasmoneans were illegitimate usurpers who "despoiled the throne of David" (5–6). Again as in psalms 2 and 8, the overthrow of the Hasmoneans is God's own work, working through "a man alien to our race" (7). It is somewhat unclear, however, how to understand the reference to God's "uprooting their descendants from the earth" and (God or "the alien one") "hunting down their descendants" (7, 9). Pompey ended the Hasmonean kingship but restored Hyrcanus to the high priesthood. The "man alien to our race," however, is more likely Herod, whose father Antipater was Idumean, not Judean. Like Pompey before him, Herod also laid siege to and conquered Jerusalem (Josephus, *Ant.* 14.468–91). And it was Herod who, according to Josephus's accounts, hunted down and executed the last of the Hasmoneans (*Ant.* 14:487–91; 15:5–10, 164–78).[14]

The Arrogance of the Dragon 153

Parts of the extensive description of how "the lawless one laid waste our land, so that no one inhabited it" (17:11–20) also might fit Pompey's actions in the initial Roman conquest of Jerusalem. His soldiers did carry out a "massacre" in the storming of the temple; he took Aristobulus and his family prisoners "to the west," and he "acted arrogantly" in invading the inner sanctuary (11–13). If "the lawless one" is a reference to Pompey, then psalm 17, like psalm 2, parallels the interpretation of the Qumranites, that the conquest by the Kittim (code for the Romans) was the Hasmoneans' just deserts for their previous conquests of nearby peoples: "the last priests of Jerusalem, who will accumulate riches and loot from plundering the nations. However, in the end of days their riches and loot will be given into the hands of the army of the Kittim" (1QpHab 9:4–7, to Hab 2:8a).

Most of the acts of desolation of Jerusalem and the Judeans mentioned in 17:11-20, however, fit Herod's conquest of his own people with the aid of Roman troops and his tyrannical rule of Judea, as known primarily from the accounts of Josephus (see ch. 7 above).[15] After being appointed "king of the Judeans" by the Roman Senate, Herod literally "laid waste the land" and "massacred young and old" (11; cf. *Ant.* 14.479–80, 482–86) in his three-year conquest of the people and on several occasions during his reign.

To the tradition-minded, he would have seemed "a stranger alien to our God" (13; *Ant.* 14.403). As the king appointed by the Romans and the face of Roman imperial rule in Judea, he constructed alien institutions in Jerusalem, such as a hippodrome (*Ant.* 15.268, 364; 17.255). The centerpiece of his many huge construction projects was the massive reconstruction of the Temple in grand Hellenistic style, which became one of the great wonders of the Roman imperial world (*Ant.* 15.380–425). Among other departures from strictly scriptural tradition, Herod erected a golden Roman eagle above the main gate of the great new Temple complex (17.151). But this was exactly what other "nations did for their gods in their cities" (14). In addition to lavish gifts to the imperial family, Herod made many extravagant gifts to various cities of the Roman Empire, especially where there were communities of Judeans (*Ant.* 15.326–30; 16:146–49). Posing as the patron of "the children of the covenant [living] among the nations" (15), Herod may well have led them into "alien" practices.

In Judea itself, Herod ruled with an iron fist, imposing repressive measures to control the people and to stifle dissent. At several points, people would have become "refugees in the wilderness to save their lives" (17). Drought ("springs were stopped," v. 19) and famine occurred during Herod's siege of Jerusalem and later during his reign (*Ant.* 14.475; 15.299–304). Under Herod, finally, "the king was [indeed] a criminal" (20). At his death, massive protests by scribal groups and the people of Jerusalem erupted, followed by widespread revolt in the countryside.

The focus on an "anointed king, son of David (17:21-44), moreover, seems more likely to be a response that would have emerged after Herod's tyrannical reign as "king of the Judeans" than after the later Hasmoneans, who had added the title king to that of high priest. Apart from the Qumran texts produced by a utopian community that had withdrawn into the wilderness, there is a paucity of Judean texts that express any interest in an "anointed king," or a "messiah." *Psalm of Solomon* 17 (along with the brief reference in psalm 18) is not only the most prominent text, but about the only one from late Second Temple Judea to offer an extended passage on a "messiah."[16] Herod was appointed "King of the Judeans" by the Romans, and then reduced the high priesthood to relative insignificance in comparison with his power. It thus seems most likely that a focus on restoration by an "anointed son of David" emerged in response to Herod, not to the Hasmoneans. All of these considerations suggest that psalm 17 originated after and in response to Herod's kingship.

The resolution of the historical crisis that the anointed son of David is charged with accomplishing is twofold, the same two interrelated tasks that God was expected to do in earlier Judean texts, such as the surveys of history in *1 Enoch* 85–90, Daniel 7–12, and the *Testament of Moses:* the judgmental defeat of the dominant empire and the renewal of the people's life on their land under the direct rule of God. Lines from *Psalm of Solomon* 17 have long been cited as prime proof texts for the supposed "Jewish expectation" of a "militant Messiah." And indeed, the psalm has several martial images. Some of these are traditional images of Solomonic imperial kingship known from royal psalms, most obvious perhaps the "smashing of the potter's jar . . . with a rod of iron" (17:23; cf. Ps 2:9). The anointed son of David is "to shatter unrighteous rulers, to purge Jerusalem from the nations who trample her to destruction" (22). In psalm 17, however, he does not use a sword and other military weapons; he does "not rely on horse and rider and bow [or] collect gold and silver for war." Instead, he "destroys unlawful nations with the word of his mouth" (24, 33-34). Psalm 17 anticipates a scribal messiah in the tradition of the closely delimited Deuteronomic law of kingship and the utopian image of the king in Deuteronomy 17:16-17 and Isaiah 11:4, rather than a militant imperial messiah.[17]

The psalm gives far more attention to the second work of the anointed son of David, the restoration of the people in their twelve tribes on their land (17:26-44). This will indeed be a political and economic restoration of the people (28), and the people will live in justice and holiness, so that "there will be no arrogance among them, that any should be oppressed" (41). Again in the renewal of the people, the anticipated anointed one is not militant, but rather scribal in governing with wisdom by the word of his mouth in the assemblies of the tribes.

All of these psalms (2, 7, 8, 13, 15, and 17) express horror at the slaughter and destruction of the Roman conquest of Jerusalem. And they petition God to deliver Jerusalem and/or Israel from imperial domination. Also central to their concern, however, is the imperial kingship of the Hasmoneans. And in the Roman conquest, they also see the righteous judgment of God against the sins of the (later) Hasmoneans in general, or Aristobulus in particular.

Psalms of Solomon: Different from Apocalyptic Texts

While the *Psalms of Solomon* show similarities with contemporary texts from Qumran and with earlier Judean texts, they also display significant differences. The similarities should not be surprising, considering that they were rooted in the same Judean cultural traditions cultivated by various circles of scribes, and they addressed at least similar historical circumstances. The differences may be partly, or even largely, those of viewpoint. Yet they may also be due to the different situations that the texts address.

The differences that the psalms have with earlier "apocalyptic" texts that were also concerned with imperial rule are surely due to the different circumstances between the situation under the Seleucid Empire in the 170s and 160s B.C.E., on the one hand, and the situation at the beginning of Roman rule in the 60s B.C.E. and the next few decades. The Enoch and Daniel texts reflect and address the crisis of rapidly escalating violent suppression of the traditional Judean way of life by Antiochus Epiphanes. Once the Hasmoneans brought in professional mercenary troops, conquered nearby cities and peoples, and transformed the temple-state into a kingdom, however, it seemed to some circles of scribes, such as those who withdrew to Qumran and those who produced the *Psalms of Solomon*, that their own rulers in Jerusalem had picked up where the Seleucids had left off. The move by the Romans finally to take direct control of the area around the southeastern Mediterranean presented an opportunity to those who had struggled against Hasmonean tyranny to play one imperial power off against another. And for those who composed the psalms, as expressed in psalms 2 and 8, Pompey's conquest represented God's just judgment against their own oppressive Hasmonean kings, despite the horror of the imperial destruction and slaughter. Before long, however, in the rapacious acts of Roman warlords and the brutal measures of their client-king Herod, it became evident just how oppressive and repressive Roman imperial domination was. The composers and compilers of the *Psalms of*

Solomon turned from petitioning God for deliverance to direct condemnation of Roman rule and to their hope for an anointed deliverer and restoration of Israel's independence on the land (psalms 2 and 17).

More significant for the *Psalms'* difference from earlier Judean anti-imperial texts, however, is their orientation or viewpoint. Even more than the *Testament of Moses*, the *Psalms* are deeply rooted in a Deuteronomic view of societal life and history. What happened in people's lives depended on their adherence to the covenantal law, and God would judge on the basis of obedience or disobedience, rewarding righteousness and punishing lawlessness. The scribes who composed the psalms, moreover, believed that God's judgment, however delayed in particular circumstances, was active in current events. One of their own responsibilities as devout scribes was to justify God's judgment in current events, often through a review of God's previous acts of judgment (8:7). Thus, despite the horrific violence and slaughter involved, the Roman conquest of Jerusalem was God's judgment on the wicked Hasmonean kings for their many sins.

Given this worldview from which the composers of the psalms were working, it is not surprising that many motifs prominent in the earlier Enoch and Daniel texts are missing. For example, since God is exercising judgment in current events such as Pompey's conquest of Jerusalem or Pompey's assassination in Egypt, the psalms do not emphasize a great future judgment by God. Outside of the picture of the future restoration of Israel on the land, which involved historical defeat of the empire by the anointed king, the most sustained reference to the future is the oraclelike announcement of the ingathering of the diaspora in psalm 11, patterned after Isaiah 40. While the psalms mention such a judgment in passing at a few points, they have no scenario of future judgment, even in psalm 17, in stark contrast with Daniel 7 or the Animal Vision or the *Testament of Moses* 10.

In another difference from the Enoch and Daniel texts, although the psalms allude to particular prophetic oracles in the Judean cultural repertoire, the "psalmists" do not resort to heavenly visions from which they receive revelation about a historical crisis that is otherwise opaque to scribes undergoing persecution. There is also no need or place for an elaborate explanation of the origin of imperial violence and exploitation in the heavenly governance of the world. Although the scribes who composed the psalms interpreted current events on the basis of their reflection on God's past judgments, they felt no compulsion to construct elaborate reviews of history leading to the current crisis of oppressive imperial rule, such as in the Animal Vision and the visions in Daniel. And although the "psalmists" include a brief appeal to the regularity of the heavenly bodies at the very end of the concluding psalm

(18:10-12)—and thus clearly know their astronomical wisdom—they do not seek reassurance that God is ultimately in control of history on the basis of the "secrets" of the divine governance of the cosmos in any of the other psalms.

The scribes who produced these psalms, however, are horrified at the slaughter and destruction of imperial conquest, and they are fully aware that they are vulnerable to being simply "devoured" by the Roman Empire. This is clear in the earliest representations of the Pompey's conquest of Jerusalem, and the implications are even more clearly expressed in the later psalm 17 and the introductory first psalm. But in their pious devotion, they stress submission to God's discipline and are apparently politically quietist. That is an argument from silence, of course, since we simply do not know what action they may have taken. Their condemnation of and opposition to the Roman Empire and its client ruler Herod, however, are clear.

Chapter 9

Visions of Vindication: The Parables of Enoch and the Updated *Testament of Moses*

It is rarely noted that we do not have any Second Temple Judean texts that are classified as "apocalyptic" that are thought to have originated between the Maccabean Revolt and the imposition of direct Roman rule in the early first century C.E. Should this be dismissed as simply an accident of what texts were preserved? Or is it possible that the reemergence of Judean "apocalyptic" texts has something to do with the return of intrusive imperial rule? The only two "apocalyptic" texts we have from the end of the Second Temple period, moreover, stand in continuity with earlier texts from the escalating crisis under Seleucid rule: an "update" of the *Testament of Moses*, and the latest text included in *1 Enoch*, the Parables of Enoch (chs. 37–71). That is, they each stand in a distinctive scribal tradition of composition addressed to crises of imperial rule. With so little textual evidence for Judean and Galilean society in the late Second Temple period, interpreters of Jesus and the Gospels might want to be a little more cautious about sweeping claims about how pervasive "apocalypticism" was at the time of Jesus. The limited evidence suggests rather that only limited circles of scribes expressed their concerns in "apocalyptic" forms. The two texts that were composed in the early first century C.E., however, both focus on the problem of Roman imperial rule.*

---

* I am using the new translation of the Parables of Enoch now available in George W. E. Nickelsburg and James C. VanderKam, *1 Enoch: A New Translation* (Minneapolis: Fortress Press, 2004), and the translation of the *Testament of Moses* in J. H. Charlesworth, ed., *Old Testament Pseudepigrapha* (2 vols; Garden City, NY: Doubleday, 1983–85), 1.919–34, which should be read in connection with this chapter.

Again, to avoid taking passages out of context, we will pursue an approach that considers the overall form and flow of the texts, particularly of each of the so-called "Parables" of Enoch, difficult as they may be to discern.

The *Testament of Moses* "Updated"

At some point in the first few decades of the first century C.E., the *Testament of Moses* was "updated" to address the new situation under Roman imperial rule, by adding what appear as chapters 6 and 7 in the Latin text.[1] It was evidently standard practice in the scribal circles that cultivated such Judean texts to adapt them to shifting historical circumstances. The visions and interpretation in Daniel 8 and 10–12 presuppose the revelation in Daniel 7, and bring new revelation to bear on the rapidly escalating crisis under Antiochus Epiphanes (ch. 5 above). Texts such as Daniel underwent at least minor "updating" in early transmission. For example, the sense that the crisis would last roughly half of a seven-year period (1290 days) in Daniel 12:11 was adapted somewhat (to 1,335 days) in Daniel 12:12.[2]

There are insufficient clues in the text of the *Testament of Moses* to discern some sort of continuity between the scribes who produced chapters 1–5, 8–10 (–12) and those who produced chapters 6–7. Such continuity seems unlikely considering the historical turmoil in the temple-state and its treatment by successive imperial regimes. But the continuation of the scribal circle that originally produced the *Testament* is not a necessary social basis for the later revision of the text to address new circumstances. The presence of Enoch texts and many copies of Daniel and *Jubilees* among the Dead Sea Scrolls found at Qumran suggests that (dissident) scribal circles valued and cultivated texts produced by other (dissident) scribal circles.

The additions in chapters 6–7 do not consistently continue the Deuteronomic perspective in which kings are understood as a punishment the people deserved for violating the Mosaic covenant. The first new rulers, the Hasmoneans, are introduced with the standard phrase derived from the tradition of dynastic prophecy (familiar from Daniel), "then powerful kings shall arise over them" (6:1). Composed with many decades of retrospect and regret, the text utterly rejects the Hasmonean "kings" as illegitimate rulers over the temple-state. "They will be *called* priests of the Most High God [but are not!]. They will perform great impiety in the Holy of Holies" (6:1). Those who produced the updated *Testament of Moses* agreed with the Qumran community and the producers of the *Psalms of Solomon* in rejecting the Hasmonean priest-kings.

Even worse and more illegitimate than the Hasmoneans is Herod, although a touch of the Deuteronomic perspective returns ("he will judge them as they deserve").

A wanton king, not of priestly family . . . rash and perverse. . . . He will shatter their leaders with the sword, and he will (exterminate them) in secret places so that no one will know where their bodies are. He will kill both old and young, showing mercy to none. Then fear of him will be heaped upon them in their land, and for thirty-four years he will impose judgments upon them as did the Egyptians, and he will punish them. (6:2-6)

This brief description of Herod's tyrannical rule is similar to Josephus's portrayal of the Rome-appointed client, "King of the Judeans." As noted in chapter 7 above, the utterly paranoid Herod even had many of his family members or courtiers that he suspected of disloyalty arrested, taken to unknown places, and executed. He also treated his subjects at large tyrannically, with heavy taxation and brutal repression of any suspected trouble. The "massacre of the innocents" in Matthew's narrative of Jesus' birth (Matt 2:16-17) has full "historical verisimilitude." The focus of the additions to the *Testament of Moses* on how Herod treated the elite, with no mention of his exploitation of and brutality to the people, signals a viewpoint we would expect from scribes who were oriented toward the operations of ruling circles whom they served or from whom they were alienated. Scribal circles, who had experienced (in effect) a "demotion" in status that corresponded to the diminished role of the temple-state in the rule of Judea and outlying districts, knew only too well the risks of opposing Herod. Some of the Pharisees had evidently plotted against him and suffered severe consequences. And the two revered teachers Judas and Matthias and their disciples had risked the bold stroke of cutting down the Roman eagle from above the gate of the Temple—and Herod had them burned alive in front of the officers of his court (*Ant.* 17.149–67; *War* 1.648–55; see further ch. 10 below).

"The powerful king of the West who will subdue them" after Herod's death is clearly the Roman general Varus. As the governor of Syria, based in Antioch, he led an army to put down the widespread revolt that had erupted in the countryside as well as Jerusalem following Herod's death in 4 B.C.E. The brief account in *Testament of Moses* 6:8-9 corresponds with many of the major actions he took in reconquering Galilee and Judea, according to the accounts in Josephus. In addition to slaughtering the people in several villages and towns, Varus did indeed "take away captives," for example, the inhabitants of the town of Sepphoris in Galilee (*Ant.* 17:289; *War* 2.68). The "part of the Temple burned with fire" in the course of the revolt and Roman reconquest was done by troops under the procurator Sabinus, but also under Varus's overall command (*Ant.* 17.254–64; *War* 2.49–50). And indeed Varus "crucif[ied] some of them around their city," to the number of two thousand, according to Josephus's accounts (*Ant.* 17.295; *War* 2.75). The updated text of the *Testament of Moses* does not mention the initial Roman conquest by Pompey in 63 B.C.E. But the reconquest by Varus was far more violent (and far more recent), and was followed ten years later by direct Roman rule.

The statement that Herod "will beget heirs who will reign after him for shorter periods of time" (6:7) seems to be oriented to events in Judea (again only to be expected from scribes who [had] served the Jerusalem temple-state). Archelaus, whom the Romans placed over Judea and Samaria after Herod's death, lasted only ten years. Both Antipas and Philip, whom they set, respectively, over Galilee and Perea and the area north and east of the Sea of Galilee, both ruled longer than their father's thirty-four years. This also suggests that the additions to the *Testament of Moses* were addressed to the situation in Judea in 6 C.E. and immediately afterwards, when the Romans deposed Archelaus and reimposed the tribute, in response to which the "fourth philosophy" organized resistance.

The following clause, "when this has taken place, the times will quickly come to an end" (the first clause in 7:1), reinforces the sense that the additions address the situation of the early first century C.E. The next few clauses (7:1b-2) are impossible to reconstruct from the remaining fragments of the text. The subsequent account of the "destructive and godless men" is both stereotypical and vitriolic. But a combination of factors, including the historical situation evidently addressed and some comparative material, indicates that the text is speaking of the Judean priestly aristocracy. Their supposed warning, "Do not touch me, lest you pollute me in the position I occupy," indicates that they are priests, evidently in high position. After they deposed Archelaus, the Romans placed four high-priestly families in power as client rulers of Judea under the oversight of the Roman governor in Caesarea. Aristocrats in most societies, certainly those who are also the highest-ranking priests of the gods, represent themselves as "righteous" (7:3) by virtue of their ancestry and office, and in their wielding of power. The charge that the "destructive men" love "gluttonous feasts," "winings and dinings" (7:4, 8), could certainly refer to what the wealthy priestly families were doing in the lavish mansions they were constructing in Herodian times in the "New City" to the West, across the valley from the Temple Mount, according to archaeological excavations. Similar charges of indulgence in wealth and of violating proper holiness, while hiding behind their supposed sanctity and righteousness, were leveled against the Hasmonean high priests by the Qumranites (see esp. CD 6:12-17; 1QpHab 8:8-13; 11:4-15; 12:1-10; cf. *Ps. Sol.* 2:3; 4:24).

The charge that they were "consuming the foods of the (poor)" and thus "committing criminal deeds" parallels both Josephus's accounts of the predatory actions of the high-priestly families and the complaints about their

Visions of Vindication

actions that survive in rabbinic texts. Powerful high-priestly figures would send their servants to the threshing floors to (forcibly) expropriate the tithes that were due to the priests, leaving the ordinary priests starving, according to two accounts in Josephus (*Ant.* 20.181, 206–7). The lament included in the Talmud contains the names of the high-priestly families:

> Woe to me because of the house of Baithos;
>   woe to me for their lances!
> Woe to me because of the house of Hanin, . . . Ismail ben Phiabi,
>   woe to me because of their fists.
> For they are high priests and their sons are treasurers
>   and their sons-in-law are Temple overseers,
>   and their servants smite the people with sticks! (*b. Pes.* 57a)

Josephus recounts such high-priestly actions as examples of how Judean society was disintegrating in the decade preceding the great revolt of 66–70. But his accounts are meant to illustrate the extremes to which the high priests resorted in arrogant abuse of their power that had started long before.[3] It is clear from his accounts of earlier decades that they had been the object of complaints, demonstrations, and riots from at least the end of Herod's reign (see ch. 6 above).

That the *Testament of Moses* was "updated," rather than a new text composed, means that at least some scribes found the previous text applicable to the new circumstances of Judea under Roman rule in the early first century C.E. This is pertinent mainly to chapters 8–12, which come after the updating insertion of chapters 6–7. And in looking for possible points of application of the earlier version of the *Testament of Moses*, we should also consider points at which that text may have been adapted to the new situation. The reconquest by Varus may well have appeared to repeat the violent invasion by Antiochus Epiphanes as portrayed in chapter 8. We might well suspect that the statement that Antiochus "will crucify" some of the people (8:1) was "updated" to fit the brutal repression by Varus.

As noted in chapter 4 above, the text of 10:7, alluding to Yahweh's deliverance of the people on eagle's wings in Deuteronomy 32:11-13, evidently refers to the people again "mounting up on the wings of an eagle" as the Most High delivers them from oppression. The image of an eagle would immediately have resonated with scribal circles in the aftermath of Herod's brutal martyrdom of the revered teachers and their students who had cut the golden Roman eagle down from above the gate of the temple (see ch. 10 below). In the tradition of Israel (Deut 32:11-13), however, Israel's divine King was also symbolized by the wings of an eagle. And, with double entendre, delivered by the Most High, the subject Judeans could prevail over the "necks" of the Roman imperial eagle. Israelite tradition, after all, included a command by Joshua, to whom the whole *Testament of Moses* is ostensibly delivered, to the Israelites to place their feet on the necks of the kings (Josh 10:24). And another circle of scribes, in the Qumran community, had anticipated that God would "lay Thy hand on the necks of the enemies//smite the nations" (1QM 12:11; 19:3).

The latter (speculative) reading, moreover, would fit another allusion to the Israelite tradition of Joshua and the end of Deuteronomy after which the *Testament of Moses* was patterned. Moses had charged Joshua with driving out the nations (see esp. Deut 31:3-8). Toward the end, the *Testament of Moses* refers directly to this prophetic commission. Previous interpreters, keying from Taxo's admonition to his sons, have argued that the *Testament of Moses* takes a pacifist stance toward imperial domination. The reference to Joshua's charge by Moses makes the stance appear a bit more active. If the updating of the *Testament of Moses* was done, as it appears, in the aftermath of Varus's reconquest and the scribal organization of resistance to the Roman tribute, then the more activist stance of the fourth philosophy may have influenced the revision, particularly in chapter 12.

The Parables of Enoch

In the Book of Parables, as in the Book of Watchers, the antediluvian wise scribe Enoch again steps into the role of a prophet. In three "oracles" (cf. Num 23:7, 18; 24:3, 15, 29, 21, 23), he speaks "the words of the Holy One" that he claims are an unprecedented revelation of wisdom (37:2-5). The wisdom that "Enoch" "sees" is primarily cosmological (more specifically, astronomical and meteorological). Building on the tradition of prophetic audition of judgments in the heavenly court of "Yahweh of hosts," most of what he "sees" consists of scenarios of judgment in the heavenly court of "the Lord of the spirits." "Enoch" speaks three "parables/oracles." As stated at the outset of each parable, the first two (*1 Enoch* 38–44; 45–57) focus on the judgment of "the kings and powerful," when "the congregation of the righteous and chosen" and "the Chosen One" appear in the divine judgment. The third (*1 Enoch* 58–63 [with 69:26-29?]) purportedly concerns the destiny of the righteous and chosen, but devotes as much or more attention to the judgment of "the kings and powerful." The Parables are dated to the early first century C.E. on the basis of the reference to the Parthians and Medes (56:5-7), who invaded Syria-Palestine in 40 B.C.E. In contrast to the Enoch texts from the late third and early second centuries, no copy of the Parables was among the Dead Sea Scrolls found at Qumran. The Parables are available

Visions of Vindication

only in Ethiopic, but the original language was probably Aramaic, as in the earlier Enoch texts.[4]

To avoid taking terms and motifs out of their "literary" context and to enhance the possibility that we are following "Enoch's" revelation as it unfolds in each parable and sensing the principal concern(s) of the text, we begin with an overview of the parables.

The first "parable" (and the whole sequence of parables) opens with an oracle that asks rhetorically, "Where (will be) the resting places of those who have denied the Lord of spirits," and declares that "the kings and powerful" will perish and be given into the hand of the righteous and holy (38:1-6). Enoch is then snatched up in a whirlwind to the end of the heavens where he sees a vision of the dwellings of the holy ones and the place of the Chosen One and the righteous, where those who never sleep praise the Lord of spirits (39:3-14). Then he sees the four highest-ranking heavenly messengers of the Lord of spirits, whose identities and functions in protection of the (Judean) people are explained by the messenger of peace who accompanies him (40:1-10). The first "parable" appears to conclude (with an *inclusio*) when, among "all the secrets of heaven," Enoch sees "the dwelling places of the chosen" (with those of the holy ones), and the sinners being driven away by the scourge that came forth from the Lord of the spirits (41:1-2). The lengthy sections of astronomical and meteorological "secrets" about the sun, moon, stars, winds, and hail have been (awkwardly) inserted after this apparent conclusion with no apparent connection, perhaps as paradigms of faithful obedience to the commands of the Lord of spirits by the cosmic forces (41:3-9 with 43:1—44:1). Even more awkward is the insertion of the stanza about Wisdom not finding a dwelling place among people (42:1-2).

"The second parable concerning those who deny . . . the Lord of spirits" is a sequence of anticipatory visions of the judgment of the kings and the powerful. It begins with the declaration by the Lord of the spirits that the sinners will be banned from the earth on "that day" when my Chosen One sits on the throne of glory to dwell among the chosen on a renewed earth under a transformed heaven (45:1-6). Enoch then tells of his vision of the divine court in which "the son of man" who accompanies the "Head of Days" will "overturn the kings from their thrones and kingdoms," and "the blood of the righteous which had been shed" will be required by the Lord of spirits (46:1-8; 47:1-4).[5] Enoch also sees that "the son of man"/Chosen One was named before the Head of Days, even before the sun and moon and stars were created, as the vindicator of the righteous, into whose hand the kings of the earth would be delivered, so that they would have rest upon the (rejoicing) earth (48:1—51:5). Having been carried off in a whirlwind, Enoch again sees all the secrets of heaven, now focusing on mountains of metals used (by kings) for stockpiling wealth or making instruments of war, which will melt before the coming of the Chosen One, and deep valleys of punishment. These valleys, the messenger of peace explains, will be the means by which the kings and powerful will be punished and the rebel heavenly forces behind them be bound (52:1—56:4).[6] And indeed, the heavenly messengers stir up the kings to destroy one another—with an assist from the heavenly host of chariots (56:5—57:2).

The third parable is difficult to follow because of several longer or shorter interpolations. On the basis of his close examination of the manuscripts, George Nickelsburg has very helpfully identified the interpolated passages. Most obvious are the traditions of Noah in chapters 65–68. Also chapter 64 and the various pieces of 69:1-25 have no clear connection to their context. The materials in 60:1-10 interrupt two blocks of astronomical and meteorological secrets that should be taken together (59:1-3 + 60:11-23). Because of the reference to "my great-grandfather who was taken up" in 60:8, Nickelsburg takes 60:1-10 with 24-25 as a tradition originally ascribed to Noah.[7] But 60:7-10 with 24-25 has no connection to the theophany of the Head of Days in 60:1bce—6. The astronomical and meteorological secrets in 59:1-3 with 60:11-23 (like those in the first parable), moreover, have no obvious connection to the preceding or following materials. If we thus disregard these traditions of Noah and blocks of astronomical and meteorological secrets as later intrusions, we are left with a discernibly coherent narrative sequence in the third parable: 58:1-6; 60:1-6; 61:1-5; 61:6-13; 62:1—63:12.

The coherent sequence of the third parable can be discerned most easily by starting with its climax, the judgment of the kings and the powerful in chapters 62–63. Panicked at their forced confrontation with the Lord and the Chosen One, the kings and powerful make supplication. But the Lord of spirits delivers them to the heavenly messengers who exact retribution for their oppression of the chosen ones, while the latter put on garments of glory (62:1-16). The kings and powerful plead for a respite, glorify the Lord as if He were their own patron deity, and confess their false trust in their own power and ill-gotten wealth. But they are driven from the presence of the Lord of spirits, who pronounces "the law and the judgment of the powerful and the kings" (63:1-12).[8] The enthronement of the Chosen One and judgment of the heavenly forces in 61:6-13 forms an obvious preface to the judgment of the kings. The theophany of the Head of Days in 60:1-6, moreover, would quite appropriately have prefaced the whole scenario of judgment after the opening blessing in 58:1-6. And while somewhat awkward in sequence, 61:1-5 would be an appropriate preparation for the judgment. The two stanzas in

69:26-29, finally, could be seen as a conclusion to the climactic judgment scene of 61–63, except that they duplicate or conflict somewhat with the substance of the judgment of the kings and sinners already accomplished in chapters 62–63.

Judgment of the Kings and the Powerful

It is abundantly clear from the opening oracles of each parable, and the extensive representations of judgment presided over by the Lord of spirits and the chosen one, that the Parables of Enoch focus on oppression of the people by "the kings and powerful." Divine judgment on imperial rulers dominates the book from the beginning to the end.[9] In the climax of the opening oracle, for example, "the kings and the powerful will perish, . . . given into the hand of the righteous and holy" (38:5). The very purpose of the enthronement of "that son of man" in the heavenly court of judgment in the second parable is that

> he will raise the kings and the powerful from their couches,
>   and the strong from their thrones . . .
> And he will overturn the kings from their thrones and their kingdoms.
>   (46:4-6)

The extensive trial with which the third parable climaxes focuses on the condemnation, retribution, and punishment of "the kings and the powerful and the exalted" (62:1—63:12).

The Parables do briefly mention the holy ones who mated with humans (39:1) and (the host of) Azazel (54:5-6; 55:4) who revealed secrets that brought harm to humans, actions of rebel heavenly figures that provided the explanation of military violence and economic exploitation in the earlier Book of Watchers. In contrast to the earlier Enoch text's focus on the superhuman origins of imperial domination, however, the Parables focus directly on the imperial rulers, "the kings and the powerful ones."

How this concern dominates these "parables" can become clearer if we attend closely to the text as it expresses views of reality almost diametrically the opposite of standard older generalizations about "apocalyptic" literature. In particular, the Parables of Enoch articulate a highly positive, not negative, view of the world, including the earth, and do *not* presuppose or express a dualism of "this world" and the "heavenly" or "supernatural" world.

As in the books of the Hebrew Bible and the rest of ancient Near Eastern culture, the world consists of both the heaven(s) and the earth. There is clearly a difference. The heavens are the locus of the divine governance of the world, while earth is the setting of human and other life. In order to learn of what is happening on earth, a prophet or visionary scribe such as "Enoch" becomes swept up to heaven in an ecstatic experience or, in the Parables, by a "whirlwind" (39:3). The astronomical and meteorological wisdom that is revealed to Enoch in his visions as "the secrets" of heaven (41:3-8; 43-44; 59:1-3; 60:11-22)—wisdom long cultivated among Judean "Enoch" scribes—is all about how the sun and moon and stars and the winds, clouds, snow, and dew serve life on earth. While largely implicit, this is also stated explicitly: "nourishment for the land from the Most High who is in heaven" (60:21-22).

Heaven is where all the various messengers in charge of various aspects of world governance dwell, along with the Lord of spirits and the chosen one. But all are in interaction with and indeed responsible for life on earth. The Lord of spirits "fills the earth with spirits" (39:12). The four chief heavenly figures take care of the earth and people. Raphael takes care of the sickness and wounds of people, Gabriel is in charge of every power (that would affect people), and Phanuel is in charge of repentance for eternal life (40:9). These and other holy ones or messengers petition and pray for those who dwell on earth (40:6; 47:2). Some of the heavenly forces, "angels of power and principalities," are charged with the supervision of rulers (61:10). And in the divine heavenly governance of the earth, the deeds of people are weighed in the balance (41:1), which is what the Parables are all about.[10]

Finally, in the highly positive valuation of the earth, the result of the judgment that will finally end imperial rule will be a restoration of life on the land. Both heaven and earth will be transformed so that the chosen ones will dwell on the renewed earth (45:4-5). God will destroy the kings and powerful precisely so that there will be rest upon the earth (48:10). At one point, "Enoch's" vision even segues into a pastoral idyll that is articulated in traditional imagery from the Psalms and Prophets:

> In those days the mountains will leap like rams,
>   and the hills will skip like lambs satisfied with milk;
> and the faces of all the angels in heaven will be radiant with joy,
>   and the earth will rejoice,
> and the righteous will dwell on it,
>   and the chosen will go upon it. (51:4, 5b)

No heaven versus earth "dualism" or "cosmic catastrophe" anywhere on the scene: the judgment will bring the end of imperial domination and thus make possible a good life on a renewed earth.

Recognition of the highly positive valuation of life on earth under the direct rule of God may enable us to appreciate the sharp condemnation of imperial rule to which the Parables of Enoch are devoted. The life that God intended for the people to have on the earth has been made impossible by

Visions of Vindication

imperial rulers, as indicated in the very representation of "the kings and powerful." This is articulated in the opening oracle that introduces the whole series of parables, but so subtly, in a series of four steps, that it can be missed by modern readers who do not understand that control of land was the basis of ancient empires. In the somewhat vague first step (38:1), "the sinners" will be judged by being driven from "the face of the earth." In the somewhat more precise second step (38:2), as the righteous one appears at the judgment among the righteous who will (then) be dwelling on the earth, the oracle asks the leading rhetorical question, "where (will be) the dwelling place of the sinners?" The third step (38:3-4) indicates more precisely that the sinners are "the powerful and exalted" who had possessed the land but will no more after the judgment. The fourth step then indicates most precisely that the sinners who have possessed the earth (land) are "the kings and powerful ones," who will be given into the hand of the righteous and holy, that is, the very people whose land they have conquered and exploited. Thereafter through all three parables, the imperial rulers are represented as those who take over or trample or possess the earth (56:6; 62:1, 3, 6, 9; 63:1). Since land worked by peasants and laborers was the sole base of wealth in ancient agrarian societies, it was also the only basis on which rulers could build up empires. And insofar as the reference to "the Parthians and Medes" (56:5-7; the Parthians invaded Syria in 40 B.C.E.) is the basis of dating the Parables of Enoch to the early first century, "the kings and the powerful" in the Parables clearly refer to the Romans and their empire.[11]

It is conceivable, even likely, that "the kings and the powerful" include the Herodian kings and the high-priestly aristocracy in Jerusalem, particularly since the Romans controlled their empire in the East through just such client rulers (see ch. 6 above). Indeed, the very face of Roman imperial rule in Judea in the first century C.E. was the high-priestly aristocracy that headed the temple-state, along with the Herodian kings who exercised control directly or indirectly. Other, contemporary Judean texts produced by scribal circles condemn incumbents of the high priesthood and Herodian kings for their oppressive rule and collaboration with the Romans (see discussion of the *Psalms of Solomon* in chapter 8 and discussion of the updating of the *Testament of Moses* above). The "Wisdom-myth" that otherwise appears to be an intrusive interpolation into the first parable (42:1-2) would make sense in this connection. Ben Sira had claimed that heavenly Wisdom held dominion in the Jerusalem temple-state.[12] The statement that Wisdom did not find a resting place among humans, and hence withdrew to heaven, appears to be a diametrically opposite statement, in effect denying the legitimacy of the temple-state under its current incumbents.

The opening judgment scene in the second parable includes a telling list of the interrelated ways that Roman imperial rule impacted subject peoples, particularly the Judeans, ways that Judean scribal circles had been aware of for some time.

> The kings and the powerful
> . . . judge the stars of heaven,
> and raise their hands against the Most High,
> and tread upon the earth and dwell on it.
> And . . . their power (rests) upon their wealth.
> And their faith is in the gods that they have made with their hands,
> and they deny the name of the Lord of spirits.
> And they persecute the houses of this congregation,
> And the faithful who depend on the name of the Lord of spirits. (46:7-8)

While imperial power rested on the wealth that kings and powerholders could build up from subject lands and peoples, their conquest and control of those lands and peoples depended on their *military and political power*. This had been articulated clearly in the Book of Watchers' portrayal of the giants and their warfare. Enoch's second parable includes a similar portrayal (52:1-9; surely dependent on the earlier Enoch text). Enoch has a vision of six mountains of various metals—iron, copper, silver, gold, soft metal, and lead. In the ancient world, kings had a monopoly on metal mining, smelting, and manufacturing. The symbol of mountains suggests just this monopoly and stockpiling of metal by imperial regimes: iron for weapons of warfare, silver and gold used for décor and measures of value that demonstrated the glory of a kingdom, and so on. Judeans were particularly familiar with the military use of iron from repeated invasions and reconquests in early Roman times (see ch. 6 above). And of course, gold and silver had been stockpiled in the Temple, whence certain Roman warlords resorted for resources after their initial conquest. The declaration of Enoch's messenger of peace condemns just these imperial uses of metals.

> And in those days none will save himself either by gold or silver,
> and there will not be iron for war, nor a garment for a breastplate;
> bronze will be of no use. . . .
> All these . . . will perish from the face of the earth. (52:7-9)

Immediately following the vision of the military power of the kings and powerful comes a vision of their *economic exploitation of subject peoples*.

> There my eyes saw a deep valley, and its mouth was open,
> And all who dwell on the dry land . . . will bring it gifts . . . and tribute,

> But that valley will not become full.
> And everything that (the righteous) labor over, the sinners lawlessly devour.
>   (53:1-2)

The imperial rulers have an insatiable appetite for the produce of subject peoples that they expropriate through taxes, tithes, and obligatory gifts from client-kings such as Herod the Great to (the divine) Caesar and Roma. Rendering tribute to Caesar, however, was a direct violation of Israel's covenant with God, as we shall see again in the organized resistance of the "fourth philosophy" (ch. 10 below). Accordingly, Enoch also saw "the angels of punishment preparing all the instruments of Satan . . . for the kings and powerful of this earth, . . . [so that] the righteous will rest from the oppression of the sinners" (53:3-7). According to the traditional pattern, the imperial-scale punishment will fit the imperial-scale crime: "they threw the kings and the powerful into that deep valley" where, in their insatiable appetite for wealth and luxury they had devoured the goods of subject peoples (54:2). The kings' belated and futile repentance in the long trial scenario in the third parable reflects the same judgment about the illegitimacy of imperial tribute and its deserved punishment.

> Now they will say to themselves,
> "Our lives are full of ill-gotten wealth,
> but it does not prevent our descending into the flame of Sheol." (63:10)

The Parables of Enoch also emphasize *the pretentious arrogance of imperial rulers* that was so prominent in the tales and historical summaries in the book of Daniel. "Enoch's" indictment includes some of the same charges that "Daniel" made against the kings, particularly against Antiochus Epiphanes: "They judge the stars of heaven, and raise their hands against the Most High" (46:7). The Romans took over the standard Near Eastern ideology that their empire was not only eternal but divinely sanctioned, indeed was itself divine. Roman warlords had attacked and plundered the Temple in the first decades of their conquest of Judea. The Roman gods had defeated the god in Jerusalem. From early in his reign, Augustus was honored particularly by the Greek cities as divine, with titles such as "son of God" and with new shrines and temples. The gods that the Roman emperors and their elite collaborators "had made with their own hands" (46:7) even included the emperor himself. Herod had built whole new cities (named Caesarea and Sebaste = Augustus) and temples, and erected statues in honor of Caesar, and even placed a golden Roman eagle atop the principal gate of the grandly rebuilt Temple in Jerusalem. Rome and Augustus expected that the Judean high priests would perform sacrifices in the Temple in honor of both the imperial city and the emperor. To Judeans devoted to the Most High, perhaps particularly to scribal circles jealous for the proper operations of the Temple as the sacred place for the service of God, all of these actions by or for the Romans would have been understood as attacks on the sacred honor of God and the divine governance of the world, in which "the stars" and other holy ones participated.[13] Again in the long trial scene in the third parable, the kings on trial agonize that

> our hope was upon the scepter of our kingdom and throne of our glory, and on the day of our tribulation it does not save us. (63:7-8)

More specific to the situation in Judea, the Roman "kings and powerful" had "*persecuted the houses of his congregation*" (46:8). Enoch's vision elaborates on this in the next stanza.

> And in those days the prayer of the righteous had arisen, . . .
> The holy ones . . . were uniting with one voice . . .
> Interceding . . . in behalf of the blood of the righteous that had been shed.
> . . . and the blood of the righteous had been required before the Lord of spirits. (47:1-4)

The kings' persecution and shedding of the blood of the righteous may be closely related to the sinners' "oppression of the righteous" mentioned later in the second parable (53:7) and "the iniquity" that the kings had done "to his [the Lord's] children and his chosen ones" for which the messengers of punishment exact retribution in the long trial scene in the third parable (62:11).

It is unclear what these phrases may be referencing in the experience of Judeans under Roman imperial rule and whether these phrases are referring to the same or different forms of oppression. In its context noted just above, the "oppression of the righteous" appears to refer to economic exploitation of the Judean people generally. As indicated in the instructional speeches of Ben Sira, scribal circles were concerned about the economic exploitation of the people generally by their rulers, including the wealthy and powerful Judean aristocracy in charge of the temple-state.[14] Similarly, the kings' "iniquity to [God's] children and his chosen ones" seems to have general reference to the people as a whole as oppressed by the Romans (and their client rulers). It is more difficult to discern whether "the houses of his congregation" that had been persecuted is a reference to the repeatedly conquered Judean people generally or to the circles of scribes and teachers who had resisted Roman imperial rule in some way.

The language of God's "requiring the blood of the righteous" suggests martyrdom, and the scribal teachers and their students who had cut down the

Roman eagle from above the gate of the Temple had clearly become martyrs for their resistance to Herod's collaboration in Roman imperial rule (see next chapter). Insofar as "the righteous" and "the chosen" and "his congregation" in the Parables of Enoch seem to refer to the Judean people as a whole, however, it would be best to take these references as the "Enoch" scribal circle's concern for the Judean people as a whole, suffering under Roman imperial rule.

Deliverance of the Righteous and Chosen Ones

Yet another mark of how the Parables of Enoch is concerned primarily with imperial domination and oppression is its portrayal of the deliverance of the righteous and chosen ones. Their deliverance is nearly always portrayed in relation to the kings from whose power they must be delivered.

That the deliverance of the chosen is necessarily linked to the judgment of the kings, as well as the Parables' focus on imperial rule, has been obscured by the Christian theological investigation of the Parables primarily as a source for the supposed Jewish title "the Son of Man," used in a way that would help explain "the apocalyptic Son of Man" sayings in the Gospels. In recent years, it has finally been recognized that, for all its references to "the chosen one" and "that son of man," the Parables of Enoch simply does not attest to "the Son of Man" used as a *title* of an eschatological agent of judgment. In fact, when we focus carefully on the text of the Parables itself, it is quickly evident that "the chosen one" almost always occurs in close relationship with "the chosen ones" in need of deliverance and in relation to "the kings and the powerful" that have been oppressing them. These relationships run throughout the Parables. But they are most dramatically represented in the long final trial of the kings and powerful ones in the third parable.

However one sees the trial of the kings set up in the third parable—by the theophany of the Head of Days in 60:1-6 or by the Lord of spirit's seating the chosen one on the throne of glory to begin the judgment with the heavenly forces who unite in the harmony of heavenly blessings—it forms the climactic trial and judgment scene of the Parables (62–63). The kings and powerful ones, commanded to recognize the chosen one seated on the throne of glory, are absolutely panicked and terror stricken, even as the congregation of the chosen and the holy stand in the presence of the Most High (62:1-8). The kings and the powerful fall on their faces in last-minute obeisance to the chosen one, but the Lord of spirits himself delivers them to the angels of punishment to exact retribution for the iniquity they did to his children (62:9-12). Thus saved from the oppression by the kings and now living directly under the Lord of spirits, the chosen abide and eat with "that son of man," and put on the garment of life from the Lord of spirits, which will not wear out (62:13-16). The kings plead for a respite from their punishment, addressing the Lord of spirits as if he were *their* god: "the Lord of kings, and the Lord of the powerful, and the Lord of the rich," and confess their false hope in "the scepter of our kingdom" and "ill-gotten wealth" which do not save them in the day of tribulation. But the Lord of spirits does not relent, and drives them away to their punishment (63:1-12). There are, thus, several interrelated relationships in the final climactic scene of the trial and judgment of the kings, which also includes the deliverance of the chosen ones.

The same set of relations can be seen in other key passages in the Parables. The judgment of the kings is what constitutes, or makes possible, the deliverance of the chosen in the opening oracle and at key points throughout the Parables. The chosen ones can possess the land themselves when the kings perish or are condemned in the divine court (38; 41:2). In the opening oracle of the second parable, the judgment of the kings leads to the transformation of the earth (and the heaven) so that the chosen ones can dwell on it (45:4-5). Indeed, the kings and powerful are given into the hand of the righteous and elect ones at the judgment (38:5; 48:9). When the kings and powerful are given over to the instruments of Satan, "the house of his congregation" appears and the righteous gain rest from their oppression (53:3-7). The third parable that begins with blessings on the righteous and the chosen climaxes in the judgment and punishment of the kings that is, simultaneously, the deliverance of the chosen.

The relation of the chosen one and the chosen ones is particularly close. In effect, the chosen one is the representative of the chosen ones. He is never subjected to imperial rule, for he was hidden from the beginning for his role in the judgment, when he is seated on the throne of glory. But he repeatedly appears in intimate relation with and "in the presence of the righteous" (38:2). In Enoch's first vision of the heavenly court, the chosen ones are before him (39:6). In the opening oracle of the second parable, "my chosen one" will "dwell among them" on the transformed earth (45:4-5). Following the intercession of the holy ones for the blood of the righteous, the chosen one is named as their "vindicator" (47:1-4; 48:7).

Paralleling the close relationship between the chosen one and the chosen/righteous is the strikingly close relationship expressed between the chosen ones and the holy ones. As noted above, the chosen are delivered from imperial oppression into life with the chosen one on the transformed earth. It is all the more striking then, against the background of modern interpretation that tends to find a heaven-earth dualism in "apocalyptic" texts, that the Parables of Enoch speak of the delivered righteous as sharing the features of the "holy

Visions of Vindication

ones" and other heavenly forces. In his first vision, Enoch sees the dwellings and resting places of the righteous with those of the holy ones and the righteous heavenly messengers (39:4-5; cf. 41:2).

Even more striking is how Enoch sees the righteous in the place of the Chosen One: "all the righteous and chosen will be mighty before him like fiery lights" (39:7). Similarly, in the opening of the third parable,

> And the righteous will be in the light of the sun,
> And the chosen, in the light of everlasting life. (58:3)

These images are closely similar to the representation of the vindication of the martyred maskilim in Daniel 12:3 and the oppressed righteous in the Epistle of Enoch 104:1-6. The latter "will shine like the luminaries of heaven, . . . shine and appear, for the portals of heaven will be opened for you. . . . will be the companions of the host of heaven." Both the maskilim and the earlier "Enoch" scribes saw a close relationship between the scribes who are the recipients of heavenly wisdom and the glorious features of heavenly beings. The scribal and priestly community at Qumran spoke of the close communication back and forth between the heavenly world and the people in their community. The scribes who produced the Parables of Enoch evidently think of the new life made possible by the end of empire in terms of life on earth under an open heaven, with the illumination of heavenly wisdom as well as the Chosen One, living and eating with the righteous directly under the Lord of spirits (62:14).

Chapter 10

Demonstration, Organization, and Assassination: Parallel Scribal Resistance

While scribal opposition to "the kings and the mighty" continued in the composition of "apocalyptic" texts, it was not confined to them. We know of several scribal actions or movements of resistance to imperial rule in the early Roman period that have no evident relationship to a particular text or "apocalyptic" literature in general. Investigation of these other cases of scribal resistance can help illuminate the tense situation of Judea under Roman rule that the Parables of Enoch and the updated *Testament of Moses* addressed, and offer parallel modes of resistance with which the texts can be compared.*

There has never been any doubt among biblical interpreters and Jewish historians that there was widespread opposition to Roman rule toward the end of the Second Temple period. The previously standard construct of "Judaism," however, had this opposition pigeonholed in the concept of "the Zealots." Modern interpreters had constructed a substantial movement that agitated for insurrection against Roman rule from the death of Herod until it finally touched off widespread revolt in 66 C.E.[1] In this, they were misled by the Judean historian Josephus, who provides the principal sources for the history of this period. As he begins book eighteen of his *Jewish Antiquities* with the Roman assessment of property for payment of the tribute, and the opposition to the tribute organized by what he calls "the fourth philosophy" among the

---

* The most accessible translations of the Judean historian Josephus's accounts of these scribal groups are probably those in the Loeb Classical Library, *Josephus*, 10 vols.; ed. H. St. J. Thackeray, Ralph Markus, Allen Wikgren, and Louis H. Feldman (Cambridge, Mass.: Harvard University Press, 1930–65).

Judeans, he launches into a tirade against them for stirring up a revolutionary spirit that led to the great revolt (*Ant.* 18:6–8).

Modern historians simply neglected to distinguish critically between Josephus's flights of rhetoric against "civil strife" and his account of the "fourth philosophy." They proceeded to lump together several different groups that opposed Roman rule in one way or another, from ten years earlier to sixty years later, and named them after a coalition of brigand bands formed by refugee peasants in northwest Judea in the middle of the great revolt in 67–68 C.E., a coalition that was known as "the Zealots." Josephus's own previous and subsequent accounts, however, make clear that resistance to Roman rule in Judea and Galilee was much more complex and varied than suggested by his tirade against what he claimed were the effects of the fourth philosophy. Also clear in Josephus's accounts is that, despite his insinuations, that most resistance was nonviolent while nevertheless adamant.[2]

Two of the groups that were lumped under "the Zealots" were indeed led by, and perhaps comprised largely of, scribes: the "fourth philosophy" that organized resistance to the Roman tribute in 6 C.E., and the group called the "daggermen," the *sicarii* who began assassinating high-priestly collaborators with the Romans in the 50s C.E. Scribal acts of resistance to Roman rule had begun earlier, under Herod, and were rooted in earlier scribal resistance to Seleucid oppression and the expansionism and tyranny of Alexander Yannai. A critical examination of these scribal acts of resistance can illustrate two important matters in relation to the scribal resistance expressed in "apocalyptic" and other texts. On the one hand, these acts indicate that scribal opposition to Roman imperial rule was not limited to composing texts, a distinctively scribal mode of expression. On the other hand, they indicate that scribal resistance to Roman imperial rule was more common and persistent than is usually acknowledged.

The Heritage of Scribal Resistance Continues

The Pharisees, the most important faction of learned scribes serving the temple-state, having come to prominence early in the Hasmonean dynasty, were involved in wider resistance to the policies of Alexander Yannai, and, in a more measured way, to those of the Roman client-king Herod. It can be determined from a critical reading of Josephus's accounts that they were the most influential advisers of John Hyrcanus before being displaced by the Sadducees (*Ant.* 13.288–98).[3] That the ancestral regulations that they established for the people, supplementary to the laws of Moses that were written down, were included in official laws of the temple-state, under Hyrcanus and

Demonstration, Organization, and Assassination

again under Alexandra Salome, indicates both a central function of scribal circles and the prominence of the Pharisees (13.296–97; 14.408).

After being "demoted" by Hyrcanus in favor of the more compliant Sadducees, the Pharisees apparently became involved in the wider opposition to Alexander Yannai, probably for his imperial-like wars of expansion with a mercenary army. Yannai was a self-designated king as well as high priest. Josephus does not say explicitly that Pharisees were among those who fought against Yannai, hundreds of whom he crucified in his vengeance (*Ant.* 13.372–83). But this is the implication of the account of Yannai's supposed advice to his wife and successor, Alexandra Salome, that she should restore the Pharisees to prominence even though they had "suffered many injuries at his hands" (*Ant.* 14.401–3).

When Herod came to power, the Pharisees may have suffered a "demotion," but they did not suddenly withdraw from politics into pious eating clubs.[4] Herod kept the temple-state intact as an instrument of his own rule, headed by his own appointees. In ruling Judea through the temple-state, Herod, as well as his handpicked high priests, still needed the expertise of the Pharisees and other scribes learned in the laws and other traditions of the Judeans according to which the Temple and the society operated. Temple operations and other sacred rites were conducted according to the rulings of the Pharisees, who were thought to possess the "most accurate" knowledge of the laws, says Josephus (*Ant.* 17.149; 18.14–15, 17). That the Pharisees continued in their political role is confirmed by "the leading Pharisees" playing a prominent role in the "provisional government" headed by a few high priests during the great revolt of 66–70 (*Life* 21, 197–99). And at several points in his accounts of Herod's reign, Josephus mentions the Pharisees as a presence at court, but also as resistant to at least some of Herod's measures, perhaps even conspiring against him. We can deduce at least this much from Josephus's preface to his account of two incidents.

> There was also a party of Judeans priding itself on its adherence to ancestral customs and the laws of which the Deity approves called Pharisees, favored by the women at court. They were of great help to the king because of their foreknowledge, and yet they were intent on combating and injuring him. (*Ant.* 17.41)

In the first known case of their resistance, they refused to take the loyalty oath to his own rule and to Caesar that Herod demanded of the populace (*Ant.* 15.367–72). "Those who refused to go along with his practices he persecuted in all kinds of ways. . . . Those who objected to compulsion he got rid of by every possible means." The Pharisees obstinately refused the oath.

Yet they were punished only with a fine, which was paid for them by Herod's brother Pheroras's wife (17.42). Josephus explains Herod's leniency as due to his respect for (or superstition about) the Pharisee Pollion and/or his disciple Samaias (15.370-71). These leading Pharisees had advised the Jerusalemites to admit Herod to the city and to submit to his rule—advice surely based on a realistic assessment of the inevitability of Herod's rule backed by Roman military power (*Ant.* 15.3). And before that, Pollion or Samaias (Josephus is confused as to which) had reportedly scolded the obsequious council convened by the high priest Hyrcanus II for kowtowing to the show of force by Herod, who was supposedly on trial, and in effect prophesied that Herod would someday come to rule and persecute them all (14.268-76, 15.3-4).

In the second case of opposition, the Pharisees, "believed to have foreknowledge of things through God's appearances to them," reportedly prophesied that royal power would be taken from Herod and pass to Pheroras and his wife. Convinced that the Pharisees had corrupted some of the people at court, Herod killed those Pharisees most to blame and all those who approved of what the Pharisees had said (17.43-44).

Attacking a Symbol of Roman Domination

The most dramatic and public act of defiance of Roman imperial rule under Herod was the cutting down of the golden Roman eagle that he had erected above the great gate of the Temple as the king lay dying (*War* 1.648-55; *Ant.* 17.149-67).[5] According to Josephus's accounts, this brazen action was inspired by two learned teachers, Judas son of Sariphaeus (or Sepphoraeus) and Matthias son of Margalothus (or Margalus). These scholars were revered as "the most knowledgeable expounders of the ancestral laws" and "the most accurate expounders of the ancestral traditions in the city, with the highest esteem of the whole people" (*Ant.* 17.149; *War* 1.648). That second description makes them sound like Pharisees, insofar as Josephus uses the similar terms to characterize them as "the most accurate in knowledge of the laws." Although Josephus does not explicitly identify them as "Pharisees," they were clearly the most highly regarded professional scribes of their time, in the tradition witnessed by Ben Sira of scholars *(exegētai)* and teachers *(sophistai)* thoroughly knowledgeable in the laws and other traditions. We may suspect that Josephus exaggerates the number of those who were attendant on their teaching (*War* 1.649), but they evidently had a faithful following of eager students.

According to Josephus's longer account, Judas and Matthias and their circle had previously criticized Herod for his actions contrary to the law (*Ant.* 17.151). Emboldened by reports of Herod's declining health, the scholars suggested to their students that they should "pull down all the works built by the king in violation of the ancestral law" (150). Herod's erection of the golden eagle over the great gate of the Temple was a prime example of the many imperial symbols he had displayed in public places to keep the populace constantly aware of their subjugation to Rome. The eagle, symbol of Rome's sovereignty, was precisely the sort of image or dedication in the likeness of living creatures prohibited in the second commandment and related laws. The teachers urged their students to pull down the eagle, despite the risk of being apprehended and executed for the act (152).

The scholars' students appear to have undertaken the action as a symbolic demonstration of opposition to Roman rule as well as defiance of Herod. The perpetrators could not have been bolder or more flagrant in carrying out the operation. The action was no mere matter of spontaneous youthful heroics. The great gate formed the principal entrance to the massive new temple complex that Herod was constructing, almost certainly intended to be what it became, one of the wonders of the Roman imperial world. The eagle was symbolic of imperial domination, hence of the deep conflict between the empire and Judean tradition. The students pointedly timed the action for midday, to attract maximum public attention, as they let themselves down from the roof with ropes and began hacking down the golden eagle with hatchets (*War* 1.651). And given Herod's usually tight security measures, the operation clearly involved considerable organization and discipline on the part of the large number of demonstrators involved. When the king's officer hastened to the scene with military force, the student demonstrators, along with their teachers, calmly awaited capture while the crowd fled (*Ant.* 17.157).

Josephus's portrayals of the confrontation between the furious king and the scholars and their students resemble the encounters between martyrs and the tyrants who are torturing and killing them in Jewish martyrological stories, such as 2 Maccabees 7.[6] In the latter account, one or another of the seven brothers being tortured says, "We are ready to die rather than transgress the laws of our fathers. . . . I will not obey the king's command, but I obey the command of the law that was given to our fathers through Moses. . . . I, like my brothers, give up body and life for the laws of our fathers" (2 Macc 7:2, 30, 37). In some martyr stories, the reward is exaltation, as in the anticipated vindication of the maskilim. In others, the martyrs express confidence in an afterlife. Beginning at least with memory of the maskilim in Daniel 11–12, and other martyrs of the resistance to Antiochus Epiphanes, such as Taxo, a tradition had developed of faithful martyrs persisting in the traditional Judean way of life in the face of imperial repression.

Josephus's accounts locate Judas and Matthias and their students in this tradition, with emphasis on two interrelated points. We cannot know the extent to which Josephus's accounts reflect the ideas and motives of these learned teachers and their protégés. But like other Hellenistic historians, Josephus was constructing speeches that would offer the gist of what historical figures would have said in a certain situation. Their principal emphasis is on their commitment to observe the laws of their ancestors, entrusted to them by God (*Ant.* 17.158). In response to Herod's question, "Who ordered you [to cut down the golden eagle]?" they reply "The law of our fathers" (*War* 1.653). Herod's imposition of the forms of Roman imperial rule such as the golden eagle, however, had brought about a direct, irreconcilable conflict. Given their commitment to the ancestral traditions, they were compelled to observe the laws of Moses given by God rather than the king's decrees (*Ant.* 17.159). The other emphasis is on the outcome of their dying in defense of their God-given ancestral laws. Here some of Josephus's phrases, such as "winning eternal fame and glory" and "death for a noble cause" (152–54) are directed to his Hellenistic readers. However, behind other phrases, such as "attain immortal life and an abiding sense of good," "enjoying an abundance of good," and "glory" (*War* 1.650, 653), we can detect expectations such as the renewal of the Judean people and the vindication of the martyrs familiar from earlier Judean texts (such as Dan 12:1-3; *1 Enoch* 104:1-6; and *T. Mos.* 10:8-9).

Judas and Matthias, however, may be moving a significant step beyond the motive of resistance articulated in earlier Judean texts. Assessment of this possibility, of course, depends on both how much stock we put in Josephus's accounts, and on whether, in extant texts, we possess an adequate articulation of the motives of other circles of learned scribes. According to Josephus, Judas and Matthias say, "We have come to the aid of a cause entrusted to us by God . . . and of deep concern to us who obey the law" (*Ant.* 17.158–59). They would appear to be taking action out of a sense of having been commissioned by God, either for resistance in general or for this particular bold, public, symbolic demonstration. Their action itself was not simply a persistence in obeying the ancestral laws in the face of repressive action by imperial agents, like that of Taxo. Rather, they were taking deliberate organized action against the intolerable imperial order of life imposed on the Judean people, as had the maskilim and the "lambs whose eyes were opened."

Herod thereupon orchestrated a trial in a public assembly for a demonstration effect of his own, although if it was held at the amphitheater at the royal resort in Jericho, the immediate audience would have been limited. Addressing the officers of the Judeans (priestly heads of the Temple, others?), he appealed to his glorious reconstruction of the Temple at great expense and vented his (not unjustified) paranoia about their support. On the suspicion that the high priest Matthias was implicated, he deposed him and appointed his wife's brother Joazar in his place. He ordered the scholars and their students who had cut down the golden eagle to be burned alive (*Ant.* 1.161–167).

We cannot know if the scholars and students hoped to provoke a more general resistance to the dying Herod with their dramatic and highly visible symbolic action. But this was the effect of their act of defiance of imperial rule and their ensuing martyrdom at the hands of Herod. When Herod died shortly afterward, their brutal execution quickly became a rallying cry of the Jerusalem crowd in demanding from his son and presumed successor Archelaus a reduction of taxes, the freeing of political prisoners, and the ouster of oppressive Herodian officials.

> [There began] a lamentation over the fate of those whom Herod had punished for cutting down the golden eagle from the gate of the Temple . . . mourning . . . in honor of the unfortunate men who had in defense of their country's laws and the Temple perished on the pyre. These men ought, they clamored, to be avenged by the punishment of Herod's favorites, and the first step was the deposition of the high priest whom he had appointed. (*War* 2.5–7)

When Archelaus responded with military repression, the protest intensified and spread into the countryside, becoming a full-scale popular revolt.

It Is Not Lawful to Render Tribute to Caesar

The Judean intellectuals whom Josephus refers to as the "fourth philosophy" have persistently been misunderstood as advocates and even practitioners of revolt against Roman rule, as noted above.[7] Even interpreters who recognize that they were not the founders of "the Zealots," the supposed revolutionary party in first-century Judea, describe them as advocates of revolt. A number of misreadings of Josephus's and others' accounts of particular figures and movements have contributed to this misunderstanding. It will help to clear up these misreadings in preparation for a closer consideration of what Josephus (plus a brief reference in Acts) does say about the "fourth philosophy."

First, Josephus adds to his account of this "new philosophy" a harangue about the effects of their views: They "planted the seeds of those troubles which subsequently overtook [the people]" (*Ant.* 18.6, 9). But he does not say that they engaged in revolt. In fact, at the end of his account, he blames the great revolt of 66–70 not on them, but on the last Roman governor: "The folly that ensued began to afflict the people after Gessius Florus . . . had by his overbearing and lawless actions provoked a desperate rebellion against the Romans" (18.25).

Second, in construction of the synthetic concept of "the Zealots," scholars used to assume that "Judas from Galilee," one of the leaders of the fourth philosophy, was identical with Judas, the son of Hezekiah. The latter, however, was the son of the brigand chieftain active in Galilee in the 40s B.C.E., who was murdered by the young Herod. With the resonance remaining from his father's exploits, the son was acclaimed as "king" by his followers, who rose in revolt in the area around Sepphoris in Galilee after Herod died in 4 B.C.E. Josephus refers to the Judas who helped lead the fourth philosophy ten years later as a "scholar-teacher" *(sophistēs)* who was active in Judea, not Galilee. As Josephus indicates more precisely, he had come from Gamala in Gaulanitis, a fortress hilltop town that became an important administrative and/or military town in the area east of Galilee under Herod.

Third, related to the confusion of the peasant "messiah" active in Galilee in 4 B.C.E. and the scholar-teacher active in Judea in 6 C.E. has been the notion that this synthetic "Judas" was part of a dynasty of "messianic" leaders of insurrection that included Menahem, the "messianic pretender" among the sicarii, who were active in the initial events of the revolt in Jerusalem in the summer of 66.[8] That Judas from Gamala in Gaulanitis was father, or more likely grandfather, of Menahem who led revolutionary activity briefly in Jerusalem in 66 does not mean that he also was a messianic pretender or advocated revolt in different circumstances sixty years earlier.

Fourth, some translations of both Josephus's and the book of Acts' (5:37) accounts of Judas have apparently been influenced by the modern construct of "the Zealots," which in turn further reinforced the misunderstanding of the fourth philosophy. The term *apostasis* and its variants in both accounts, for example, was used a great deal more ambiguously and vaguely than the modern English term "rebellion" or "revolt." The NRSV translation that Judas "got people to follow him" is a good deal less ominous and more appropriate than the New English Bible's "induced some people to revolt under his leadership."

Aware of these previous misreadings and misunderstandings, we can examine Josephus's account of the "fourth philosophy."

> A certain Judas, a Gaulanite from the city named Gamala, in league with the Pharisee Saddok, pressed hard for resistance. They said that [the Roman] tax-assessment amounted to slavery, pure and simple, and urged the people to claim their freedom. If successful, they argued, the Jews would have paved the way for good fortune; if they were defeated in their quest, they would at least have honor and glory for their high ideals. Furthermore, God would eagerly join in promoting the success of their plans, especially if they did not shrink from the slaughter that might come upon them. . . . Judas the Galilean established

himself as the leader of the fourth philosophy. They agree with the views of the Pharisees in everything except their unconquerable passion for freedom, since they take God as their only leader and master. They shrug off submitting to unusual forms of death and stand firm in the face of torture of relatives and friends, all for refusing to call any man master. (*Ant.* 18.4–5, 23)[9]

Both here and in his parallel account in the *War* (2.118–9), Josephus groups Judas and his associates with what he portrays as the "philosophies" of the Judeans: the Essenes, the Pharisees, and the Sadducees. Here he identifies Saddok explicitly as a Pharisee, and elsewhere he refers to Judas as a "scholar-teacher" *(sophistēs)*, like the revered Judas and Matthias ten years earlier, who inspired their students to puåll down the golden eagle from the great gate of the Temple. They were thus "intellectuals," learned scribes and teachers. If one of the leaders of the group was a Pharisee and they agreed with the views of the Pharisees in everything (except their passion from freedom), we could easily conclude that they were at least closely associated with the Pharisees, perhaps an activist spinoff of that long-established party.

If they were (like) Pharisees, however, they were intellectuals involved in public affairs. Elsewhere, Josephus refers to the Pharisees and Sadducees as "parties" or "factions" striving to implement particular religious-political policies in the Judean temple-state and with distinctive senses of the scope of Torah that they accepted as authoritative (*Ant.* 13.297–98). The Essenes, as discussed in chapter 8 above, had withdrawn to the wilderness in protest at an intransigent Hasmonean high priesthood, to set up their own separate covenantal community. Perhaps Josephus's use of the Hellenistic analogy of "philosophies" in his accounts of the events in 6 C.E. is partly a signal of how scribal circles that had served as advisers in the temple-state had been "demoted" under Herod and the Romans. It is clear in his histories, however, that the Sadducees, the Pharisees, and other scribes still had some role and responsibilities under Herod and played a significant role in the temple-state in the first century, as noted just above. The "intrusive fourth philosophy," however, was not an established "faction" among scribal circles like the Sadducees and Pharisees. They would appear to have been a smaller association of learned scribes-teachers who came together specifically in response to the imposition of direct Roman rule and the tribute-assessment in 6 C.E.

To appreciate their "views" in the context of Roman Judea, however, it is necessary to "translate" back into Israelite/Judean cultural expressions from the Hellenistic philosophical discourse in which Josephus couches his accounts. It may help, moreover, to keep in mind that particular "ideas" were integrally interrelated and can be isolated only for analytical purposes. Their most distinctive feature, says Josephus, was "their unconquerable passion for freedom." Attachment to the idea of "freedom" *(eleutheria)* was not distinctive to Judas and his circle or to the Pharisees, but widespread in Judean society. Judeans, who annually celebrated at Passover their ancestors' liberation from subjugation in Egypt, would have focused their hopes on freedom, particularly in circumstances of continuing domination by the Romans. The ideal of freedom had been articulated in one form or another by most of the circles of scribes examined in the chapters above, from the "the people of the holy ones of the Most High receiving the sovereignty" (Daniel 7) to the righteous being free of domination by "the kings and the powerful" (the Parables of Enoch). Distinctive to Judas, Saddok, and their followers, however, was their drive to act on the ideal in organizing collective resistance to the tribute.

The fourth philosophy's "unconquerable passion for freedom" was directly related to their conviction that God was "their sole ruler and master" *(monon hegēmona kai despotēn; Ant.* 18.23). Again this is hardly distinctive to them or to the Pharisees with whom they supposedly agreed in all things. It was the standard Judean confession of faith. Many prayers and psalms, such as the contemporary *Psalm of Solomon* 17, begin and/or end with the confession that God is (sole) King of Israel, indeed of the world. The phrase "*only* ruler and master" appears to allude to the first commandment of the Mosaic covenant, which demands exclusive loyalty to God in a social-political sense inseparable from the religious sense. Judas and his circle's application of it to the Roman tribute indicates that they also took seriously the economic demands of the second commandment, the prohibition of bowing down and serving another "ruler and master" with the produce of one's labor (cf. *War* 2.118). This is the clear implication of their insistence that the tribute amounted to slavery, that is, service of a "ruler and master" other than or in addition to the God of Israel.

Although he had clearly compromised the political-economic implications of the covenantal commandment, Josephus himself explains that the Judean constitution given by Moses was a "theocracy" that placed "all sovereignty and authority in the hands of God" (*Ag. Ap.* 2.164–65), and that the God-given "laws" were their "masters" *(despotas)* just as God was their true "ruler" *(hegemon; Ant.* 4.223). We saw expressions of this conviction that God was the true Lord and King in texts from the tales of Daniel to the Parables of Enoch. In regard to God as sole ruler, the fourth philosophy was hardly innovative and "intrusive." In terms of the seriousness with which they took the conviction politically and economically, however, they went beyond the compromises made by most Pharisees and Sadducees.

Judas's and Saddok's sense that God would be helping or concurring in their action sounds like an "activist" variation on the Pharisees' belief that, in Josephus's Hellenistic terms of fate and free will, "to act rightly or otherwise rests, indeed, for the most part with men, but that in each action Fate cooperates" (*War* 2.163). This is evidently the Greek philosophical attempt at stating the more subtle Pharisaic (or perhaps more general Judean scribal) understanding of a certain synergism between God's and people's actions, God taking action through human action and interaction. Israelite tradition was rich in stories of God effecting liberation through the action of the people. God led the people out of bondage in Egypt, but only when the people finally fled, following Moses' lead. In the Animal Vision and the ten-week vision of "Enoch," the lambs sprouted horns and the sheep or the righteous were given a sword. As evident in their War Scroll, the Qumranites were rehearsing war maneuvers in anticipation that God would do mighty deeds by the hands of his people. Perhaps there were some Judean scribes who were standing around waiting for "signs" that God was taking action. But the maskilim in Daniel 11–12, the "Enoch" scribes in the Animal Vision, and Taxo and sons all engaged in resistance in the expectation that God was about to take action in judgment of imperial rulers and at least to vindicate their resistance if not also to restore the people's sovereignty.

Judas, Saddok, and company differed from the Pharisees in being ready to die for their beliefs. Rather than preparing to engage in violent revolt, they were prepared to suffer violent repression, even the torture and death of themselves, relatives, and friends. Their passion for freedom did not overwhelm their realistic assessment of the political situation. They evidently understood that the Romans, for whom failure to render up the tribute was tantamount to revolt, would take severe repressive action. They and others would have remembered Cassius's enslavement of the residents of Emmaus and three other district towns for failure to raise an extraordinary levy of tribute in timely fashion (*War* 1.220–22; *Ant.* 14.271–76). In their readiness to face death for disciplined persistence in their exclusive loyalty to their divine Lord and master, the adherents of the fourth philosophy again stood in a scribal tradition. When imperial rule under Antiochus Epiphanes had become unacceptably intrusive and overbearing, learned scribes such as the maskilim had resisted and faced torture and martyrdom at the hands of the rulers they refused to obey.

What was distinctive about the fourth philosophy in comparison with both the Pharisees with whom they agreed, and earlier circles of scribes who also engaged in resistance, was their organization of wider resistance. They preached and planned an organized action of nonviolent noncooperation with the assessment for the tribute. Just before discussing the appearance of Judas and Saddok, Josephus explains that the Romans' imposition of the assessment for the tribute shocked the Judeans in general, but that they were persuaded by the high priest Joazar not to pursue their opposition (18.2–3). What Judas and Saddok did that was "intrusive" and perhaps unprecedented was to urge others to refuse to participate, that is, to refuse payment of the tribute. And since "Judas persuaded not a few Judeans to refuse to enroll themselves" for the tribute (*War* 7.253), the plan of collective refusal, a "tax strike," made serious progress (*Ant.* 18.6).

We may wonder why, when Judea had been subject to Roman rule for well over two generations and, with the end of client-kingship, there was now one less layer of rulers and taxes, activist Pharisees and other scholar-teachers suddenly organized resistance to the Roman tribute in 6 C.E. The removal of client-kingship, with the high priesthood now running domestic affairs directly under the supervision of a governor, would presumably have offered an opportunity for some scribes to regain a degree of influence in the operation of the temple-state. The legacy of Herodian client-kingship may have been a factor in the emergence of the fourth philosophy, having evoked deep resentment against Roman rule generally, especially with visual reminders of subjection to Augustus Caesar on Herod's many buildings. The crucial factor, however, was that Judea had suddenly been placed under direct Roman rule, with a governor overseeing public affairs. The high priesthood and priestly aristocracy, co-opted and weakened under Herod, now formed less of a buffer or shield from the imperial use of force. Administration of the assessment for the tribute brought Judeans face-to-face with Roman domination and exploitation.

Weapons of the Weak: The Counterterrorism of the Sicarii

Fifty years later, as Judean society slipped into chronic social turmoil, with repressive Roman governors, a predatory high priesthood, a worsening famine, and both escalating banditry and popular prophetic movements in the countryside, the sicarii sent shock waves through the families of the elite.[10]

> When [the brigands] had been cleared from the countryside, a different kind of banditry sprang up in Jerusalem, known as the *sicarii*, who murdered people in broad daylight right in the middle of the city. Mixing with the crowds, especially during the festivals, they would conceal small daggers beneath their garments and stealthily stab their opponents. Then, when their victims fell, the murderers simply melted into the outraged crowds, undetected because of this plausible behavior. The first to have his throat cut was the high priest Jonathan, and after him many were murdered daily. (*War* 2.254–56)

The sicarii persisted in their violent resistance to Roman rule for well over a decade and attempted to take over leadership of the great revolt when it erupted in Jerusalem in the summer of 66, before withdrawing to Masada where they sat out the rest of the war.

As Josephus explains, their name (a Latin loanword) came from their chosen weapon, "daggers resembling the scimitars of the Persians in size, but curved and more like the weapons called *sicae* by the Romans" (*Ant.* 20.186). Like the fourth philosophy, these "daggermen" have been lumped together with other resistance groups and movements into "the Zealots." This is partly because Josephus refers to them as "bandits," a term used by the Romans for anyone rebelling against the Roman imperial order. But Josephus is more precise in his references. The "bandits" that the Roman governor Felix had recently captured and crucified were what scholars such as Eric Hobsbawm refer to as "social bandits," who form bands in the countryside in times of war and/or economic hardship.[11] Such "Robin Hoods," moreover, often have the sympathy and support of the villages from which they have fled in desperation, as Josephus indicates in this case (*War* 2.253). By contrast, says Josephus, the sicarii were "a different kind of bandits" who operated in the city carrying out assassinations. This was evidently something unprecedented in Judean society, for which Josephus has no distinctive term. In the anticolonial and anti-imperial agitation of recent history, it has come to be called terrorism. And in recent history as well as Roman-ruled Judea, it was both preceded by and a response to the colonial-imperial terrorism of brutal conquest and repression.

The aggressive assassinations carried out by the sicarii were dramatically different tactics from the defensive resistance organized by the fourth philosophy. Yet there was evidently some continuity, at least in the leadership of the two. One of the only events that merits mention during the governorship of Tiberius Alexander, a prominent Alexandrian Jew who rose to this high level in the Roman imperial administration, was that he crucified two sons of Judas of Galilee, James and Simon (*Ant.* 20.102). That the latter were crucified, a form of execution that the Romans used on those who rebelled against the imperial order, indicates that they had been engaged in some sort of resistance. Josephus also refers to Menahem, the leader of the sicarii who posed as a messianic pretender at the beginning of the revolt, as the "son of Judas of Galilee" (more likely the grandson?) and calls him a "scholar-teacher" *(sophistēs)*, the same term he used for Judas (*War* 2.445). Josephus also suggests that there was continuity between the fourth philosophy and the sicarii in his concluding harangue against the rebel groups (*War* 7.253–54). On the basis of these links, we can reasonably conclude that the sicarii, like the fourth philosophy, were scribal, at least in their leadership.

The historical circumstances in which assassinations and other acts of terror arise are generally situations in which all avenues of protest or the redress of grievances have been closed off to subjugated people. Feeling powerless, with no possibility of organizing wider resistance, and seeing no other way in which they can change an utterly intolerable situation, people take desperate action. Acts of terror are "weapons of the weak."

To Judean scholar-teachers in the 50s C.E., their situation may well have appeared desperate, calling for desperate actions. Exploitation by the wealthy and powerful Herodian and high-priestly families, compounded by a drought and famine in the late 40s, had weakened the position of the Judean peasantry, leading to spiraling debt, loss of land, disintegration of village communities, and an epidemic of banditry. The response of the Roman governors was brutal suppression of the brigands and attacks against their village sympathizers, further exacerbating the social-economic turmoil (*War* 2.228–31, 253). Given their social location as scribes trained to serve the temple-state, they had no connections with the desperate peasantry through which they could organize a wider movement. Their predecessors had tried and failed to organize a wider movement of resistance to the tribute. High-priestly and Herodian families had become increasingly predatory in their treatment of the people. And the leading high-priestly figures, including former high priests and power brokers such as Jonathan, were collaborating closely with the Roman governors and imperial court against the interests of the Judean people. With Roman governors and the high priesthood alike impervious to appeals and protests from the scribal advisers, some of the latter evidently moved toward desperate measures.

While regular bands of brigands operating in the hill country sometimes attacked Roman supply trains, the scribal "bandits of a different kind," with no way of attacking Romans directly, focused on the collaborating Jerusalem aristocrats who made Roman rule effective in Judea. Thoroughly familiar with the Temple complex and the procedures of the priesthood, they could exploit the vulnerability of the high-priestly officers and send a message of desperation by acts of desperation. They carried out three particular sorts of actions: selective symbolic assassinations, more general assassinations along with plunder of the property of powerful figures, and kidnapping for ransom.

First, like recent terrorists, the sicarii appear to have carried out selective, symbolic assassinations for their "demonstration effect," both on the ruling high-priestly families and Herodians and on the Judean people generally. In attacking prominent high-priestly figures, they chose targets with maximum symbolic value: the sacred officers of the Temple. But many of the priestly aristocrats, including current and former presiding high priests, had become symbols also of collaboration with the Roman overlords, not simply as the collectors of the tribute but also in their close cooperation with the Roman governors. Whether or not he was the first victim, Jonathan was a powerful figure and power broker in Jerusalem for twenty years after serving as high priest in the later 30s (*Ant.* 18.95, 123; 19.313–16; 20.162–64; *War* 2.240–42, 256).

It seems likely that the assassinations were intended as punishment of the high priests for previous exploitation and collaboration and as a warning about their future actions. The assassinations would presumably have demonstrated to the high priests and Herodians their own vulnerability and the inability of the Romans to protect them. Josephus is fully aware of these effects on the ruling elite.

> The fear of attack was worse than the crimes themselves. . . . Men watched their enemies from a distance, and not even approaching friends were trusted. Yet despite their suspicions and precautions they were laid waste, so suddenly did the conspirators strike and skillfully avoid detection. (*War* 2.256–57)

Another effect on the high-priestly elite was further fragmentation, as particular figures and families were now all the more looking out for themselves. The people would have seen their religious-political overlords and economic oppressors punished and warned. Similarly, they would have seen how vulnerable the elite figures really were.

Second, the sicarii extended their assassinations to the estates of the pro-Roman aristocracy in the countryside.

> The *Sicarii* conspired against those who wished to obey the Romans and treated them as enemies in every way, plundering their goods, rounding up their cattle, and setting fire to their buildings [killing the powerful rich and plundering their houses; *War* 2.265]. They declared that such persons were no different from foreigners, sacrificing the hard-won freedom of the Judeans, preferring servitude to the Romans. (*War* 7.254–55)

The learned scribe Ben Sira had criticized the priestly aristocracy for oppressing the people, and the "Enoch" scribes had pronounced God's condemnation on them for building their estates by sin and violence (*1 Enoch* 94:6-7; 99:12-13).[12] The sicarii attacked the wealthy and their estates alike, presumably as a combination of punishment, warning, and deterrence. It is conceivable that their attacks may also have had the effect of loosening the powerful elite's hold on the tenant farmers and landless laborers who had lost control of their land to these wealthy creditors.

Third, in another tactic typical of modern terrorist groups, the sicarii kidnapped important persons in order to extort the release of some of their own members who had been captured. At festival time, under the governor Albinus (62–64 C.E.),

> the *Sicarii* sneaked into the city by night and kidnapped the secretary of the high priest Ananias, and spirited him away in bonds. They then made contact with Ananias and said they would free the secretary into his custody if he would persuade Albinus to release ten of their imprisoned fellows. Having no option, Ananias successfully persuaded Albinus to make the exchange. But this was just the beginning. In various ways the brigands managed to kidnap a string of members of Ananias' household and held them until ransomed for some of their own *Sicarii*. (*Ant.* 20.208–9)

The sicarii clearly contributed to the spiral of violence that climaxed in the revolt in Jerusalem and the countryside in the summer of 66 C.E. Contrary to the previously standard construction of the course of the revolt against Roman rule that identified them with "the Zealots," however, the sicarii did not initiate the revolt, nor was the messianic pretender Menahem the principal leader at the outset. Acts of rebellion were already well underway when the sicarii managed to sneak into the Temple, where they were recruited by the already active rebels. They helped with, but did not lead, the torching of the royal palaces, the mansion of the high priest Ananias, and the archives that housed the records of debts (*War* 2.422–27). Only after other rebel groups had taken the fortress of Masada, overlooking the Dead Sea, from the Roman garrison did some of the sicarii raid Herod's old armory there to arm themselves (2.408, 433–34). Menahem, at the beginning of the revolt not clearly the leader of the sicarii, had not posed as a messiah for very long before he was attacked by the previously dormant "citizens" of Jerusalem and tortured to death (2.444–48). Thus driven from Jerusalem, the rest of the sicarii withdrew to Masada, where they sat out the rest of the revolt.

Finally, contrary to the previously standard view—and to decades of religious-nationalist propaganda—it is now clear that there was no such event as "the Zealots' last stand" against the attacking Roman army at Masada. Rather, when the Romans besieged Masada as part of their "mopping up" operations in southern Judea, the sicarii offered no active resistance and finally committed mass suicide (*War* 7.309–401). This scribal (-led) group, however, before withdrawing to Masada, had maintained a highly disciplined resistance to Roman rule by attacks on the Judean elite collaborators for a decade.

Conclusion
Rethinking "Apocalyptic" Texts

Our examination of the contents and principal concerns of the Second Temple Judean texts customarily classified as "apocalyptic" indicates that they are all responses to imperial rule. Their authors are all struggling to understand the origins of the destruction and exploitation of Judeans at the hands of Hellenistic or Roman rulers in relation to God's sovereignty over history, which was central to traditional Judean faith. Many of these texts focus on the historical crisis of Antiochus Epiphanes' invasion of Jerusalem in support of the Hellenizing reform that threatened the traditional Judean way of life. All of them anticipate God's judgment of the oppressive empires and restoration of the Judean people.

The Book of Watchers (*1 Enoch* 1–36), often considered the earliest Judean "apocalyptic" text, explains the origins of imperial violence and exploitation from the rebellion of heavenly watchers. These watchers generated a warring race of giants who forged metals into weapons (symbolizing the Ptolemic and Seleucid empires). But Enoch is commissioned as a prophet to announce that God is still ultimately in control of history; that the destructive power of rebel heavenly forces has been checked; and that the people will be restored on a renewed earth. The visions-and-interpretations in Daniel 7–12 present the violent attack by Antiochus Epiphanes as arising from an escalating sequence of destructive empires. In God's judgment, however, imperial domination will be terminated, the people restored to sovereignty, and the wise teachers who were martyred in resistance vindicated. "Enoch's" Animal Apocalypse places Antiochus's attack on the traditional Judean way of life in even wider historical perspective. The predatory enemies of Israel originated from rebellious heavenly forces; heavenly "shepherds" allowed far more imperial violence to the Judeans than God intended as punishment for disobedience. But God will sit in judgment on the oppressive heavenly and imperial agents and their Judean collaborators and will restore the Judean flock as the house of God (but without the Temple).

Against Roman rule, scribal successors of the Enoch traditions articulated scenarios of God's judgment of "kings and mighty" for their devastation of the earth. What is evidently the latest "apocalyptic" text from Second-Temple Judea, the Parables of Enoch (*1 Enoch* 37–71), focuses on the divine judgment of the destructive "kings and the mighty" (the Romans) and the restoration of the people. Other scribes expanded "Moses's" survey of history to apply to the new empire. Still other circles of scribes expressed their opposition to Roman rule in newly composed psalms. And the renegade scribal-priestly community at Qumran articulated its rejection of the Romans in its distinctive "interpretation" of the prophetic statements of Habakkuk and even rehearsed its anticipated battle against "the Kittim," as indicated in the War Rule.

In addition to explaining the origins of imperial rule and pronouncing God's condemnation of oppressive rulers, Judean "apocalyptic" texts also represent their composers as engaged in resistance. The scribal actions mentioned in these texts, moreover, fit into a wiser resistance by scribal circles that was sustained over several generations. And the texts themselves played a significant role in the sustained scribal opposition to Hellenistic and Roman rule.

Resistance by Circles of Scribes

Most of the "apocalyptic" texts focused on Antiochus Epiphanes present active scribal opposition to his attacks on Jerusalem as one of the key events in the climax of their survey of history. In some cases their opposition began earlier and persisted against Antiochus's measures to suppress it. Some texts even present scribal resistance as the turning point of history. The acts of opposition by the scribal circles that produced these texts were paralleled by other scribal resistance to Antiochus. In the ensuing century and a half, such resistance persisted, first against the imperial pretensions of the later Hasmonean high priests and then against the Romans and their client rulers, both in other kinds of texts and in actions by groups that did not (also) produce texts.

As discussed in the introduction, scribes were conservative by training and disposition. Their training to serve as intellectual and legal advisers in the temple-state focused on learning obedience to the priestly aristocracy as

Rethinking "Apocalyptic" Texts

well as on learning the various components of the Judean cultural repertoire. Their dependence on the temple-state for their economic support, moreover, compounded their conservative bent. But scribes were also committed to the values and ideals carried in the Torah, prophecies, and various kinds of wisdom of which they were the professional guardians. Moreover, insofar as the Torah and prophecies were understood to come from God, scribes looked to a divine authority independent of and higher than that of their aristocratic patrons who headed the temple-state. Given their conservative character, most scribes probably either remained loyal to their aristocratic patrons no matter what course they pursued or kept their own counsel in a crisis. When the heads of the temple-state collaborated too closely with the dominant imperial regime, however, other scribes objected. When the dominant aristocratic faction substituted a Hellenizing constitution for Jerusalem that replaced the traditional Judean way of life, they resisted, in their "conservative" loyalty to the higher authority of God. And after the scribes of the early second century B.C.E. had shown the way, when Herod and the high priests became, only too transparently, instruments of Roman rule, later intellectuals devised new tactics of protest and defiance.

There are sufficient clues in these texts, especially the Enoch texts, to suggest that scribal resistance to imperial rule did not develop suddenly only in response to Antiochus Epiphanes. The development and ongoing cultivation of the tales of Daniel (so that they were available for merger with the visions and interpretations in the same document) indicates that conflict between Judean cultural traditions and ideals and imperial policy and practice had been a frequent problem for the scribes who retold them. The insistence in the Daniel tales on God's sovereignty over imperial kings provided a paradigm of scribal loyalty to God and to Judean traditions. The sharp condemnation of the Second Temple as having polluted bread and the omission of the Temple in the restoration of the people in the Animal Vision (*1 Enoch* 89:73; 90:29), combined with Enoch texts that contemporary specialists date to the mid- or late third century B.C.E., suggest that a circle of "Enoch" scribes may have rejected the legitimacy of the Temple and its dominant priesthood earlier in the second-temple period. The Book of Watchers indicates that their "dissident" stance included acute awareness of and opposition to Hellenistic imperial rule for its destruction and exploitation of the people. The portrayal of the actions of the "lambs whose eyes were opened" at the center of the climactic events of the Animal Vision seems to be a clear self-reference to the "Enoch" scribes' active, organized resistance to the Hellenizing reform that was backed by Antiochus. The "ten-week" survey (*1 Enoch* 93:1-10 and 91:11-17) also indicates active opposition by "Enoch" scribes to the Hellenizing reform; indeed, it appears to have been composed at the beginning stage of resistance, prior to the intervention of Antiochus to enforce that reform.

Both the *Testament of Moses* and the survey of Second Temple history in Daniel 10–12 focus specifically on resistance in the face of Antiochus's violent measures to enforce the Hellenizing reform. The "Moses" text offers only a general statement of "the Orderer (Taxo) and his disciples" determined to continue in the traditional covenantal way of life despite their sure martyrdom at the hands of Antiochus's soldiers. The account of the maskilim in Daniel 10–12 indicates that they had been involved in conflict with those who had abandoned the covenant and had steadfastly persisted in the traditional Judean way of life against imperial orders. The sequence of "visions-and-interpretations" in Daniel 7, 8, and 10—12 (Daniel 7 evidently having been composed before Antiochus's military invasion of Jerusalem and the abomination on the altar of the Temple) indicates that the maskilim had sustained their opposition for some time. Because of their resistance, the maskilim were being hunted down, imprisoned, tortured, and executed. Through this ordeal they not only remained personally stalwart in opposition to Antiochus's measures, but attempted to "make many understand" what was happening and, presumably, to join in the resistance. That the lambs who began to open their eyes in the Animal Vision sprouted "horns" suggests more "militant" opposition than that mounted by the maskilim or by Taxo and his sons, pointed acts of resistance sufficiently serious to provoke military action against them. The concluding section of the Animal Vision, moreover, was evidently expanded to include further resistance by the "Enoch" scribes, as they joined in the wider revolt led by Judas the Maccabee.

Other sources for these events, the books of the Maccabees and some of the texts composed by the Qumran community, indicate that yet other circles of scribes in addition to the "Enoch," "Moses," and "Daniel" scribal circles also became engaged in resistance to Seleucid imperial rule. A generation ago, a standard explanation of the origin of "apocalyptic" texts as well as of the "Jewish sects" (Sadducees, Pharisees, and Essenes) was that they all originated from the *hasidim* mentioned briefly in passing in 1 and 2 Maccabees, but there is insufficient evidence to sustain this hypothesis. Although the hasidim may have included a wider range of Judeans who rose against the Hellenizing reform and particularly against the imperial invasion, it is clear that scribes were involved, perhaps in leadership roles. They, like the awakened "lambs" of the Animal Vision, eventually joined the wider Maccabean revolt. According to the reconstruction in chapter 7 above, the scribal-priestly group that eventually withdrew to Qumran in adamant rejection of the Hasmonean seizure of the high priesthood originated earlier, as a protest against the Hellenizing reform under Antiochus Epiphanes.

There appears to have been little or no coordination between these various scribal circles. This is only what we would expect, given the political-economic structure indicated in several instructional speeches of Ben Sira and the factions that emerged in the priestly aristocracy under the Ptolemaic and Seleucid regimes. Insofar as scribes served, and were economically dependent on, the aristocracy that headed the temple-state, factions would have developed among the scribes corresponding to factions in the aristocracy. His famous "hymn to the ancestors" makes it clear that Ben Sira was a staunch supporter of the incumbent Oniad dynasty at the beginning of the second century B.C.E. The "Enoch" scribes had evidently become alienated from the controlling faction of the high priesthood some generations earlier. In the crisis that climaxed in the Hellenizing reform and imperial military enforcement, other circles of scribes also evidently moved into opposition, but each with its own separate tactics. The maskilim steadfastly resisted Antiochus's invasion and repressive action, communicating with others and resolutely facing martyrdom. "Enoch's" lambs who grew horns moved into more aggressive activity that provoked military action, and eventually joined the Maccabean Revolt.

Resistance by circles of scribes continued under Hasmonean rule and became widespread again under direct Roman rule. The one case of clear continuity from opposition to the Hellenizing reform to a break with the upstart Hasmonean high priesthood and sharp opposition to Roman domination is the large group of scribes and priests who withdrew into the wilderness to form their own covenantal community at Qumran. Far more vividly than any other scribal group of which we have knowledge, the Qumranites anticipated, indeed, apparently rehearsed a decisive holy war in which they would attack the Roman army, a way in which God would finally intervene to give them victory. Specialists surmise that the Qumranites did engage the Roman forces who attacked as part of their "mopping up" operations in the Judean wilderness after they had destroyed Jerusalem and the Temple.

Under Hasmonean rule many scribes must have resumed some sort of service in the restored temple-state. The Pharisees evidently formed some sort of association or "party" well before the end of the second century, their influence in temple-state operations being countered by the Sadducees, who were more closely aligned with the new priestly elite. After a period of favor under John Hyrcanus, however, the Pharisees were evidently among those who mounted active opposition to his son Alexander Yannai, partly because of his empirelike wars of expansion using mercenary troops. While they continued to wield at least some influence even under Herod, they did refuse the loyalty oath to his own and Roman imperial rule.

The devout scribes who composed and used the *Psalms of Solomon*, while clearly condemning the destruction and exploitation of Judea by Roman warlords, give no indication that they were about to engage in any particular acts of opposition. But there were other learned scribes who did. Taking the declining health of Herod as the opportune moment they had been waiting for, Judas and Matthias and their disciples carried out their well-planned protest of Roman imperial domination, the toppling of the Roman eagle above the gate of the Temple, with maximum impact on the Jerusalem populace. Victims of gruesome execution on Herod's order, their martyrdom became a rallying point for a wider surge of protest in Jerusalem and popular revolts in the countryside. We have no particular reason to connect the martyrdom of these teachers and students with the updating of the *Testament of Moses* sometime in the following decades. But just such acts of resistance to Roman rule would have made the earlier defiance and martyrdom of "the Orderer and his disciples" again pertinent for Judeans who now stood directly under the Roman governors who carried out harsh military action against any disruption.

While most Pharisees and other scribes evidently settled into a new *modus operandi*, subordinate to the newly restored priestly aristocracy who collaborated in direct Roman rule, activist Pharisees and other learned teachers responded by organizing a collective refusal to pay the tribute. Their insistence that Judeans could not render up produce in tribute to Rome since, according to the covenantal commandments, God was their exclusive Lord and master was a more radical statement than any of the reaffirmations of God's ultimate sovereignty in "apocalyptic" texts, with obvious implications for active resistance to imperial demands. Perhaps their passion for their principles slackened as they faced the implications, since the Romans viewed failure to pay the tribute as tantamount to rebellion and would again have devastated the country and enslaved or crucified their fellow Judeans. The Parables of Enoch (*1 Enoch* 37–71) voice an equally blunt and adamant opposition to Roman rule, with their scenarios of God's judgment against "the kings and the mighty," but give no hint of corresponding acts of opposition.

The frustration of learned scribes passionately opposed to Roman rule must have festered over the next several decades as popular protest was put down by repressive violence. As priestly aristocrats turned to predatory acts against their own people, matching the repressive violence of the Roman governors, scribes could see no way to mitigate the worst effects of imperial rule. As in similar imperial situations in other times, the closing off of any avenue of protest must have been what led to the desperate acts of terrorism by the sicarii, particularly their assassinations of collaborationist high priestly figures.

None of these instances of scribal resistance to imperial rule amounted to what could be called a movement, except perhaps for the Qumran community and its satellites in Judean towns. The acts of opposition to imperial invasion and exploitation were undertaken by relatively small groups of scribes (hence the term "circles"). If the population of Judea was around a hundred thousand people, then the scribes would have numbered in the hundreds or a few thousand. Josephus, who often exaggerates, lists the disciples of Judas and Matthias who were apprehended at around forty. A scribal circle may have counted no more than a dozen or two.

Through all of these instances of resistance to imperial rule by circles of learned scribes, there are precious few indications of direct links or close collaboration with popular resistance. The "lambs" whose eyes were opened (in the Animal Vision) appear to have eventually joined in the Maccabean revolt. But Daniel 11 gives no hint of a connection with Judas Maccabeus, but rather says that the maskilim received "little help" (from anyone). The bold removal of the golden eagle from the great gate of the Temple by Judas, Matthias, and their disciples, and especially their subsequently being burned alive by Herod, helped to inspire wider protests after Herod's death. But there is no indication of scribal leadership in these popular protests, much less in the revolts that followed. Josephus's accounts of the fourth philosophy's attempts to organize a collective refusal to pay the tribute give little indication of whether they attempted to mobilize popular participation. The apparent attempt of the sicarii to step into the leadership of the widening revolt in Jerusalem in the summer of 66 was a failure, as Jerusalemites turned on them and killed the messianic pretender Menahem. In fact, separate and sometimes parallel action by scribal circles and the peasantry is what we would expect given the political-economic structure. Scribes centered in Jerusalem had little or no connections with people who lived in outlying village communities upon which they might have built in mounting potential common causes. Scribal resistance to imperial rule was usually separate from popular protest or revolt, which seems usually to have erupted without scribal provocation or leadership.

The Role of Texts in Resistance to Imperial Rule

In addition to the actions taken by certain circles of scribes, "apocalyptic" texts played an important role in scribal opposition to Hellenistic and Roman imperial rule. That role was closely connected with the political-economic location of the scribes.

Prior to recent sociological analysis in biblical studies, many Christian interpreters believed that "Judaism" at the time of Jesus was pervaded by "apocalypticism" on the basis of texts classified as "apocalyptic." The discovery of the Dead Sea Scrolls reinforced this impression insofar as the Qumranites were interpreted as an "apocalyptic" community. Historical sociological analysis shows that this standard scholarly belief rested on the unwarranted assumption that ancient Judean texts are good sources for ideas in Judean society generally. Given that literacy was limited primarily to professionally trained scribes, however, nearly all texts were composed and cultivated in scribal circles. Scribal texts, including those classified as "apocalyptic," are thus not good guides to the perspective and attitudes of ordinary people.[1]

As Ben Sira states explicitly, scribes were sympathetic with the people and critical of their exploitation by the powerful. Yet they understood themselves as a considerable cut above the rural peasants and urban artisans who labored with their hands (as discussed in the introduction). Scribes, trained to serve as advisers and assistants in the temple-state, lived and worked in Jerusalem and had little interaction with the peasants in outlying villages who comprised the vast majority of the people. Anthropologists have long pointed out that in traditional agrarian societies peasants were unlikely to share the ideas of professional intellectuals, perhaps particularly if the latter were identified as representatives of their rulers.[2] The harangue against the views and practices of "the scribes and Pharisees" in the Gospels, which emerged from a movement among ordinary people, signals just such a division in late Second Temple Judean society (see Mark 7:1-13; 12:38—13:2; Luke 11:39-52).

Nor, in considering the influence of texts, should we think that "apocalyptic" texts attest to a crystallized ideology or distinctive worldview that pervaded scribal circles generally or led to certain attitudes and actions in opposition to imperial rule. Scribal groups that articulated closely similar perspectives on the crisis under imperial rule took different stances and actions in resistance to it. Both the Enoch scribes and the maskilim were convinced that their acts of resistance would be followed by divine judgmental action to terminate the oppressive rule of Antiochus Epiphanes. The Enoch scribes, however, seem to have taken more aggressive action in opposition ("sprouted horns") to Antiochus Epiphanes and joined the wider popular revolt. Nor did strong beliefs necessarily lead to action on the basis of those beliefs—particularly where economic dependency and/or coercion were involved. According to Josephus, the Pharisees in general, like all of the scribal circles discussed, believed strongly in "freedom." Yet only some of them joined in the organization of collective refusal to "render to Caesar" led by the "fourth philosophy"

Rethinking "Apocalyptic" Texts

who shared the Pharisees' beliefs. Scribal actions in a given crisis situation may have been determined as much by social-political factors as by particular ideas.

The important role played by "apocalyptic" texts in resistance to imperial rule lies less in the ideas they spread than in their effect within scribal circles involved in resistance and their successors. Texts, like certain forms of speech more broadly, have recently come to be understood not just as the sources of ideas that may lead to action, but as particular forms of action or practice. This may be best explained by illustration. When a prophet such as Amos or Jeremiah delivered a public pronouncement of God's condemnation of the king or chief priests for exploiting the people, it was understood as a threat to the regime, an action that warranted forcible suppression (Jeremiah 26:1-23; Amos 7:10-17). The incorporation of such prophetic condemnations of rulers into texts henceforth easily recited again, even if only in scribal circles, nurtured a critical awareness of rulers' abuse of their power. Scribes became the heirs of the prophetic message and, potentially, of the prophetic role, as in the cases of the Enoch and Daniel texts.

With a far more ominous scope of God's judgment but a more limited audience of scribes themselves, texts such as the Animal Vision and the visions and interpretations in Daniel 7–12 pronounced God's condemnation, not only of the Judean rulers, but of the imperial regime that was keeping them in power. This was equivalent to a "declaration of independence" in an imperial system that brooked no independence among subject peoples. But it was more. It was virtually "a declaration of war" in the form of God's anticipated judgment. In these texts a circle of scribes was declaring, at least to themselves and perhaps more widely to other scribes (and perhaps factions in the aristocracy as well), that they stood in opposition to the empire as well as to its local clients, their previous patrons. In an ancient society where writing had connotations of permanence and irrevocability (partly because it was rare), the writing of a text was a decisive enactment of their resistance, their "putting it in writing." And even though texts were cultivated by recitation from memory rather than by physically reading from a cumbersome scroll, continuing recitation of their declaration was all the more powerful because "it is written."[3] Indeed, the text that was inscribed on the scroll(s) in the possession of an "Enoch" or "Daniel" scribal circle would have been understood as the same as, a copy of, what was written on "the heavenly tablet" that Enoch had read (*1 Enoch* 93:2) or "the book of truth" communicated to Daniel (Dan 10:21).

The texts of these "declarations of independence" would have been all the more powerful for the scribal circles for which they were composed because they were statements of the revelatory breakthrough that they themselves had experienced in a desperate situation. Judean scribes must have felt not just "caught in the middle" between loyalty to their patrons and commitment to covenantal law, but in what appears to have been a classic "catch-22" situation. Obedience to God and the covenant meant condemnation to death by the imperial order; disobedience to God's covenant to avoid death meant abandoning and being abandoned by God. As guardians of the tradition of covenantal Torah and prophecy and personally obedient to covenantal commandments, Judean scribes must have come to an acute crisis of faith. As the Judeans who were the most faithful to God and the commandments, they had been suffering the apparent divine curses for disobedience of covenantal law. Had God become so remote as to lose control of history, of the universal governance established in the creation? In the strength of their faith, however, they could not entertain the notion that God had abandoned them or lost control of history. Enoch and Daniel texts are breakthrough revelations of why history seemed so out of control and assurances that God was still in control. God would resolve the historical crisis in decisive termination of imperial rule and restoration of the people on a renewed earth.

There would also have been an intimate relationship between the text and the formative experience of resistance that had closely bonded the circle of scribes, a relationship perpetuated in the continuing recitation of the text. Perhaps the most obvious example is the experience of some of their number having been martyred in resistance to imperial violence, as with the maskilim who composed the narratives in Daniel and the "Moses" scribes who focused on "the Orderer and his disciples." Not only did those texts retell the history in which imperial oppression had intensified, but they commemorated their associates' death in defense of their faith and commitment. In both texts, as in the Animal Vision, the death of close associates leads directly to God's judgment, and in Daniel 11–12, the judgment itself focuses on the vindication of the martyrs (as part of the general restoration of the people).

Another effect of these texts, closely related to the ones just discussed, would have been to motivate the circles of scribes and perhaps others to further resistance. Through the revelation provided in the text, the scribes now understood "what was happening" and, in the midst of that, their own role as the recipients of heavenly wisdom. The survey of history in Daniel 10–12 and the "ten-week" review of "Enoch" indicate this explicitly (the wise who make many understand; the chosen who have received sevenfold wisdom). Indeed the scribes stand at the turning point in history, as in the Animal

Rethinking "Apocalyptic" Texts

Vision as well as the ten-week review and Daniel 11–12. They are thus called to mobilize and to continue resistance.

This effect of motivating continuing resistance is attested in the continuity of later texts with earlier ones. The maskilim and probably others found inspiration in the oft-told tales of the legendary Judean scribal hero, Daniel. The Enoch texts included in the later collection known as *1 Enoch* offer a remarkable example of continuity, from the third-century B.C.E. Book of Watchers through the Animal Vision composed in the crisis under Antiochus Epiphanes, to the Book of Parables in the early first century C.E.[4] Each of these texts was a composition addressed to a particular crisis of imperial rule. But each successive text drew inspiration as well as ideas from the previous one(s). The *Testament of Moses* was so compelling in its pertinence to domination by a new empire that it required only the updating of historical events that led up to the new crisis of repressive violence.

The Daniel and Enoch texts also had a continuing effect on other scribal circles in the decades following the crisis to which they were originally addressed. Many copies of Daniel and multiple copies of the earlier Enoch books were found among the Dead Sea Scrolls. Qumran specialists regard the number of copies of a given book as a mark of its influence and importance for the breakaway covenantal community living there. Judging from the number of copies found there, Enoch texts and particularly the book of Daniel were relatively more important for the Qumran community (more "scriptural") than some books later included in the Hebrew Bible. Daniel and the Enoch texts helped shape the continuing dissent and eventual withdrawal of the scribal-priestly Qumran community and, perhaps, its continuing opposition to imperial rule once the Romans conquered Judea.

Then and Now

One of the principal reasons that we conduct critical historical investigations of texts and history is their potential relevance for issues we face today. A closely related reason is to gain at least some critical perspective on how standard concepts and constructions of the past may be problematic and may stand in the way of fresh historical investigations. With regard to Judean "apocalyptic" texts, Christian biblical scholarship has not been critically aware enough of the ways in which it may have reinforced popular understanding of "apocalypticism" and the use of "apocalyptic" images.

It is sobering to remember how often popular movements in the European Middle Ages turned "apocalyptic" themes against Jews, whom they attacked as scapegoats for their own frustration in the face of exploitation by both ecclesial and "secular" Christian rulers.[5] Such events, which have only escalated in more recent history, should lead to continuing scrutiny of the residual anti-Judaism that persists in the assumptions, approach, and conceptual apparatus of established biblical studies. Scholarly views of Judean scribes has often bordered on a Christian stereotype of "scribes and Pharisees" as hypocrites. This stereotype draws upon—but goes far beyond—the portrayal of the "scribes and Pharisees" in the Gospels, which (as we have seen) probably reflects the attitudes of Galilean villagers critical of representatives of the Judean temple-state. The previous reading of "apocalyptic" texts in terms of "(early) Judaism," pervaded with eschatological expectations of the end of the world and of "the Jews" calculating the time of the end, is a variation on this Christian stereotype.

Closer examination of the texts composed by Judean scribes, however, enables us to appreciate them on their own terms and in the difficult historical circumstances they faced. We can begin to appreciate how they were "caught in the middle" between their service of the heads of the temple-state who adopted imperial political-cultural forms, on the one hand, and their commitment to the Torah and prophecies of which they were the guardians, on the other. Particularly striking in the Judean texts classified as "apocalyptic" and certain others is how at least a substantial minority of scribes chose, at great personal risk and in many cases in the knowledge that they would surely be killed, to oppose the imperial regimes that had become so exploitative of Judeans and destructive of their traditional way of life.

Awareness of how at least some circles of ancient Judean scribes gained critical perspective on and actively resisted imperial destruction and exploitation might well lead contemporary biblical interpreters and other intellectuals to consider our own mediating location and role as the guardians of cultural tradition today. Contemporary intellectuals, such as teachers and clergy (among others), have responsibility to conserve and pass on the cultural repertoire, just as Second Temple Judean scribes did. Rooted in the prophetic tradition as well as the heritage of the Enlightenment, however, contemporary intellectuals also see themselves as having responsibility to question and to criticize the tradition and its current use and abuse. It may be instructive, therefore, to appreciate how some of their ancient Judean counterparts dealt with situations in which the power-holders on whom they were dependent compromised traditional values to flow with the dominant new political-economic culture. Might contemporary intellectuals also have a role, with significant historical precedent, in discerning how imperial political-economic forces cause destruction and exploitation of people subject to their power, and in resisting those forces as well as in "giving understanding to many," as did the maskilim in ancient Judea?

Rethinking "Apocalyptic" Texts

As mentioned at the outset, previous scholarly interpretation of "Jewish apocalypticism" emphasized its focus on a forthcoming "cosmic catastrophe," thus reinforcing the popular sense that "apocalypticism" is about the end of the world. "Apocalypticism" supposedly held that history is hopeless, under the control of evil forces, and that the earth itself, having become corrupted, will be destroyed in a coming "cosmic dissolution." The explorations in the preceding chapters, of course, indicated that the virtual opposite is true with regard to both history and the earth, with potentially profound implications pertinent to the historical situation in which intellectuals find themselves today.

The principal message of the Second-Temple Judean texts usually classified as "apocalyptic" is that, despite appearances, history is not hopeless. As we have noted in each case, the texts focus on how imperial rulers have done violence to subject people and taken their resources. The pressures to conform to the values and practices of the dominant order have become severe, including pressures exerted by those who hold immediate power over the scribes themselves. A key part of the revelation these texts disclose is that these predatory rulers have been generated by beastly superhuman forces that have rebelled against God's intended governance of human life on earth. But God and other superhuman forces are struggling to regain control of history. God will being an end to imperial oppression and restore the sovereignty of the people. Hence the scribes who face a seemingly impossible situation will not be alone in insisting on living according to their traditional covenantal principles. Indeed, persisting in their principles may turn out to be the turning point of history (as in the Enoch texts), or else the faithful scribes may be vindicated (Dan 12).

It is at least conceivable that intellectuals today could learn from their ancient counterparts, first, to identify those contemporary imperial political and economic forces that correspond to the Hellenistic and Roman empires, and second, to discern what (seemingly) superhuman forces—those of global capitalist civilization—may be driving their destructive and oppressive effects. More difficult will be to recognize the pressures we are under to cooperate with the dominant order and to figure out how it might be possible to resist.

Closely related to the message that history is not hopeless is the revelation that, far from being destroyed, the earth will be renewed. As noted in our discussion of the Book of Watchers, the *Testament of Moses*, and the Parables of Enoch, the construction of "apocalypticism" by an earlier generation of biblical scholars tended to take representations of God's coming in judgment somewhat literally as metaphysical statements. Like the same representations in prophetic oracles from which they were derived, however, theophany in "apocalyptic" texts was expressed in "earthshaking" metaphor and hyperbole. And the theophany was God's coming in judgment on imperial rulers who had destroyed the earth or the watchers whose rebellious actions had generated destructive imperial warfare. Coupled with the message of the end of empire in both of those Enoch texts, moreover, was the reassurance that God would renew the earth as the context of independent and abundant life of the people.

Again, intellectuals today can learn from the ancient Judean scribes to discern and name the imperial forces that have destroyed the earth and that it is not God's will that the earth be destroyed, but rather that it be renewed, as the nurturing context of human life, through the necessary historical action.

Finally, it may be well to look critically at the messages and images of these texts for the ways in which they project onto God's action of judgment and renewal some of the same kinds of action for which imperial rulers are being condemned. That is, both Enoch and Daniel texts represent the Most High as a powerful emperor, somewhat remote from history in which the human emperors have wrought such destruction. While both the maskilim and Taxo and his sons resist non violently, inviting martyrdom by refusing to obey imperial orders, both the Animal Vision and the ten-week survey describe a large sword being given to the "sheep" or the "righteous" to execute righteous judgment. The Animal Vision, moreover, represents the Lord as destroying the heavenly forces and "shepherds" by fire, just as Hellenistic kings and Roman warlords destroyed conquered cities and villages by fire. The Book of Watchers, on the other hand, offers an alternative means of restoring the heavenly governance of the universe, by consigning the forces that caused destruction by their rebellion against the divine order to the chaos beyond that order. Daniel's visions and interpretations, the *Testament of Moses*, and the *Psalms of Solomon* all focus the resolution of the historical crisis narrowly on the independence or restoration of Judean society. The Book of Watchers and Parables of Enoch expand the scope of future fulfillment to the renewal of the earth, however. The Enoch historical surveys add fulfillment of a more universal scope to the restoration of Judean society, with all species becoming white cattle, like the primordial ancestors at the beginning of history prior to the appearance of the predatory violence of rulers, or all peoples being taught the torah of justice.

A closer examination of late Second Temple "apocalyptic" texts in their historical context thus indicates that the concerns of the learned scribes who composed them were very different from how they appeared in the standard scholarly construct of "apocalypticism." Far from having turned away from history in despair, they had identified the forces that were at work in the oppression of the Judean people through their interpretations of visions and prophetic oracles. Far from looking for the end of the world, they were looking for the end of empire. And far from living under the shadow of an anticipated cosmic dissolution, they looked for the renewal of the earth on which a humane societal life could be renewed.

Abbreviations

Bar	Baruch
BO	*Bibliotheca orientalis*
CBQ	*Catholic Biblical Quarterly*
CBQMS	Catholic Biblical Quarterly Monograph Series
CD	Cairo Genizah copy of the *Damascus Document*
ConBOT	Coniectanea biblica: Old Testament Series
CP	*Classical Philology*
CQS	Companion to the Qumran Scrolls
FOTL	Forms of the Old Testament Literature
HDR	Harvard Dissertations in Religion
HSM	Harvard Semitic Monographs
HTR	*Harvard Theological Review*
HTS	Harvard Theological Studies
IDB	*The Interpreter's Dictionary of the Bible.* Edited by G. A. Buttrick. 4 vols. Nashville, 1962.
JBL	*Journal of Biblical Literature*
JCS	*Journal of Cuneiform Studies*
JJS	*Journal of Jewish Studies*
JSJ	*Journal for the Study of Judaism in the Persian, Hellenistic, and Roman Periods*
JSJSup	Journal for the Study of Judaism Supplement
JSOT	*Journal for the Study of the Old Testament*
JSOTSup	Journal for the Study of the Old Testament: Supplement series
Jub.	*Jubilees*
NovT	*Novum Testamentum*
1QH^a	*Hodayot^a* or *Thanksgiving Hymns^a*
1QM	*Milhamah* or *War Scroll*
1QpNah	Pesher on Nahum (from Qumran)
1QS	*Serek Hayahad* or *Rule of the Community*
Sir	Sirach/Ecclesiasticus
SBLEJL	Society of Biblical Literature Early Judaism and Its Literature
SBLSCS	Society of Biblical Literature Septuagint and Cognate Studies
SCI	*Scripta Classica Israelica*
SJLA	Studies in Judaism in Late Antiquity
STDJ	*Studies on the Texts of the Desert of Judah*
SVTP	Studia in Veteris Testamenti pseudepigraphica
T.Mos.	*Testament of Moses*
ZAW	*Zeitschrift für die alttestamentliche Wissenschaft*

Notes

Introduction

1. Albert Schweitzer, *The Quest of the Historical Jesus* (New York: Macmillan, 1962; orig. 1906), saw Jesus caught up in Jewish apocalyptic doctrine in which "the final tribulation" would lead into "the cataclysm" (esp. 362, 367–68, 389). Rudolf Bultmann, *Theology of the New Testament* (2 vols., New York: Scribner, 1951–55), 1.4–5, finds in "apocalyptic" literature the expectation of a "cosmic catastrophe" that will "do away with all conditions of the present world," which stands under "Satanic corruption."

2. Among the important studies are John J. Collins, *The Apocalyptic Imagination* (New York: Crossroad, 1984); and *Daniel* (Hermeneia; Minneapolis: Fortress Press, 1993); George W. E. Nickelsburg, *Jewish Literature between the Bible and the Mishnah* (2nd ed.; Minneapolis: Fortress Press, 2005); and *1 Enoch 1* (Minneapolis: Fortress Press, 2001); Patrick A. Tiller, *A Commentary on the Animal Apocalypse on 1 Enoch* (SBLEJL 4; Atlanta: Scholars Press, 1993); and James C. VanderKam, *Enoch and the Growth of the Apocalyptic Tradition* (CBQMS 16; Washington, D.C.: Catholic Biblical Association, 1984). I am dependent on and deeply indebted to the work of these scholars and friends in my "revisionist" explorations.

3. John J. Collins, ed., *Apocalypse: The Morphology of a Genre* (Semeia 14; Missoula, Mont.: Scholars Press, 1979), which Collins then refers to in other important works, such as *Apocalyptic Imagination*, 2–6; "From Prophecy to Apocalypticism: The Expectation of the End," in Collins ed., *The Origins of Apocalypticism in Judaism and Christianity.* Vol.1 in *The Encyclopedia of Apocalypticism* (New York: Continuum, 2000), 146. Collins defines apocalypse as "a genre of revelatory literature with a narrative framework, in which a revelation is mediated by an otherworldly being to a human recipient, disclosing a transcendent reality which is both temporal, insofar as it envisages eschatological salvation, and spatial insofar as it involves another, supernatural world."

4. Collins, *Apocalyptic Imagination*, 7; "From Prophecy to Apocalypticism," 147.

5. See, for example, the discussions by Collins in *Apocalyptic Imagination*, ch. 1, and the more recent statement in "From Prophecy to Apocalypticism"; and Nickelsburg's systematic exposition in *1 Enoch 1*, 37–42.

6. Collins, "From Prophecy to Apocalypticism," 138.

7. The classic, magisterial work pursuing this approach is Martin Hengel, *Judaism and Hellenism: Studies in Their Encounter in Palestine during the Early Hellenistic Period* (2 vols.; Philadelphia: Fortress Press, 1974). The many works of John J. Collins on "apocalyptic" literature in general and on Daniel in particular also focus on cultural conflict and the history of ideas; for example, *Apocalyptic Imagination*, 18–28.

8. See especially George W. E. Nickelsburg, "Social Aspects of Palestinian Jewish Apocalypticism," in *Apocalypticism in the Mediterranean World and the Near East* (ed. David Hellholm; Tübingen: Mohr, 1983), 641–54; Philip Davies, "The Social World of Apocalyptic Writings," in *The World of Ancient Israel: Social, Anthropological, and Political Perspectives* (ed. R. E. Clements; Cambridge: Cambridge University Press, 1989), 251–71.

9. See Susan Niditch, *Oral World and Written Word* (Louisville: Westminster John Knox, 1996); William V. Harris, *Ancient Literacy* (Cambridge: Harvard University Press, 1989); Catherine Hezser, *Jewish Literacy in Roman Palestine* (Tübingen: Mohr-Siebeck, 2001).

10. Fuller analysis and discussion in Richard A. Horsley, "The Politics of Cultural Production in Second Temple Judea," in *Conflicted Boundaries in Wisdom and Apocalypticism* (ed. Benjamin G. Wright III and Lawrence M. Wills Symposium Series 35; Atlanta: Society of Biblical Literature, 2005). While biblical scholars are not always focused on the issue, Jonathan Z. Smith is clear that "apocalyptic" literature was produced by scribes, in "Wisdom and Apocalyptic," in *Map Is Not Territory: Studies in the History of Religion* (Leiden: Brill, 1975), 67–87. For a discussion of how scribal "apocalyptic" texts do not necessarily provide windows onto the views of ordinary people, see Richard A. Horsley, *Jesus and the Spiral of Violence: Popular Jewish Resistance in Roman Palestine* (San Francisco: Harper & Row, 1987), 129–46.

11. The articles in *The Sage in Israel and the Ancient Near East* (ed. John Gammie and Leo Perdue; Winona Lake, Ind.: Eisenbrauns, 1990) are helpful. Niek Veldhuis, *Elementary Education at Nippur* (Groningen: Styx, 1997), presents breakthrough research on ancient Mesopotamian scribes. David Carr, *Writing on the Tablet of the Heart: Origins of Scripture and Literature* (Oxford: Oxford University Press, 2005) summarizes recent scholarship on scribal training and practice in Mesopotamia and Egypt and discusses scribes in ancient Israel. Building on these studies, I have examined scribal training and practice in Second-Temple Judea, in Richard A. Horsley, *Scribes, Visionaries, and the Politics of Second Temple Judea* (Louisville: Westminster John Knox, 2007), chs. 4 and 5.

12. The following discussion depends on Richard A. Horsley and Patrick Tiller, "Ben Sira and the Sociology of the Second Temple," in *Second Temple Studies III: Studies in Politics, Class, and Material Culture* (ed. Philip R. Davies and John M. Halligan; JSOT SS340; Sheffield: Sheffield Academic Press, 2002), 74–107; and Richard A. Horsley, *Scribes, Visionaries*, chs. 3 and 4.

13. Victor A. Tcherikover, *Hellenistic Civilization and the Jews* (repr.; New York: Atheneum, 1959), 149. Similarly, Hengel, *Judaism and Hellenism*, 32–55.

14. The various collections of laws later included in the Pentateuch had been designed to legitimate and guide the operations of the temple-state that was also a local instrument of Persian rule. Ezra, the great scribe "skilled in the law of Moses" (Ezra 7:6), who presented and ceremonially recited the book of Mosaic Torah that was to govern Judean society, was an envoy sent by the Persian court. The law he was to impose in Judea was simultaneously the law of the king as well as the law of God (Ezra 7, esp. 7:26). From the extensive discussion of the laws that were taken up into the Pentateuch, see the essays in James W. Watts, ed., *Persia and Torah* (Atlanta: Society of Biblical Literature, 2001).

15. More fully explored in David Carr, *Tablet of the Heart*, ch. 6; and Horsley, *Scribes, Visionaries*, ch. 6.

16. See further the typology of wisdom in John J. Collins, "Wisdom, Apocalypticism, and Generic Compatibility," in *In Search of Wisdom: Essays in Memory of John G. Gammie*, ed. Leo

Notes to Chapter 1

Perdue et al. (Louisville: Westminster John Knox, 1993), 168; and its adaptation on the basis of information in Sirach, Daniel 1, and Enoch literature in Horsley, *Scribes, Visionaries*.

Chapter 1

1. These interrelated conflicts between aristocratic factions in Jerusalem and the conflicts between and within the Hellenistic imperial regimes are discussed more fully, with extensive references, in Richard A. Horsley, *Scribes, Visionaries, and the Politics of Second Temple Judea* (Louisville: Westminster John Knox, 2007), 33–49, 69–70.

2. For summaries of this history, see Peter Schaefer, *The History of the Jews in Antiquity* (Luxembourg: Harwood, 1995), 15–24; and Lester L. Grabbe, *The Persian and Greek Periods*. Vol. 1 of *Judaism from Cyrus to Hadrian* (Minneapolis: Fortress Press, 1992), 212–14.

3. While the account of Hecataeus cannot be taken at face value, it may well reflect how the priestly aristocracy viewed itself, since they would presumably have been his informants, directly or indirectly. Critical discussions of the text in Frances H. Diamond, "Hecataeus of Abdera and the Mosaic Constitution," in *Panhellenica: Essays in Ancient History and Historiography in Honor of Truesdell S. Brown* (ed. S. M. Berstein and L. A. Okin; Coronado, 1980), 77–95; Doron Mendels, "Hecataeus of Abdera and a Jewish 'Patrios Politeia' of the Persian Period (Diodorus Siculus 40.3)," *ZAW* 95 (1983): 96–110.

4. David Goodblatt, *The Monarchic Principle* (Tübingen: Mohr/Siebeck, 1994), 29–35.

5. Dov Gera, *Judaea and Mediterranean Politics, 219 to 161 B.C.E.* (Leiden: Brill, 1998), 212–14; Roger S. Bagnall, *The Administration of the Ptolemaic Possessions outside Egypt* (Leiden: Brill, 1976), 14–15, 219; cf. Grabbe, *Judaism*, 1:190–91.

6. On Tobiah's gifts, see Victor Tcherikover and A. Fuks, *Corpus Papyrorum Judaicarum* (3 vols.; Cambridge: Harvard University Press, 1957–64), 1, # 4, 5.

7. Critical examination of the Tobiad romance in Daniel Schwartz, "Josephus on the Jewish Constitution and Community," *SCI* 7 (1983–84): 30–42; Dov Gera, "On the Credibility of the History of the Tobiads," in *Greece and Rome in Eretz Israel*, ed. A. Kasher, U. Rappaport, and G. Fuks (Jerusalem: Israel Exploration Society, 1990), 211–38. The figures and events portrayed in Josephus's reproduction of the Tobiad romance belong to the time of Ptolemy II Euergetes (246–21 B.C.E.) rather than of Ptolemy V Epiphanes (204–180 B.C.E.), when the Ptolemies no longer controlled Syria-Palestine.

8. See Michael Rostovtzeff, *The Social and Economic History of the Hellenistic World* 1 (Oxford: 1953), 335, 338.

9. Schaefer, *History*, 13; Martin Hengel, *Judaism and Hellenism: Studies in Their Encounter in Palestine during the Early Hellenistic Period* (2 vols.; Philadelphia: Fortress Press, 1974), 1:53, 106. By contrast the Tobiad romance portrays Joseph as ruthlessly exploitative and mercilessly brutal.

10. Hengel, *Judaism and Hellenism*, 1:53.

11. See Victor A. Tcherikover, *Hellenistic Civilization and the Jews* (Philadelphia: Jewish Publication Society, 1959; repr.; New York: Atheneum, 1970), 127–42, 153–74; and Martin Hengel, *Judaism and Hellenism*, 1:267–83.

12. Gera, *Judaea*, 28–32.

13. See further Grabbe, *Judaism*, 1:240–41, 246; Goodblatt, *Monarchic Principle*, 15.

14. Tcherikover, *Hellenistic Civilization*, 403–4; Hengel, *Judaism and Hellenism*, 1:279.

15. For a concise summary of scholarly discussion of the Hellenizing "reform," see Uriel Rappaport, "Maccabean Revolt," *IDB* 4:437–8, concentrating on the important analysis by Elias Bickerman, *The God of the Maccabees* (Leiden: Brill, 1979; orig. 1937); and Victor Tcherikover, *Hellenistic Civilization and the Jews*.

16. Hengel, *Judaism and Hellenism*, emphasizes the cultural change.

17. See the careful study by Robert Doran, "Jason's Gymnasion," in *Of Scribes and Scrolls: Studies on the Hebrew Bible, Intertestamental Judaism, and Christian Origins Presented to John Strugnell*, ed. Harold W. Attridge, J. J. Collins, and T. H. Tobin (Lanham, Md.: University Press of America, 1990), 99–109.

18. See the studies by Fergus Millar, "The Phoenician Cities: A Case Study," *Proceedings of the Cambridge Philological Association* 209 (1983): 55–71; Seth Schwartz, "The Hellenization of Jerusalem and Shechem," in *Jews in a Graeco-Roman World* (ed. Martin Goodman; Oxford: Clarendon, 1998), 37–45.

19. Similarly, Tcherikover, *Hellenistic Civilization*, 166, 169.

20. The most careful and convincing analysis of the escalating crisis in Jerusalem, particularly the motives of Antiochus's attacks, is Erich Gruen, "Hellenism and Persecution: Antiochus IV and the Jews," in *Hellenistic History and Culture* (ed. Peter Green; Berkeley: University of California Press, 1998), on which I rely heavily in the following sketch.

Chapter 2

1. Lawrence M. Wills, *The Jew in the Court of the Foreign King: Ancient Jewish Court Legends* (HDR 26; Minneapolis: Fortress Press, 1990), 55–70, provides a very helpful discussion of the form of the tales.

2. Wills, *Jew in the Court*, 39–40, 43; John J. Collins, *Daniel* (Grand Rapids: Eerdmans, 1984), 45; and more recently, Karel Van Der Toorn, "Scholars at the Oriental Court: The Figure of Daniel against Its Mesopotamian Background," in *The Book of Daniel: Composition and Reception* (ed. John J Collins and Peter W. Flint; Leiden: Brill, 2001), 37–54. See further Richard A. Horsley, *Scribes, Visionaries, and the Politics of Second Temple Judea* (Louisville: Westminster John Knox, 2007), ch. 3.

3. Wills, *Jew in the Court*, 68.

4. John J. Collins, *Daniel* (Hermeneia; Minneapolis: Fortress Press, 1993), 36–38.

5. Wills, *Jew in the Court*, 86. Collins, *Daniel* (1984), 46, sees a narrower scope: "the problems the heroes encounter are specifically religious, . . . the traditional tale type is being adapted in Daniel for specifically religious ends."

6. In a critical analysis of the Old Greek version of the tales in Daniel 4–6, Wills, *Jew in the Court*, 87–152, concludes that they represent an earlier stage in the development of the tales than does the Masoretic text of the later rabbis that is the basis of the English translation(s) in our Bibles. Moreover, these earlier versions exhibit even sharper political conflict than the evidently "toned down" Masoretic version. Since the later and less politically conflictual version in the Masoretic text on which the NRSV is based is more accessible to readers, we focus on it here.

7. W. L. Humphreys, "A Life-style for Diaspora: A Study of the Tales of Esther and Daniel," *JBL* 92 (1973): 211–23 ("the possibility of a creative and rewarding interaction with the foreign environment that could work for the good of the Jew," 213); followed by Collins, *Daniel* (1984) 51, and elsewhere. Wills, *Jew in the Court*, 35, 197, suggests rather that the tales reflect the orientation of the administrative class, and probably did not pertain to the lower class.

8. Collins, *Daniel* (1993), 146, suggests that the emphasis on education here reflects the ideal of the Judean sage. He also thinks (p. 138) that the literature of the Chaldeans must be the professional literature of the soothsayers. See further Horsley, *Scribes, Visionaries*, ch. 4.

9. Replacing the NRSV's "magicians and enchanters" with the more appropriate translation in Collins, *Daniel* (1993). In other tales as well, the general term of "the wise" seems to include those who possess particular skills, such as "dream interpreters, exorcists, Chaldeans, and diviners," 4:6-7; cf. 5:7-8, 11; although "dream interpreters" may also be used as a term

that covers other skills, since the widely competent Daniel is called "chief of the dream interpreters" in 4:9.

10. The doxologies may be "redactional," included when the tales were "collected," as suggested by Collins, *Daniel* (1984), 35. Yet what they make explicit is already at least implicit in the tales, as the ensuing discussion of the tales will show.

11. Collins, *Daniel* (1984), 161.

12. The Roman chronicler Aemilius Sura, in Velleius Paterculus; *Sibylline Oracles* 4:49–101; and the Persian Bahman Yasht. This scheme and other political oracles in Hellenistic times (for example, Egyptian Potter's Oracle, Oracle of Hystaspes, and Babylonian Dynastic Prophecy) concerned the rise and fall of kingdoms. See further the important discussions of this background to the succession of empires in Daniel 2 and 7 by Joseph Ward Swain, "The Theory of the Four Monarchies: Opposition History under the Roman Empire," *CP* 35 (1940): 1–21; David Flusser, "The Four Empires in the Fourth Sibyl and in the Book of Daniel," *Israel Oriental Studies* 2 (1972), 148–75; Collins, *Daniel* (1984), 166–70.

13. Evident in Hesiod, *Works and Days*, 106–201, and the Persian Zand-i *Vohuman Yasn*.

14. The combination of "dream interpreters" and "exorcists" (2:2, 10) points to the practice of dream interpretation in the Near East. According to Collins, *Daniel* (1984), 156–57, the latter included a therapeutic removal of the evil consequences of the dream. Nebuchadnezzar's own telling of the dream would thus have been part of the therapy. The tale in Daniel 2 thus represents Nebuchadnezzar as exacerbating the implication of the dream about which he is already troubled.

15. Collins, *Daniel* (1984), 53.

16. To think that the story encourages the belief that "religious fidelity was compatible with the royal service [and] could ultimately lead to advancement" (Collins, *Daniel* [1984], 59) is a modern Western theological interpretation that assumes the separation of religion and politics and the reduction of religion to personal faith. On the latter, see Talal Asad, *Genealogies of Religion: Discipline and Reasons of Power in Christianity and Islam* (Baltimore: Johns Hopkins University Press, 1993). The story does not portray "the conversion of the king" (Collins, Daniel [1984], 59) it mentions only an imperial decree of toleration for the Judeans' worship of their god.

17. "[T]here is no objection to Gentile rule as such" (Collins, *Daniel* [1984], 65); "the legitimacy of gentile rule is not in doubt" (Collins, *Daniel* [1993], 51, to Dan 4).

18. Collins, *Daniel* (1984), 63.

19. As Collins explains, *Daniel* (1984), 62–63; *Daniel* (1984), 216–19.

20. Matthias Henze, *The Madness of King Nebuchadnezzar: The Ancient Near Eastern Origins and Early History of Interpretation of Daniel 4* (Leiden: Brill, 1999), esp. 98–99, 204–6.

21. It is not clear in the story that the vessels represent idolatry (Collins, *Daniel* [1984], 69). Rather, they represent imperial subjugation and humiliation of the Judeans as symbolized by their temple regalia.

22. Philip R. Davies, "Daniel in the Lions' Den," in *Images of Empire* (ed. Loveday Alexander; JSOTSS 122; Sheffield: Sheffield Academic Press, 1991), 161, who discerns the political conflict in the Daniel tales that many simply miss. However, it does not seem that the tales give "qualified approval" of empire. And if the tales portray "resistance" to empire, it is only ideological, not actively political, in contrast to the maskilim in Daniel 10–12.

23. Cf. Davies, "Daniel in the Lions' Den," 163.

24. In this connection we could apply some of the insights about the "hidden transcript" in which subordinated people communicate "off-stage" out of the hearing of the dominant, which is very different from the "public transcript" in which communication is conducted between subordinates and the dominant. See James C. Scott, *Domination and the Arts of Resistance:*

Hidden Transcripts (New Haven: Yale University Press, 1990). Daniel "speaks truth to power" at points *in the tales*, which were then cultivated in Judean scribal circles as part of the "hidden transcript" of the cultural elite of a subject people. But their hidden transcript thereby became what Scott would call a "well-cooked" discourse of dignity cultivated among themselves—and a cultural reservoir of strength and resolve from which they could draw when the conflict in which they lived came again to a head.

Chapter 3

1. Typical of many interpreters hesitant to see relations between symbols in the text and the historical situation is John J. Collins, *The Apocalyptic Imagination* (New York: Crossroad, 1984), 38–39, 46.

2. James C. VanderKam, *Enoch and the Growth of an Apocalyptic Tradition* (CBQ MS 16; Washington, D.C.: Catholic Biblical Association, 1984), 37–42; W. Lambert, "Enmeduranki and Related Matters," *JCS* 21 (1967): 126–38.

3. On questions of genre, including the applicability of "apocalypse" and "testament," see George W. E. Nickelsburg, *1 Enoch 1* (Minneapolis: Fortress Press, 2001); the debate between John Collins and George Nickelsburg in *George W. E. Nickelsburg in Perspective: An Ongoing Dialogue of Learning* (ed. Jacob Neusner and Alan J. Avery-Peck; Leiden: Brill, 2003), 2.373–78, 410–11; and a critical response in Richard Horsley, "Of Enoch, Nickelsburg, and Other Scribes of Righteousness," *Review of Rabbinic Judaism* 8 (2005): 250–56.

4. See especially the magisterial recent commentary on *1 Enoch* by Nickelsburg.

5. Collins, *Apocalyptic Imagination*, 37, insists that "the day of distress" refers to the eschatological judgment. The references cited by Nickelsburg, *1 Enoch*, 136n6, however, indicate that this "biblical cliché" refers rather to times of historical distress for the whole people or individuals.

6. Laid out in detail in Nickelsburg, *1 Enoch*, 138; and VanderKam, *Enoch*, 116.

7. Enoch literature elsewhere doubles or triples the sources of revelation; e.g., 93:2.

8. VanderKam, *Enoch*, 117.

9. On the inscriptions of Balaam "the seer" discovered at Tell Deir 'Alla in the east Jordan valley dating to the end of the eighth century B.C.E., see Joanne A. Hackett, "Some Observations on the Balaam Tradition at Deir 'Alla," *BA* 49 (1986): 216–22.

10. Cf. "cosmic dissolution," Nickelsburg, *1 Enoch*, 147.

11. Illustrations printed out in Nickelsburg, *1 Enoch*, 153–54.

12. It would seem a bit of a stretch to see this as "universal judgment" or an indictment of "humanity's" disobedience, *pace* Nickelsburg, *1 Enoch*, 149, 157. And while Nickelsburg, *1 Enoch*, 133, argues that the "sinners" addressed include (some of) the "Enoch" people, he admits that "it is difficult to imagine the sharp language of the curses in 5:5-7 being directed in a definitive way toward those who are present at a communal reading of the book."

13. Biblical scholars who have studied the Book of Watchers tend to believe that *1 Enoch* 6–11 "is, in some sense," an "interpretation" of Genesis 6–9; see Nickelsburg, *1 Enoch*, 166; and James VanderKam, "The Interpretation of Genesis in *1 Enoch*," in *The Bible at Qumran: Text, Shape, and Interpretation* (ed. Peter Flint; Grand Rapids: Eerdmans, 2001), 129–48. The verbal parallels, say, between *1 Enoch* 6:1—7:6 and Genesis 6:1-4, 7, 11-12, however, are not that close. Longer or shorter references to the story of the giants in several Judean texts (Sir 16:7; Bar 3:26-28; *Jub.* 7:2-23) indicate that it was a standard item in the cultural repertoire of various scribal circles. And the fragments of copies of The Book of Giants found among the Dead Sea Scrolls attest to yet another version of the story of the rebellion of the watchers,

the birth of the giants, and their destructive deeds on the earth (see excursus in Nickelsburg, *1 Enoch*, 172–73).

14. Cf. Collins, *Apocalyptic Imagination*, 4, 5, 10, et al.

15. Nickelsburg, *1 Enoch*, 170.

16. In the political and economic system of the ancient Near East, the only way for an imperial regime to "grow its wealth" was to expand its control over subject peoples who produced crops and/or to demand increased amounts of taxes and tributes from subject people.

17. Skittish about a more precise political reading of the text, Collins, *Apocalyptic Imagination*, 46, reduces the violence and destruction mentioned in the story of the watchers and subsequent sections of the book into indications of a crisis of a general nature, such as the spread of Hellenistic culture in the East.

18. The "house" in which God is seen is also holy; the "high heaven" where the holy ones operate is an "eternal sanctuary" (15:3). But this should not lead to narrowing "the great house" and "a house greater than the former one" in which Enoch saw the "lofty throne" on which the Great Glory sat to only or mainly a temple. It is more broadly the divine palace at the pinnacle of heaven from which the universe is ruled. The heavenly houses in *Enoch* 14 do not correspond to any temple (including Solomon's) in "biblical" texts, as pointed out by Martha Himmelfarb, *Ascent to Heaven in Jewish and Christian Apocalypses* (Oxford: Oxford University Press, 1993), 15. The vision of the chariot throne in Ezekiel 1–2 dissociates God's heavenly dwelling from the Temple in Jerusalem (11–12). Ezekiel saw the Temple defiled, no longer suitable to host the glory of God. Another Enoch text, the Animal Vision, clearly suggests that the "Enoch" scribes stood in a tradition that remained critical of the reestablished Temple (see ch. 5 below).

19. Nickelsburg, *1 Enoch*, 254–55, provides an elaborate chart of the parallels and sketches the close similarities with Ezekiel 1–2.

20. Whether the "Enoch" scribes were simply working creatively from the tradition of revelatory prophetic commissioning and visions, or were themselves caught up in visionary experiences that took the traditional form they knew about and provided the source for such creativity, may be impossible to judge. While it would be uncritical to take the text at face value as a record of a vision, it would be potentially reductionist for a modern interpreter to deny the possibility that the "Enoch" scribes might have had visions—which would surely have been deeply rooted in and shaped according to the long-standing tradition of such visions that was cultivated in scribal circles, as exemplified in Micaiah's vision (1 Kings 22).

21. Somewhat similarly, Collins, *Apocalyptic Imagination*, 45: "The comprehensive tour of the cosmos is designed to show that the destiny of humanity is not left to chance but is built into the structure of the universe"—except that the scope of the "Enoch" scribes' concern appears to have been a good deal narrower than humanity in general.

22. E.g., that chapters 21–23 are "primarily eschatological" or that much of chapters 21–27 is "eschatological material" (Collins, *Apocalyptic Imagination*, 42–43), leading to the suggestion that the Book of Watchers is "our earliest extant example of a Jewish text that is governed by a full-blown apocalyptic worldview," characterized by "imminent future judgment" (Nickelsburg, *Jewish Literature*, 52).

23. Collins, *Apocalyptic Imagination*, 45, also argues that the Book of Watchers does not convey the sense of an imminent ending. "It is sufficient that there is an eventual judgment. It is also important that the places of judgment are there in the present and can be contemplated through the revelation of Enoch."

Chapter 4

1. The following investigation, especially of Enoch's Animal Vision, is deeply indebted to the probing and magisterial scholarship of George W. E. Nickelsburg, *1 Enoch 1* (Hermeneia; Minneapolis: Fortress Press, 2001); Patrick A. Tiller, *A Commentary on the Animal Apocalypse of 1 Enoch* (SBLEJL 4; Atlanta: Scholars Press, 1993); and Patrick A. Tiller, "Israel at the Mercy of Demonic Powers: An Enochic Interpretation of Postexilic Imperialism," in *Conflicted Boundaries in Wisdom and Apocalypticism* (ed. Benjamin G. Wright III and Lawrence M. Wills; Symposium Series 35; Atlanta: Society of Biblical Literature, 2005), 113–21.

2. See especially John J. Collins, *The Apocalyptic Imagination* (New York: Crossroad, 1984), 2–8; and Collins, *Daniel* (Hermeneia; Minneapolis: Fortress Press, 1993), 52–60.

3. Collins, *Daniel*, 60. The suggestive comparative study by Paul Niskanen, *The Human and the Divine in History: Herodotus and the Book of Daniel* (London: Clark, 2004), questions the characterization of Daniel as deterministic and eschatological in ways complementary to my argument.

4. Similarly, Tiller, *Animal Apocalypse*, 101. In traditional Christian theological terms, the beasts and birds that violently attack the sheep are "Gentiles." See, for example, Nickelsburg, *1 Enoch*, 354–55, 383, 398.

5. Nickelsburg (*1 Enoch*, 355–56 and throughout the commentary) emphasizes the cultic aspects of the tower and house, an interpretation rooted in the standard synthetic construct of Second Temple "Judaism." The only sign in the allegory that seems to signify cultic activity, however, is the "table" in the tower (89:50, 73). In the Animal Vision, the sheep repeatedly going astray may include cultic aspects, although they are never signified explicitly (except for the table with polluted bread). But the blindness and straying of the sheep throughout the allegory appears to be a more general departure from the path they were taught by Moses and their cohesion as a people, as Tiller suggests, *Animal Apocalypse*, 331.

6. Following Tiller, *Animal Apocalypse*.

7. As Tiller argues (*Animal Apocalypse*, 49–51), the meaning of a sign such as the house must be established on the basis of how it functions in the overall story, not primarily by reference to biblical texts.

8. As Tiller explains, *Animal Apocalypse*, 43–45.

9. Tiller, *Animal Apocalypse*, 49, makes a persuasive argument that "the house" represents the covenantal relationship between Israel and God.

10. Nickelsburg (*1 Enoch*, 355, 384) takes this to signify the northern Israelites' withdrawal from Jerusalem.

11. "Shepherds" was a standard metaphor for Israel's rulers, particularly in prophetic oracles that condemned disobedient and negligent shepherds who, for example, had fed themselves on the flock (Isa 56:11; Jer 23:2; Zech 10:3; Ezek 34). One oracle even has God delivering the flock to shepherds for destruction (Zech 11:15-17). Jeremiah refers to the Babylonian kings as "shepherds" in oracles that decry their violence against the sheep (Jer 25:30-38). The Animal Vision combines the metaphor of shepherds with the idea that God had assigned particular peoples to the jurisdiction of certain "sons of God" (Deut 32:8). See further Nickelsburg, *1 Enoch*, 391; Tiller, "Israel at the Mercy," 117–19; Paul A. Porter, *Metaphors and Monsters: A Literary-Critical Study of Daniel 7 and 8* (ConBOT 20; Uppsala: Gleerup, 1983).

12. Tiller, "Israel at the Mercy," 117.

13. Nickelsburg, *1 Enoch*, 396.

14. As carefully laid out and explained by Nickelsburg, *1 Enoch*, 396–97.

15. Tiller, *Animal Apocalypse*, 36–38, 48, argues that the camp of all Israel was the historical ideal. Nickelsburg thinks that the new house has the characteristics of the temple as well as the city of Jerusalem (404–5).

Notes to Chapter 5

16. Tiller, "Israel at the Mercy," 120–21, reaches a similar conclusion.

17. Critical discussion in Nickelsburg, *1 Enoch 1*, 414–45.

18. *1 Enoch* 93:7, following the textual variant in Nickelsburg's note, p. 436, instead of his translation, p. 434. "House" is the symbol for the people of God centered in Jerusalem here as well as in the Animal Vision, which uses "tower" as a symbol for the Temple.

19. Again following Nickelsburg's textual note, p. 437, rather than his translation on p. 434. Nickelsburg surely represents the majority of interpreters (rooted in the synthetic construct of "Judaism" centered in the Temple) in finding a reference to "the eschatological temple" in 91:13 (*Jewish Literature between the Bible and the Mishnah*, [2nd ed.; Minneapolis: Fortress Press, 2005], 111). The sharp criticism of the Second Temple and noticeable lack of an "eschatological temple" in the Animal Vision (89:73; 90:28-36) makes it difficult to imagine that another Enoch text so close in date would project a rebuilt Temple at the center of the restoration of Israel.

20. Collins, *Apocalyptic Imagination*, 51, quoting 91:14, says that in the ninth week, "the world is written down for destruction." But this must be dependent on older English translations based on only the Ethiopic version of the text. Nickelsburg, *1 Enoch*, has a more critical reconstruction of the text, and the much more "historical" as opposed to "cosmological" translation, "all the deeds of wickedness will vanish from the whole earth and descend to the eternal pit" (434). Efraim Isaac's earlier translation, in *The Old Testament Pseudepigrapha*, ed. James H. Charlesworth (2 vols.; Garden City, NY: Doubleday, 1983), 1.72, was also more "historical": "all the deeds of the sinners shall depart from upon the earth, and be written off for eternal destruction."

21. "Moses'" survey parallels both of "Enoch's" surveys in using the terms "house" and "kingdom," separately or in combination, for the establishment of Israel as a cohesive independent people in their land (*T. Mos.* 2:2; *1 Enoch* 89:36 and following, 93.7).

22. Discussion and other references in Sigmund Mowinckel, *He That Cometh* (Nashville: Abingdon, 1954), 300–301, on the basis of an earlier article; and Frank Moore Cross, *The Ancient Library of Qumran* (New York: Doubleday, 1961), 226–28, esp. n. 73.

23. Collins, *Apocalyptic Imagination*, 104, sees in Taxo's appeal to God's vengeance a good deal more: a "way to bring about change in the course of history . . . by moving God to action." Similarly Nickelsburg, *Jewish Literature*, 76, sees "the innocent deaths of the pious" as "the event precipitating the judgment." Some martyrs may well have been motivated by such "logic." But the text (even the "at once" in 10:2) does not seem to imply a causative relationship between Taxo's statement of faith in God's vengeance and the ensuing oracle of God's appearance in judgment.

24. Further discussion in Nickelsburg, *1 Enoch*, 146, and in the discussion of the parallel theophany at the beginning of the Book of Watchers in ch. 3 above.

Chapter 5

1. George W. E. Nickelsburg, *Jewish Literature between the Bible and the Mishnah* (2nd ed.; Minneapolis: Fortress Press, 2005), 77; John J. Collins, *The Apocalyptic Imagination* (New York: Crossroad, 1984), 82, 92.

2. Nickelsburg, *Jewish Literature*, 79; Collins, *Apocalyptic Imagination*, 84; John J. Collins, "From Prophecy to Apocalypticism," in *Encyclopedia of Apocalypticism* (ed. John J. Collins; New York: Continuum, 2000), 1:147.

3. In Daniel 9, the "word" given to the prophet Jeremiah, that seventy years must be fulfilled for the devastation of Jerusalem, takes the place of a vision (9:2), with "the man Gabriel" giving the "wisdom and understanding" of how the seventy "weeks of years" would unfold (9:24-27).

Notes to Chapter 5

4. Collins, *Apocalyptic Imagination*, 4–6; John J. Collins, *Daniel* (Hermeneia; Minneapolis: Fortress Press, 1993), 54.

5. Early rabbinic sources also count Daniel among the prophets, as noted by Collins, *Daniel*, 52n426.

6. On the development of the vision form, see Susan Niditch, *The Symbolic Vision in Biblical Tradition* (HSM 30; Chico, Calif: Scholars Press, 1980); Klaus Koch, "Vom profestischen zum apokalyptischen Visionsbericht," in *Apocalypticism in the Mediterranean World and the Near East* (ed. David Hellholm; Tübingen: Mohr/ Siebeck, 1983), 387–411; Philip Davies, *Daniel* (Sheffield: JSOT Press, 1985), 69–70.

7. A. Leo Oppenheim, *The Interpretation of Dreams in the Ancient Near East* (Philadelphia: American Philosophical Society, 1956), 187.

8. A. K. Grayson, *Babylonian Historical-Literary Texts* (Toronto: University of Toronto Press, 1975), 24–37; W. G. Lambert, *The Background of Jewish Apocalyptic* (London: Athlone, 1978), 9–10.

9. See discussion in Richard A. Horsley, *Scribes, Visionaries, and the Politics of Second Temple Judea* (Louisville: Westminster John Knox, 2007), 126–28.

10. Cf. Collins, *Daniel*, 319: the dream images of "teeth of iron" and "claws of bronze" were "not in [themselves] pejorative." The narrative context, however, represents them as "exceedingly terrifying."

11. Collins, *Daniel*, 296; M. C. Root, *King and Kingship in Achaemenid Art* (Acta Iranica 19; Leiden: E. J. Brill, 1979), 81.

12. Collins, *Daniel*, 299, and see his notes 194–98.

13. Quotes from ibid., 289; "a powerful portrayal of chaos unleashed," p. 296.

14. Quotes from ibid., 324.

15. Collins appears to recognize this, in comments such as "The description of the individual beasts, however, cannot be explained from any Canaanite sources now available. . . . the portrayal of the specific beasts is probably determined by biblical tradition" (*Daniel*, 289).

16. There is no reason in the account itself to divide the dream into a "throne vision" separate from the vision of the beasts and the vision of judgment, versus the segmentation of the account in Collins, *Daniel*, 299–311.

17. That the account of both dream and interpretation are so clearly focused on the divine judgment make it seem unlikely that what was still a vision of the throne of God in Daniel 7:9-10 and *1 Enoch* 14:8-23 had already moved into "speculation about the divine throne" (Collins, *Daniel*, 300), as attested in *2 Enoch* and later Merkavah mysticism (see Gershom Scholem, *Jewish Gnosticism, Merkabah Mysticism, and Talmudic Tradition* (New York: Jewish Theological Seminary, 1965).

18. Discussion of the kinds of writing and their functions in Horsley, *Scribes, Visionaries*, ch. 5; and more general discussion in Susan Niditch, *Oral World and Written Word* (Louisville: Westminster John Knox, 1996).

19. See references in Collins, *Daniel*, 292.

20. Collins, *Daniel*, 313–18.

21. Some texts from the Dead Sea Scrolls represent a very close relationship between the members of the Qumran community and the holy ones, with both interaction and synergism of action between their respective heavenly and earthly levels (1QH 3:21–22; 11:11–12). The War Scroll from Qumran expresses confidence that "the multitude of the holy ones [with God] in heaven" will fight for and with them against the armies of the Kittim (Romans; 1QM 12:1-7). See further ch. 7.

22. John J. Collins, *The Apocalyptic Vision of the Book of Daniel* (HSM 16; Missoula, Mont: Scholars Press, 1977), 132–47, argues that "one like a human being" in Daniel 7 is a reference

Notes to Chapter 5

to Michael, identified in Daniel 10:13, 21; and 12:1 as one of the principal heavenly figures charged with the protection of Judean society. Nothing in the text of Daniel 7 itself, however, suggests this identification. Collins's argument assumes a consistency of images and the same pattern of relationships across the different visions and interpretations of Daniel 7; 8; and 10–12. This procedural assumption is surely unwarranted. Dream imagery is notoriously inconsistent from vision to vision. And it seems clear from both internal and external indications that the visions and interpretations of Daniel 8 and 10–12 originated after and addressed situations somewhat different from Daniel 7.

23. Collins, *Daniel*, 322, 324, who takes the interests of the visionary here as "rather mystical, focusing on the heavenly throne and the angelic world."

24. References in ibid., 330.

25. On the details: for the visionary falling prostrate in 8:17, see Ezekiel 1:28, 3:23; on the human appearance of the messenger in 8:13, see Ezekiel 8:2; on that of one messenger instructing another to instruct the visionary, see Zechariah 2:8. For such details, I am dependent on the phrase by phrase commentary of Collins, *Daniel*, 337, et al.

26. See "the Day Star, son of Dawn," Isaish 14:12-15, behind which stands a Ugaritic or Babylonian myth of the Day Star, as discussed by Collins, *Daniel*, 332. Antiochus Epiphanes' arrogance was well-known, as attested in 2 Maccabees 9:10: he "thought he could touch the stars of heaven."

27. Pace Collins, *Daniel*, 343.

28. Ibid., 338–39—but imperial, not "gentile" rule.

29. Interpreters of "apocalyptic" texts, taking somewhat literally these numbers, along with the "time, two times, and a half a time" in 7:25 and 12.7, the "half a week" in 9:27, and 1,290 and 1,335 days in 12:11-12, claim that "calculation" of the "end-time" was a standard practice in such literature. As indicated in Daniel 9, however, the "Daniel" scribes were thinking in terms of seventy "weeks of years." In that way of thinking, these figures, as explicitly stated in "half a week," are symbolic, code for being in the middle of the last week of history. If we are sensitive to the desperate situation of the Daniel people, who were undergoing martyrdom for their resistance to the imperial suppression of their way of life, we can better appreciate these figures as part of the exhortation to persevere rather than a crude calculation.

30. The form and features of the appearance of the heavenly messenger is particularly influenced by portrayals of the revealer and the divine throne itself in Ezekiel (see esp. 1:7, 13, 16, 27; 9:2, 3, 11; 10:2, 6, 7). While the revelations in Daniel 10–12 are communicated orally, like those in Daniel 7 and 8, writing is also prominent, as the heavenly messenger narrates what is "inscribed in the book of truth" and Daniel himself records the revelation in a sealed book (Dan 10:1, 21; 12:1; cf. *1 Enoch* 83:1-2). As with the heavenly books in the introduction to the ten-week survey (*1 Enoch* 93:1-2), the contents of the heavenly "book of truth" consist of the sequence of historical events.

31. Collins, *Daniel*, 377.

32. Similarly, ibid., 61. This worldview would have been shared at least by scribes and priests.

33. In the War Scroll from the Qumran community, the four high-ranking heavenly officers are all lined up to fight for the remnant of Israel (1QM 9:15-16), and after the final battle against "the prince of the kingdom of wickedness," the kingdom of Michael will be raised up in the midst of the gods, corresponding to that of Israel among human beings (1QM 17:6-8).

34. Collins, *Daniel*, 383–85, focuses on matching up the narrative in Daniel 11 with events according to other sources and later interpreters, in effect ignores the term and its potential significance.

35. Collins, *Daniel* (FOTL; Grand Rapids: Eerdmans, 1984): 101-2, says that "Daniel's perspective is that of the world-kingdoms rather than of the internal Jewish tensions." Daniel's perspective is rather that of God's transcendent sovereignty over all kingdoms, and his main concern is coming to understand and oppose the overwhelmingly destructive imperial rule of Judea, which had resulted in a sharp conflict between factions in the temple-state, which the narrative focuses on in 11:20-35.

36. Collins, *Daniel*, 385, the "common people" is too broad. That the same combination of terms, *maskil* and *rabbim* (the many), were used for the master and the members of the group/community suggests that "the many" in Daniel 11:33 also would have been a more confined group than "the common people" in general.

37. Ibid., 386.

38. In this regard there may be a suggestive parallel with the later and more extreme circle of intellectuals who formed the sicarii, who launched an early attack on the collaborationist high priestly families in Jerusalem during the summer of 66 C.E., yet gained no support from the populace, who drove them out of the city. See further ch. 10 below.

39. George W. E. Nickelsburg, *Resurrection, Immortality, and Eternal Life in Intertestamental Judaism* (Cambridge: Harvard University Press, 1972), 12; summarized by Collins, *Daniel*, 390.

40. The many inconsistencies and qualifications evidently necessary in critical discussions of "resurrection" indicate just how slippery and elusive the construct is. See the careful critical discussion in Collins, *Daniel*, 392, 394-98.

41. It is unclear, according to Collins' discussion in *Daniel*, 392, how scholars claim that Dan 12:2 "is referring to the actual resurrection of individuals from the dead, because of the explicit language of everlasting life" when "the precise understanding of 'everlasting' is open to question" (392). The Hebrew Bible passages claimed as evidence for awakening as resurrection (Job 14:12; Jer 51:39, 57) do not attest it. The Pseudepigrapha passages (*1 Enoch* 91:10; 92:3) adduced for awakening as resurrection are read quite differently by Enoch scholars. See Nickelsburg, *1 Enoch*, ad loc. If Daniel 12:2-3 "does not address the form of the resurrection," it is not clear how it can nevertheless give "information about the resurrected state" (Collins, *Daniel*, 392).

42. It would thus be going too far to say that Daniel 12:3 anticipates that humanity would be brought into the place of God, with Nickelsburg, *Jewish Literature*, 82.

43. Collins, *Daniel*, 393.

Chapter 6

1. The sources for the Maccabean Revolt are 1 Maccabees 2:1—9:22 and 2 Maccabees 8-15. 1 Maccabees was probably the official history of the Hasmoneans monarchy, clearly glorifying Judas and his brothers who succeeded him in leadership. See, briefly, Lester L. Grabbe, *The Persian and Greek Periods* (vol. 1 of *Judaism from Cyrus to Hadrian;* Minneapolis: Fortress Press, 1992), 222-24. On 2 Maccabees, a condensation of a five-volume work, see Robert Doran, *Temple Propaganda: The Purpose and Character of 2 Maccabees* (CBQMS 12; Washington, D.C.: Catholic Biblical Quarterly, 1981).

2. For a somewhat fuller summary of this history, see Grabbe, *Judaism*, 285-99.

3. Close analysis of these references in Hanan Eshel, *The Dead Sea Scrxolls and the Hasmonean State* (Grand Rapids: Eerdmans, 2008), ch. 6.

4. Robert M. Kallet-Marx, *Hegemony to Empire: The Development of the Roman Imperium in the East from 148-62 B.C.* (Berkeley: University of California Press, 1995), gives a detailed critical treatment of the Roman expansion into the eastern Mediterranean.

5. Among the recent studies of Roman imperialism that offer a more critical and blunt portrayal than did earlier treatments of the impact on conquered peoples are Susan P. Mattern, *Rome and the Enemy: Imperial Strategy in the Principate* (Berkeley: University of California Press, 1999); and J. E. Lendon, *Empire of Honor* (Oxford: Oxford University Press, 1997). Standard histories of Judea under Roman rule include the revision of Emil Schürer, *The History of the Jewish People in the Age of Jesus Christ* (175 B.C–A.D. 135), ed. Geza Vermes et al. (Edinburgh: T. & T. Clark, 1986–87), 233-454; and E.. Mary Smallwood, *The Jews under Roman Rule* (SJLA 20; Leiden: Brill, 1976), 1–200.

6. Peter Richardson, *Herod: King of the Judeans and Friend of the Romans* (Columbia: University of South Carolina Press, 1996), is an extensive, thoroughly researched recent account of Herod that sees much less conflict between the Roman client-king and the Judeans.

7. For a summary of Herod's building projects in honor of the emperor Augustus, see Richardson, *Herod*, 184–85. On his building projects generally, see Duane W. Roller, *The Building Program of Herod the Great* (Berkeley: University of California Press, 1998).

8. The key studies are Simon R. F. Price, *Rituals and Power: The Roman Imperial Cult in Asia Minor* (Cambridge: Cambridge University Press, 1984); and Paul Zanker, *The Power of Images in the Age of Augustus* (Ann Arbor: University of Michigan Press, 1987); both excerpted for pertinence to New Testament studies in Richard A. Horsley, ed., *Paul and Empire: Religion and Power in Roman Imperial Society* (Harrisburg, Pa.: Trinity, 1997).

9. On these monuments, see Richardson, *Herod*, 61–63, 183–84, with references to the archaeological as well as the limited literary evidence.

10. On the high-priestly families under Herod and under the Roman governors, see James Vanderkam, *From Joshua to Caiaphas: High Priests after the Exile* (Minneapolis: Fortress, 2004), 337–436.

11. See further Richard A. Horsley, "Popular Messianic Movements around the Time of Jesus,"*CBQ* 46 (1984): 471–93.

12. See further Richard A. Horsley, "High Priests and the Politics of Roman Palestine," *JSJ* 17 (1986): 23–55.

13. For more elaborate treatment of Judea in the first century C.E. prior to the great revolt, see Richard A. Horsley, *Jesus and the Spiral of Violence: Popular Jewish Resistance in Roman Palestine* (San Francisco: Harper & Row, 1987; Minneapolis: Fortress Press, 1993), chs. 1–2; Martin Goodman, *The Ruling Class of Judea* (Cambridge: Cambridge University Press, 1987).

14. For a fuller analysis of the many Roman provocations and Judean protests and movements arising out of this conflict, see further Horsley, *Jesus and the Spiral*, chs. 3–4.

15. See the critical reconstruction of these events through a critical analysis of Josephus's accounts in Richard A. Horsley, "The Zealots, Their Origins, Relationships, and Importance in the Jewish Revolt," *Novum Testamentum* 28 (1986): 159–92.

Chapter 7

1. This is standard in work on Qumran and the Dead Sea Scrolls, as exemplified in introductions such as Lawrence H. Schiffman, *Reclaiming the Dead Sea Scrolls: Their True Meaning for Judaism and Christianity* (New York: Doubleday, 1994); James C. VanderKam, *The Dead Sea Scrolls Today* (Grand Rapids: Eerdmans, 1994); and the introduction in Geza Vermes, *The Complete Dead Sea Scrolls in English* (London: Penguin, 1997).

2. Critical treatment of archaeological finds and their pertinence to the Qumran texts in Jodi Magness, *The Archaeology of Qumran and the Dead Sea Scrolls* (Grand Rapids: Eerdmans, 2002).

3. References and quotations of Dead Sea Scrolls are from the translation (sometimes adapted) by Vermes, *The Complete Dead Sea Scrolls in English*.

Notes to Chapter 7

4. Recent introduction to the Community Rule in Michael A. Knibb, "The Rule of the Community," *Encyclopedia of the Dead Sea Scrolls*, ed. Lawrence H. Schiffman and James C. Vanderkam (2 vols.; New York: Oxford University Press, 2000), 2:793–97.

5. Among the substantial critical studies of the Damascus Document are Philip R. Davies, *The Damascus Covenant: An Interpretation of the "Damascus Document"* (JSOT Sup 24; Sheffield: Sheffield Academic Press, 1983); Charlotte Hempel, *The Damascus Texts* (CQS 1; Sheffield: Sheffield Academic Press, 2000) and *Laws of the Damascus Document: Sources, Traditions, Redactions* (Leiden: Brill, 1998). Maxine L. Grossman, *Reading for History in the Damascus Document* (STDJ 29; Leiden: Brill, 2002), raises serious questions about the use of the Damascus Document as a source for historical reconstruction.

6. Vermes, *Dead Sea Scrolls*, 43–44.

7. Convenient summary in VanderKam, *Dead Sea Scrolls Today*, ch. 3.

8. The scribal orientation of the Qumran community is sometimes obscured by emphasis on its priestly, specifically Zadokite character. For example, Schiffman, *Dead Sea Scrolls*, 113–14, states that "the sect was initially formed by Zadokites, who were joined by others." The principal passage from which this claim is derived, however, takes the terms for the various classifications of priests in Ezekiel 44:15 figuratively, not literally, as referring to the members of the movement in general. "The *priests* are the converts of Israel who departed from the land of Judah, and (the *Levites* are) those who joined them. The *sons of Zadok* are the elect of Israel, the men called by name who shall stand at the end of days" (CD 3:20—4:6). In other passages, the sons of Zadok and/or priests are always mentioned together with "the multitude of men of the community/covenant" (1QS 5:2–4, 8–9). That the Zadokites are mentioned first may well indicate that they are first in rank in the community, as in Judean society generally. But the community/movement does not appear to have been composed primarily of priests, much less of Zadokites.

9. Nothing in the passage about the two spirits suggests that they are among the heavenly forces that participate in the governance of the universe, as in earlier Judean texts. It is not clear what their relationship is with "the holy ones."

10. The most recent and detailed analysis of Dead Sea Scroll texts and their matches with other sources and historical persons and events, including Jonathan as the wicked priest, is Hanan Eshel, *The Dead Sea Scrolls and the Hasmonean State* (Grand Rapids: Eerdmans, 2008), ch 2.

11. Vermes, *Dead Sea Scrolls*, 60.

12. Many of the connections made by Eshel, *Scrolls and Hasmonean State*, ch. 1, would support this conclusion.

13. See now the extensive critical discussion by Eshel, *Scrolls and Hasmonean State*, ch. 9.

14. Vermes, *Dead Sea Scrolls*, 56, 59.

15. John J. Collins, *Apocalypticism in the Dead Sea Scrolls* (London: Routledge, 1997), locates Qumran texts critically in relation to "apocalyptic" texts and the standard interpretive concepts of "apocalypticism." In chapter 6 he discusses the War Rule as being about "the eschatological war." For different points of view, see Philip R. Davies, *1QM, the War Scroll from Qumran: Its Structure and History* (BO 323; Rome: Biblical Institute Press, 1977), and Jean Duhaime, *The War Texts: 1 QM and Related Manuscripts* (CQS 6; London: T. & T. Clark, 2004).

16. Collins, *Apocalypticism*, 99–106, sees some of the ways in which the concept of dualism does not fit comfortably onto the War Rule, yet attempts to defend its applicability in nuanced form. "The dualism of the War Rule differs from that of the Instruction on the Two Spirits only in its emphasis" (p. 105).

17. Summary of evidence on the dating of 1QM and related MSS in Collins, *Apocalypticism*, 95.

18. On the similarity of the military formations in 1QM to Roman, compared with Maccabean, military practices, see Collins, *Apocalypticism*, 97–99; Vermes, *Dead Sea Scrolls*, 162–63;

and the extensive earlier investigation by Yigael Yadin, *The Scroll of the War of the Sons of Light against the Sons of Darkness* (Oxford: Oxford University Press, 1962).

19. Among others finding the "eschatological war" in the War Rule are Schiffman, *Dead Sea Scrolls*, 380, and Collins, *Apocalypticism*, 93. Collins cites passages from several other scrolls as referring to "the final conflict" at "the end of days," but offers none from 1QM itself. Collins's earlier discussion (pp. 56–58) of the Hebrew phrase (*'aharit hayyamim*) translated "end of days," however, suggests that it refers to a future time less ominous than an "eschatological" ending of time.

20. The War Rule has been the principal text quoted to attest the intimate relationship between the Qumranites and God's angels or "holy ones," despite the limited basis in the text. But other Qumran texts, such as 1QS 11:7–8 and CD 15:16–17 also presuppose and give expression to the close relationship. See, for example, John J. Collins, *Daniel* (Grand Rapids: Eerdmans, 1984); George W. E. Nickelsburg, *Jewish Literature between the Bible and the Mishnah* (2nd ed.; Minneapolis: Fortress Press, 2005), 146.

Chapter 8

1. On introductory matters such as language and dating, see George W. E. Nickelsburg, *Jewish Literature between the Bible and the Mishnah* (2nd ed.; Minneapolis: Fortress Press, 2005), 238–47.

2. The classic statement is by H. E. Ryle and M. R. James, *Psalmoi Solomontos: Psalms of the Pharisees, Commonly Called the Psalms of Solomon* (Cambridge: Cambridge University Press, 1891). On more recent scholarship, see J. L. Trafton, "The Psalms of Solomon in Recent Research," *Journal for the Study of the Pseudepigrapha* 12 (1994): 3–19.

3. The many penitential psalms in the collection, for example, are similar to the psalms in the Hymn Scroll (1QH) and other texts found at Qumran.

4. The psalms are also full of language drawn from or alluding to passages in the prophets and Psalms, which the scribes, along with the priests, learned and recited as part of the Judean cultural repertoire of which they were the professional guardians.

5. Characterization of the community behind the psalms is the major concern of Kenneth Atkinson, *I Cried to the Lord: A Study of the Psalms of Solomon's Historical Background and Social Setting* (SJSJ 84; Brill: Leiden, 2004). See especially his "Conclusion," where he argues for a "sectarian community, meeting in their own synagogues [buildings] in Jerusalem (214, 218).

6. Sketched more fully in Richard A. Horsley, *Scribes, Visionaries, and the Politics of Second Temple Judea* (Louisville: Westminster John Knox, 2007), ch. 3.

7. See further the analysis and discussion of "synagogues" in Richard A. Horsley, *Galilee: History, Politics, People* (Valley Forge, Pa.: Trinity Press International, 1995), ch.10.

8. Atkinson, *I Cried to the Lord*, 201, takes the "synagogues of Israel" as "the physical locale" (buildings), despite their representation as "glorifying the Lord," that is, congregations of people engaged in hymns or prayers of praise.

9. Rodney A. Werline, "The *Psalms of Solomon* and the Ideology of Rule," in *Conflicted Boundaries in Wisdom and Apocalypticism* (ed. Benjamin G. Wright and Lawrence M. Wills; Symposium Series 35; Atlanta: Society of Biblical Literature, 2005), 69–88, offers a very suggestive analysis and interpretation of the "ideology of rule" in psalms 1, 2, 8, and 17.

10. See A. A. Bell Jr., "Fact and *Exemplum* in Accounts of the Deaths of Pompey and Caesar," *Latomus* 53 (1994): 824–36; and such texts as Dio Cassius, *Roman History*, 42:5-6; Caesar, *Civil Wars* 2.86; Lucan, *Pharsalia* 8.521–22, 605–8, 708–11; Velleius Paterculus, *Roman History*, 2.53.3; Seneca, *Marcia*, 16.

11. Eyal Regev, "How Did the Temple Mount Fall to Pompey?" *JJS* 48 (1997): 276–89, argues that the partisans of Aristobulus in the siege of Jerusalem in 63 B.C.E. were Sadducees.

12. *Pss. Sol.* 2:6 also stands parallel to the interpretation of Nah 3:10 in 1QpNah 4:2–4, where "Manasseh" is a code word for the Sadducees and (closely allied with) Aristobulus, "whose reign over Isr[ael] will be brought down [. . .] his wives, his children, and his infants will go into captivity. His warriors and his honored ones [will perish] by the sword."

13. See the extensive, although not always apt, discussion of texts from the Dead Sea Scrolls on charges such as sexual impurity among ruling priests, with many references to scholarly literature, in Kenneth Atkinson, *I Cried to the Lord*, 66–83.

14. So also Kenneth Atkinson, "On the Herodian Origin of Militant Davidic Messianism at Qumran: New Light from *Psalm of Solomon* 17," *JBL* 118 (1999): 441–44, with discussion of text and with references to pertinent scholarly discussion.

15. For an even-handed historical treatment of Herod's conquest and rule, see Peter Richardson, *Herod: King of the Jews and Friend of the Romans* (Columbia, SC: University of South Carolina Press, 1996).

16. *Psalm of Solomon* 17 was the prime proof text for the older Christian construct of the "Jewish expectation" of a "militant messiah." Since the 1960s, there has been extensive critical discussion of the limited evidence for expectations of one or more "anointed" figures in Jewish texts. The Christian construct of a "militant messiah" who will lead a violent rebellion, however, is still perpetuated, for example, by Atkinson, "On the Herodian Origin," and *I Cried to the Lord*, 139–44.

17. On the Deuteronomic ideology in the *Psalms of Solomon*, see Werline, "Ideology of Rule," esp. 72–74.

Chapter 9

1. The Latin text is a translation of a Greek translation of an original Aramaic or Hebrew manuscript. The most accessible translation and critical introduction to the text of the *Testament of Moses* is that of John Priest, in *Apocalyptic Literature and Testaments* (vol. 1 of *The Old Testament Pseudepigrapha*, ed. James H. Charlesworth; Garden City: Doubleday, 1983), 919–34; Johannes Tromp, *The Assumption of Moses: A Critical Edition with Commentary* (SVTP 10; Leiden: Brill, 1993) is a new edition of the Latin text, with translation, introduction, and commentary.

2. Among the limited critical works on the *Testament of Moses* are George Nickelsburg, ed., *Studies on the Testament of Moses* (SBLSCS 3; Cambridge: Society of Biblical Literature, 1973), esp. the articles by John Collins, George Nickelsburg, and Jonathan Goldstein, pp. 15–52; Adela Yarbro Collins, "Composition and Redaction of the Testament of Moses 10," *HTR* 69 (1976): 179–86; Norbert J. Hofmann, *Die Assumptio Mosis: Studien zur Rezeption massgültiger Überlieferung* (JSJSup 67; Leiden: Brill, 2000); and Nickelsburg, "Testament of Moses—Revised," in *Jewish Literature from the Bible to the Mishnah* (2nd ed.; Minneapolis: Fortress Press, 2005).

3. See Richard A. Horsley, "High Priests and the Politics of Roman Palestine," *JSJ* 17 (1986): 23–55; and Martin Goodman, *The Ruling Class of Judea: The Origins of the Jewish Revolt against Rome* (Cambridge: Cambridge University Press, 1987).

4. In the following discussion of the Parables of Enoch, I am dependent on and deeply indebted to the meticulous and magisterial scholarship on the Enoch texts by George W. E. Nickelsburg in many articles and books. His updated introduction to the Parables of Enoch is included in his *Jewish Literature*, 248–56; and his detailed commentary will soon be completed, *1 Enoch 2* (Hermeneia; Minneapolis: Fortress Press, forthcoming).

5. The vision of the divine heavenly court set up for judgment of the oppressive imperial kings (46:1) builds on the same prophetic tradition as the vision in Daniel (7:9-14). The vision with the appearance of a man that accompanies the wooly-haired Ancient of Days is now a

revealer and mainly an agent of judgment, although still representative of the people who will be restored to life directly under the rule of God on the earth.

6. Nickelsburg, *Jewish Literature*, 252, judges "the tradition about the flood, 54:7—55:2, as an interpolation that interrupts the vision and explanation of the angels' punishment; 55:3 picks up where 54:6 left off."

7. Nickelsburg, *Jewish Literature*, 252.

8. Nickelsburg, *Jewish Literature*, 252–53, argues that the description of the judgment in chapters 62–63 adapts "a traditional judgment scene, attested also in Wisdom 4–5, which expanded Isaiah 52:13—53:12 with material from Isaiah 13 and 14," with the kings and mighty in the Parables being the counterparts of the audience (evidently kings) in Isaiah 52–53, et al. "Chapter 63 is the counterpart of the confession in Isaiah 53:1-6." He is surely right that the judgment scene in chs. 62–63 builds on a traditional scene that can be seen in Isaiah 52–53 and Wisdom 4–5. But the portrayal of the kings who have already been delivered to the heavenly messengers for punishment appealing for a respite by confessing their false trust in scepters and ill-gotten wealth seems quite different from the kings' recognition that the servant of the Lord "was wounded for our transgressions" in Isaiah 52:1-6.

9. John J. Collins, *The Apocalyptic Imagination* (New York: Crossroad, 1984), 145–46, finds that "the major focus of the Similitudes is on the destiny of 'the righteous and the chosen,'" but must then note that the descriptions of their opponents ("the kings and the powerful") are "more frequent." It is the oppression of the righteous by the kings and the powerful, however, that has raised the issue of the destiny of both and drives Enoch's visions of the judgment.

10. Previous interpretation, which has tended to impose a dualism of heavenly or "supernatural" world versus earthly world onto apocalyptic texts must therefore be revised. Collins, *Apocalyptic Imagination*, 145, for example, states that "the revelations [to Enoch] concern the transcendent world of the heavens." The revelations take place in heaven, seat of the divine governance of the world, but they concern what is happening on earth in "international relations," i.e., that imperial rulers are attacking and/or oppressing the Judean people. The visions seek resolution of the historical crisis in the divine judgment.

11. The "waters" that heal "the kings and powerful and exalted" but will be transformed into a fire of punishment in 67:5-13 would provide another historical reference for dating the Parables. Chapters 65–68, however, appears to be an interpolated Noah tradition, although it does share many of the terms, cast of characters, and concerns of the Parables and other Enoch texts.

12. See the discussion in Richard A. Horsley, *Scribes, Visionaries, and the Politics of the Second Temple* (Louisville: Westminster John Knox, 2007), 146–47.

13. Collins, *Apocalyptic Imagination*, 146, following the standard assumption that the Parable of Enoch and other "apocalyptic" texts are (only or primarily) about religion (understood as separate from politics and economics), states that "the issue that divides the righteous and the wicked is belief in the heavenly world of the Lord of Spirits and the Son of Man." If we acknowledge the full scope of reality covered by the text, however, it is clear that what "divides" the righteous from the kings and the powerful includes the latter's denial and active attack on the Lord of spirits as well as their military conquest and economic exploitation.

14. Discussed in Horsley, *Scribes, Visionaries*, 69, 139–40, 166–72.

Chapter 10

1. The most substantial presentation is Martin Hengel, *Die Zeloten* (Leiden: Brill, 1961); more popular presentations can be found in Hengel, *Victory over Violence* (Philadelphia: Fortress Press, 1973); Oscar Cullmann, *Jesus and the Revolutionaries* (New York: Harper & Row, 1970).

2. See Solomon Zeitlin, "Zealots and Sicarii," *JBL* 81 (1962): 395–98; Morton Smith, "Zealots and Sicarii: Their Origins and Relation," *HTR* 64 (1971) 1–19; and Richard A. Horsley, "Josephus and the Bandits," *JSJ* 10 (1979): 37–63; "The Sicarii: Ancient Jewish Terrorists," *JR* 59 (1979): 435–58; "The Zealots: Their Origins, Relationships, and Importance in the Jewish Revolt," *Nov T* 27 (1986): 159–92. The diversity of resistance and types of movements are laid out precisely and systematically in Richard A. Horsley, with John S Hanson, *Bandits, Prophets, and Messiahs* (Minneapolis: Winston, 1985; Harrisburg, Pa.: Trinity Press International, 1999).

3. On the political role of the Pharisees under the Hasmoneans, see Jacob Neusner, *From Politics to Piety* (Englewood Cliffs: Prentice Hall, 1973); Steve Mason, *Flavius Josephus on the Pharisees* (Leiden: Brill, 1991).

4. A thesis of Neusner's, in *Politics to Piety*.

5. The following paragraphs depend on, while shifting the perspective and emphasis in, Richard A. Horsley, *Jesus and the Spiral of Violence: Popular Jewish Resistance in Roman Palestine* (San Francisco: Harper & Row, 1987), 71–77.

6. George W. E. Nickelsburg, *Resurrection, Immortality, and Eternal Life in Intertestamental Judaism* (HTS 26; Cambridge: Harvard University Press, 1972), 42.

7. This section builds on, but shifts the perspective and makes corrections to, my previous treatments of the "fourth philosophy" in *Bandits, Prophets, and Messiahs*, 190–99; and *Jesus and the Spiral*, 77–89.

8. On Menahem, the sicarii, and their relationship to Judas and the fourth philosophy, see Richard A. Horsley, "Menahem in Jerusalem: A Brief Messianic Episode among the Sicarii—Not 'Zealot Messianism,'" *NovT* 27 (1985): 334–48.

9. Translation adapted from that of John S. Hanson, in Horsley with Hanson, *Bandits, Prophets, and Messiahs*, 191–92.

10. This section depends partly on, while changing the perspective and emphasis in, my previous analysis and interpretation in "The Sicarii" and *Bandits, Prophets, and Messiahs*, 200–216. Translations of Josephus's accounts of the sicarii are those of John Hanson in *Bandits, Prophets, and Messiahs*.

11. E. J. Hobsbawm, *Bandits* (New York: Pantheon, 1981).

12. See further the discussion of the Epistle of Enoch (*1 Enoch* 92-105) in Richard A. Horsley, "Social Relations and Social Conflict in the *Epistle of Enoch*," in *For a Later Generation*, ed. Randall A. Argal et al. (Harrisburg, PA: Trinity Press International, 2000), 100–103, 110–115.

Conclusion

1. See the explanation in Horsley, *Jesus and the Spiral of Violence: Popular Jewish Resistance in Roman Palestine* (San Francisco: Harper & Row, 1987), 140–43.

2. Corresponding to the clear divisions in the political-economic structure of ancient agrarian societies such as Judea were differences between the elite culture cultivated by the scribes and popular culture cultivated in peasant villages. Anthropologists and others conceptualize this in terms of the differences between the parallel "great tradition" and "little tradition." Of particular pertinence to late Second Temple Judea is James C. Scott, "Protest and Profanation: Agrarian Revolt and the Little Tradition," *Theory and Society* 4 (1977), 1–38, 211–46.

3. On the aura surrounding writing in a society where writing was rare, see Susan Niditch, *Oral World and Written Word* (Louisville: Westminster John Knox, 1996); and Richard A. Horsley, *Scribes, Visionaries, and the Politics of Second Temple Judea* (Louisville: Westminster John Knox, 2007), ch. 5.

4. In his detailed commentary, George W. E. Nickelsburg, *1 Enoch 1* (Hermeneia; Minneapolis: Fortress Press, 2001), traces numerous examples of the continuity between earlier and later Enoch texts, which suggests continuity between those who produced the various texts.

5. Norman Cohn, *Pursuit of the Millennium* (Oxford: Oxford University Press, 1957).

Index

Page numbers in bold type indicate sustained discussion of key subjects.

Alexander Yannai (Hasmonean king-high priest), 109–10, 178–79
Animal Vision (*1 En.* 85–90), 63, 64, **65–73**
  summary, 66–67
anointed king, son of David, 154–55
Antiochus III, 26–27, 95
Antiochus IV Epiphanes, 28–31, 77, 84–85, 89–91, 92–94, 95–99, 102
  attacks on Jerusalem, 85, 89–90, 92–94, 96–99, 102–3
apocalypse (genre), 5–6
apocalyptic, apocalypticism, 1–2, 4–7, 159
  recent interpretation of, 4–7
aristocracy (Judean priestly), 9–16, 96, 116, 118
  factions, 15–16, 21, 22–32, 96
  as Roman client rulers, 118, 120, 162–63, 190–92
assassinations, 188–91
assemblies (synagogues), 146

Balaam, Balaam's oracles, 51–52
beasts (symbols of military power), 86–87, 89, 91
Ben Sira (Jesus), 9–14, 16–17

Caesar as lord, 118
chosen one/ righteous one/ son of man, 173–75
chosen ones, 173–75
Community Rule, 124–25
court legends/tales, 33–35

covenant, 12–15, 31–32, 64–66, 68, 74–75, 76–77, 96–97, 100, 102–3, 125, 127–28, 133–35, 137–38, 144–45, 186, 196–98, 202

Damascus Document, 125–26
Daniel (book)
  tales, chs 1–6, **33–45**
  Daniel 1, **35–37**
  Daniel 2, **37–39**
  Daniel 3, **39–40**
  Daniel 4, **40–41**
  Daniel 5, **41–42**
  Daniel 6, **42–43**
  visions and interpretations, chs 7–12, **81–104**
  Daniel 7, **85–91**
  Daniel 8, **91–94**
  Daniel 10–12, **94–101**
Daniel (figure), 82–83, 84
  in the lions' den, 42–43
  prophet, 82–83
Dead Sea Scrolls, 123
dream(s), 34, 37–39, 40, 43–44, 57, 82–83, 84–88
  interpretation of, 34, 36, 37–39, 43–44, 51, 82–83, 84–88

earth, 167–69
  renewal of, 54, 57, 62, 79, 108, 168, 174
empires/emperors/kings, 87, 89, 92, 170

Index

arrogance of, 39–41, 42, 61, 171
economic exploitation, 56, 95, 136, 170–71
judgment of, 87–88, 99, 102, **167–73**, 173–74
military-political power, 55–56, 86, 91, 170
repression/persecution by, 90, 93–94, 172
Enoch (figure), **48–49**
1 Enoch, **47–48**
"Enoch" scribes, 49, 52, 56–61, 69, 71–73, 75–76, 175
Epistle of Enoch (*1 En* 92–104), 63
Essenes, 126. *See also* Qumran community

fiery furnace, 39–40
focal plot and characters (of texts), 2–3, 8
four-empires scheme, 38, 86
fourth philosophy, **183–88**

giants, 53–57, 58–59, 60–62
God/ the Most High
as heavenly emperor, 14, 56–57, 69, 88
as King, Lord, 14, 118, 119, 149, 185–86
sovereignty of, 14–15, 35, 37, 38, 39–40, 43–44, 90–91, 95, 102–3, 149, 185–86
God's appearance in judgment, 52, 78

handwriting on the wall, 41–42
Hasmonean high priesthood, 107, 149–50, 155, 160
expansion by, 108–109
hasidim, 98, 198
heavenly book(s), 87–88, 99–100
heavenly forces, messengers, 54–55, 59–60, 90, 94–95, 101, 166, 168. *See also* holy ones
heavenly governance, 54–55, 59, 71, 94–95, 167–68
Hellenistic empires, 22–32, 56–57, 58–59, 61–62, 69–70, 91–92, 95
Hellenizing reform, 28–32, 74–75, 96–97
Herod (Roman client king), 114–17, 152–54, 160–61, 179–80, 181–83
Roman orientation of, 114–15
lack of legitimacy of, 115–16, 153
rebuilding of Temple by, 116, 153
tyranny of, 117, 153–54, 160–61
high priest, high priesthood, 23–30. *See also* aristocracy
historical approach, **4–8**
historical apocalypses, 6, 64–65
historical crisis, 27–31, 70–71, 74, 93, 102

history, historical events, 37, 63–65, 66–69, 73–76, 77–79, 84–85, 93, 94–95
turning point in, 72–73, 75, 103, 202
holy ones (of the Most High), 89–91, 101, 139, 174–75
the people of, 89–91
house (Israel/the people), 67–68, 71–72, 74
new, 71–72
"human-like one," 88–89

idolatry, 39–40
imperial rule
conflict inherent in, 14–16
interpretation of visions. *See* visions, interpretation of. *See also* dreams, interpretation of
interpreter, 64–65, 83

Jason (high priest), 28–30, 133–34
Jerusalem
attacked by Antiochus IV, 85, 89–90, 92–94, 96–99, 102–3
conquest by Pompey, 111–12
Jonathan, Hasmonean high priest, 109, 132–35
Joseph Tobiad, 23–24
Judas and Matthias (scribal teachers), **180–83**
Judas of Gamala, 184–88
Judean society, 8–14, 31–32, 107, 145–46
judgment of God, 6, 34–35, 62, 67, 71, 87–88, 99–101, 151, 156, 167–73

"Kittim" (= the Romans), 135–41

lambs, 70, 72

Maccabean revolt, 70, 134
martyr stories, 181
martyrs, martyrdom, 77–78, 100–101, 172–73, 181–82, 187
maskilim/ "Daniel" scribes, 84–85, 97–98, 100–101, 103
Menelaus (high priest), 30–31, 96

Nebuchadnezzar, 37–41, 43–44

Parables of Enoch, **164–75**
overview, 165–67
persecution, 145, 171–72
pesher (interpretation) of Habakkuk, 131–32, 135–37

Index

Pharisees, 110–11, 178–80, 185
Pompey (Roman warlord), 111–12, 148–53
   conquest of Jerusalem by, 111–12
prophetic commission (in vision), 57–58
prophetic oracle, 49–50, 51–54, 78
prophetic role, 48, 54, 58, 87, 164
prophetic tradition, 44, 57–58, 78, 83–84, 86, 93–94, 101
prophetic visions, 57–58, 83, 87
prophets, 12, 53, 68, 82–83, 131
Ptolemaic empire, Ptolemies, 22–24, 56, 69–70
purity codes, 151

Qumran community/movement, **123–41**
   covenant community, 127–28, 135
   opposition to incumbent high priesthood, **131–35**
   opposition to Roman rule, 135–41
   origins of, 131–35
   two-spirits teaching, 129–30
   war against the Romans, 135–40

reform, Hellenizing, **28–29**, 74–75, 103, 132–35
restoration of the people (Israel/Judeans), 71–72, 75, 78, 90–91, 99–100, 102, 108, 154–55, 173–75
righteous one, 173–75
Roman conquest and reconquest, 107, 111–12, 117, 121, 147–48, 150–51, 152, 155, 157
Roman eagle (over gate of Temple), 116, 172–73, 181–82
Roman governor(s), 117–18, 119–20, 190
Roman rule, 170–72, 181–82, 184–88
Roman tribute, 118, 184–88
Roman warlords, 111–13, 148–49, 155

Saddok, 184–85
scribal piety, **144–47**
scribes, 8, 9–17, 29, 33–37, 48, 49, 72, 144–45, 180, 185, 194–99
   caught in conflict, 14–16, 29, 31–32, 43–45, 103, 195
   cultural repertoire of, 16–17, 36
   social location and role of, 8, 9–15, 33–37
Seleucid empire, Seleucids, 22, 25–27, 56
Sicarii, **188–92**
son of David, 154–55
son of man, 173–75
statue, 37–38, 39–40
survey of history, 63–65, 73–74, 82

synagogues (= assemblies), 146
synergism between God's and people's actions, 186–87

Taxo (staff, orderer) and his sons, 77–78
Temple, 22, 26–27, 29, 30–31, 31–32, 67–68, 71–72, 74, 85, 97, 103–4, 109, 111–12, 116, 121, 125, 135, 171–72, 180–83, 190
temple-state, 9–15, 23–24, 179, 188
   criticized/ opposed, 69, 71–72
   subordinate to empire, 14–16, 21, 22–30, 116, 118
ten-week vision (*1 En* 93:1-10 + 91:10-17), 63, 64, 73–76
terrorism/counter-terrorism, 188
Testament of Moses, 64–65, **76–79**
   updating (chs 6–7), **160–64**
theophany, 52, 78. *See also* God's appearance in judgment
Tobiad romance, 23–35
Tobiah, Tobiads, 23–25
tower (Temple), 67–68, 71
two-spirits teaching (in Community Rule), 128–29

Varus (Roman general), 161, 163
vindication (of martyrs/ Israel), 78–79, 100–101, 175
violence, imperial, 55–56, 58, 59, 60, 66, 68–69, 85–87, 88, 90, 93, 117, 136
   escalation of, 66–67, 68–69, 89–90, 93
   origin of, 66, 67
   vision(s), 57–58, 82–83, 165–66
   interpretation of, 64–65, 83–85, 89–90, 91–93
visionary journey(s), 59–61

war(fare), 58, 170
War Rule, **137–41**
Watchers, Book of,
   composite text, 49–50
   Enoch's journeys, 59–61
   Enoch's oracle of judgment, 52–53
   Enoch's prophetic commission, 57–59
   introduction, 50–51
   story of the watchers, 53–57
watchers
   story of, 53–57
wisdom (heavenly), 169
Wisdom, 36, 48
   different forms of, 16, 36, 48

www.ingramcontent.com/pod-product-compliance
Lightning Source LLC
Chambersburg PA
CBHW071906290426
44110CB00013B/1299